P9-BZH-378

FIVE O'CLOCK COMES EARLY

By George Vecsey

Joy in Mudville: Being a Complete Account of the Unparalleled History of the New York Mets

One Sunset a Week: The Story of a Coal Miner

Coal Miner's Daughter (with Loretta Lynn)

The Way It Was: Great Sports Events from the Past (editor)

Kentucky: A Celebration of American Life (with Jacques Lowe)

Getting Off the Ground: The Pioneers of Aviation Speak for Themselves (with George C. Dade)

Five O'Clock Comes Early: A Young Man's Battle with Alcoholism (with Bob Welch)

Martina (with Martina Navratilova)

Sweet Dreams (with Leonore Fleischer)

Children's Books

Baseball's Most Valuable Players

Pro Basketball Champions

The Harlem Globetrotters

Young Sports Photographer with the Green Bay Packers (with John Biever)

The Baseball Life of Sandy Koufax

Frazier/Ali

The Bermuda Triangle: Fact or Fiction? (with Marianne Vecsey)

Superbowl

FIVE O'CLOCK COMES EARLY

A Young Man's Battle with Alcoholism

◆◆

BOB WELCH and GEORGE VECSEY

QUILL   WILLIAM MORROW

New York

Library of Congress Cataloging-in-Publication Data

Welch, Bob, 1956-
Five o'clock comes early.

1. Welch, Bob, 1956–   . 2. Baseball players—
United States—Biography. 3. Alcoholics—United
States—Biography. I. Vecsey, George. II. Title.
GV865.W43A33   1986   796.357'092'4 [B]   85-24455
ISBN 0-688-06273-3 (pbk.)

Printed in the United States of America

First Quill Edition

1 2 3 4 5 6 7 8 9 10

For
Lue, Ray, Die, Donnie,
and
Meri

—BOB WELCH

To Marianne Graham Vecsey

When the laughter or the tears erupted at five in the morning, during my week at The Meadows, she was with me, to share the feelings, just as she has always been with me, even before we met.

—GEORGE VECSEY

Acknowledgments

◆◆

My deep appreciation and thanks to: Lynn Brennan, a good counselor and a good friend, who helped me know more about Bob Welch and also about myself; the staff at The Meadows, for making it easy for me to be there; the patients and members of my family week, who are still a special "family" to me; the Welch family and Mary Ellen Wilson for being so open; John Newton and Don Newcombe, for their guidance; Al Campanis of the Los Angeles Dodgers, and also Steve Brener and Toby Zwikel; Ralph Brooks, my East Coast mentor; Ron Oestrike and Roger Coryell; Dale McReynolds and Rick Sutcliffe, two models of friendship when Bob Welch badly needed them; Ed Schuman, for blazing the trail with his excellent documentary, *Comebacker*. Laura, Corinna and David for their typing and/or observations. Kyle and Kay and Jim for being around. Marianne, for getting me to the rocks at Hydra.

I would like to publicly thank LeAnne Schreiber the only editor in my business who could have talked me back into writing about sports, for letting me be myself. I would also like to thank Joe Vecchione, another friend, who renewed that commitment, and Arthur Pincus, and Arthur Gelb, deputy managing editor of *The New York Times*. They all helped put me in a position to know Bob Welch and eventually to write this book.

Finally, I thank Bob Bender of William Morrow and Company, whose subtle editing and belief in quality pulled me through some troubling moments. Without him, this book could have turned out differently. He knows what I mean.

—GEORGE VECSEY

Contents

◆◇◆◇◆◇◆◇◆◇◆◇◆◇◆◇◆◇◆◇◆◇◆◇◆◇◆◇◆◇◆◇◆◇◆◇◆◇◆

FIVE O'CLOCK
COMES EARLY

Prologue

◆◆

Bob Welch is an alcoholic and a professional athlete and also a young man trying to grow up in America. Until the age of twenty-three, Bob tried to behave the way he thought other people expected him to behave, taking his signals from the family kitchen, the locker room, the neighborhood tavern, the billboards, and the newspapers and television. These signals took him as far as the pitching mound, in front of fifty thousand people, and then the signals deserted him.

Bob Welch had his own internal signals, his feelings, which he learned to ignore with the help of a drug called ethyl alcohol. The more ethyl alcohol he put into his system, the less he had to confront his own feelings about love, about anger, about success, about money, about loyalty, about sports, about sex, and most of all about himself.

He was fortunate that he worked for the Los Angeles Dodgers, the first team in professional sports associated with a corporate alcohol-treatment program. He was lucky that his company knew how to confront him, and that he decided to visit The Meadows, a drug abuse treatment center in Wickenburg, Arizona, where he could learn to break through the shell and find his feelings again. He was blessed with a friend like Mary Ellen Wilson, who let him know she was waiting for him.

He almost died young; his destruction is only one drink away, just as it is for millions of other alcoholics. Bob was already in danger in his teens, a period of life when alcohol is the largest single contributing factor to early death. According to the National Institute on Alcohol Abuse and Alcoholism, in its 1978 report to Congress, around 3.3 million teenagers—nearly 20 percent of the adolescents in the United States—are using alcohol dangerously. From his late teens until he was twenty-three, Bob Welch fit into that category.

Unlike most alcoholics, who may take ten or twenty years to ruin their friendships, family ties, eventually their health and finally their jobs, Bob Welch was going to destroy his baseball career at the age of twenty-three if he let his drinking go any farther. He had a few months in which to turn his life around.

The first time I heard of Bob Welch was on a warm October night in 1978 when I was driving my car from Boston to New York, having spent a long day inspecting New England colleges with my two daughters. The day had been arranged so that I would turn on the ignition just as the second game of the World Series began—the kind of arrangements a baseball fan learns to make.

All went well as we left Boston, cut across Rhode Island, and rolled through the hills near Hartford. As we approached the salt-water fringe of Connecticut, the game narrowed (as only baseball games can do) to a clear, slow, well-defined duel between two identifiable opponents. The batter for the New York Yankees was Reggie Jackson, the highly intelligent, highly egotistical slugger who had earned his nickname "Mr. October" for his devastating heroics in past World Series games. The pitcher for the Los Angeles Dodgers was Bob Welch.

There was a time when I knew every baseball player's name, but that was when I was young and there were only sixteen teams in major-league baseball. As a sportswriter in the 1960s, I had tried to keep pace with the expansion teams, but by 1970, I was eager to get out of sports. I covered Appalachia first and later religion, glad to be writing about country-music singers and coal miners, activist nuns and Hasidic Jews rather than athletes. By 1978 I felt like Rip Van Winkle about the new players in sports, but I still cared enough about baseball to plan a day in New England around a World Series game on the car radio.

The announcer (memory says Phil Rizzuto but I could be wrong) explained that Bob Welch was a young right-handed pitcher who had been sensational for the Dodgers since being brought up from the minors that summer.

As my car barreled along the New England coast, one of the most memorable World Series duels took place, between this savage slugger and the young pitcher whose name I had never heard before. The announcer described every snarl and flex performed by Jackson to unnerve the young pitcher; every foul ball that prolonged the tension. The announcer detailed a tall, athletic pitcher peering down at the plate, eyes blazing, throwing fast balls, one strike after another, as Jackson just managed to get a tip of it.

By now, perhaps hundreds of thousands of people will claim they were present at Dodger Stadium when Welch finally heaved one more fast ball past Jackson to end the game and induce Jackson to fling his bat down angrily and stomp off the field.

In this *People* magazine generation, when "the greatest moment in history" happens once a week, one is hesitant to indulge in superlatives, but the Welch-Jackson confrontation may have been one of the most exciting confrontations in World Series history. Whether for a father driving his daughters home from college shopping, or for millions of people who watched the game on television, Bob Welch has a fixed place in baseball history.

The next time I noticed Bob Welch was March of 1980, when a brief item in a Florida newspaper said Welch had announced to his teammates that he was an alcoholic who had just taken treatment. By this time I had been enticed back for another whirl in sports and I was curious about an athlete who could be an alcoholic at such an early age.

In my somewhat sheltered life, I have had very little personal contact with alcoholism. (Or so I imagined. I have since become much more sensitive to it being all around me.) It struck me that I had never heard of someone so young, apparently so healthy, at the start of an athletic career, willing to admit to this affliction. Alcoholics are middle-aged or older, I told myself. They are people who have suffered for decades, who take to drink as life's sorrows add up. Twenty-three was *too young* to be an alcoholic.

It also struck me that it took a tremendous amount of courage for Bob Welch to stand up in a clubhouse and admit to his alcoholism. I know a thing or two about clubhouses. In any professional sports clubhouse I have visited, there is a brutally honest focus on performance, on the next game. Individuals may vary greatly from saints and intellectuals to degenerates and dummies, but the mood rarely varies: Coarse humor is the *vin ordinaire* of the clubhouse. It washes everything else down. Nothing is sacred. A man names his new baby. What kind of stupid name is that? A man wears a pink shirt. What are you, a faggot? A man has acne. Hey, Pizza Face. A man gets divorced. You must have been bad in bed.

The common denominator is a battlefield abruptness, based on productivity. I later learned that as long as Bob Welch was winning, his drinking was regarded as funny, which coincided with my memories of the clubhouse. In my first ten years as a sports journalist, I saw athletes who gambled, drank, took drugs, had an overactive love life, and were rotten to their families, all of which were tolerated by their teammates as long as they could perform in the game.

In working with Bob Welch on this book, I have come to realize that this clubhouse tolerance is little different from the traditional attitude toward alcoholism in the office or at home. As long as Pop brings home the check most of the time, as long as Mom fixes supper most of the time, let's not say anything.

Bob Welch did say something. He stood up in the Dodger clubhouse and said, "I am an alcoholic, I will always be an alcoholic, but I am trying to combat my illness."

Before this book was ever conceived, my editors at *The New York Times* and I decided to write an article about Bob Welch, a twenty-three-year-old alcoholic. In the first week of the baseball season in 1980, I traveled to Houston and approached Welch in the Dodger clubhouse. I was very aware that some of the Dodgers had their eye on Welch as a phenomenon they had not yet appraised. Was it my imagination that a few of them were abrupt when I asked if anyone had seen Welch? Were a couple of Dodgers threatened by Welch's public statement about alcoholism? Did they think he was trying to reform the world? Did they resent the visitors asking about alcoholism in a major-league clubhouse where beer flows like tap water?

Just as important, would Bob Welch feel threatened or annoyed by one more journalist poking into his private life?

I soon discovered that Bob was more than eager to talk about himself and his illness. He arrived at the ball park many hours before the game, dressed in his blue-trimmed Dodger uniform, and pulled on a blue satin Dodger jacket. Then he armed himself with Copenhagen smokeless tobacco (the kind you keep between your cheek and your gum, not the kind you chew), pronouncing it a "filthy habit." He pointed to his long, athletic hands with the fingernails chewed to the level of flesh, saying it was "another bad habit. I've got to stop doing this." He found two empty paper cups, one to catch his spray of tobacco juice, another for coffee, and he led me through a tunnel toward the dugout. One Dodger nodded his head at the cup of coffee and asked leeringly, "Whaddaya got, Welch, some whiskey?" Welch smiled and said, "Hell, yes." He told me later that he enjoys the teasing. "I need some humor in my sobriety. I've got to be able to joke about it."

He told me how drinking had taken control of his life, how his personal cocktail hour had moved much earlier than five o'clock, how he had shown up drunk for five-o'clock batting practice late in the 1979 season. That episode in San Francisco's Candlestick Park had tipped the Dodgers off about his alcoholism, he said.

We must have talked for about an hour and a half that afternoon, sitting in a quiet dugout in the Astrodome. At times Welch would stare out at the empty field, his eyes growing distant, even vacant. But at other times his beautiful light-blue eyes would bore into mine. I felt I liked him very much and was happy for his life-saving decision, and I went back and wrote a two-part series on how Bob Welch, the Dodgers, and professional baseball were trying to tackle alcoholism. A few months later, Bob and his attorney, Robert L. Fenton of Detroit, asked me if I would like to write Bob's autobiography.

I am a journalist, not a ghostwriter, and I have considerable reservations about the proliferation of ghostwritten autobiographies. However, I had enthusiastically collaborated with Loretta Lynn on her autobiography, *Coal Miner's Daughter*, because of my love for Loretta and the Appalachian region, and my fascination with the story of a woman caught in a marriage and a career she had never anticipated. Loretta's book was really about America, and Appalachia, and women, as much as it was some star-gazer autobiography. I promised myself that I would never do another autobiography unless it had major themes underlying the individual.

Before I agreed to write this book, Bob and I met during the Dodgers' last trip to San Francisco in September 1980, while they were fighting for a pennant they would not win. We met in a restaurant, Original Joe's, where there were no tables available except in the bar. We sat a few feet from the huge oak bar, where the bartender was pouring early-afternoon shots for everyone. Bob had to eat his meal in an atmosphere where he could smell the alcohol, hear it being poured, watch it being consumed. He was clearly fascinated by the process; it was a world he knew well. It was a world of companionship and good times, but also a world that had led him to overturn cars, mistreat the woman he loves, antagonize friends, and jeopardize a career that offered fulfillment and a life of comfort. He was twenty-three years old, at crossroads many of us never face. Many alcoholics destroy their lives slowly, but a baseball pitcher could do it in a few weeks or months.

"I'm sober today," Bob Welch told me. "That's what counts. I can't make any promises about tomorrow, but I'm sober today. If I follow the things I've been taught, I know I won't die of alcoholism."

At that lunch, I asked Bob if he were willing to tell everything about himself, to expose himself. I realize now that I grossly underestimated what he had gone through in his treatment, how he learned to be brutally honest with himself and others. He convinced me that he wanted to talk about alcoholism so that others would know. As an athlete in a nation that makes an industry, nearly a religion, of professional sports, he had a rare opportunity to tell a story. If he talked about alcoholism, people would listen.

In the past year, I have spent hundreds of hours with Bob Welch, mostly sitting across a table with a tape recorder between us. I have watched him saunter into the room with his athlete's poise, calculatingly loose, tossing off short, hip phrases that are the language of the playgrounds of Hazel Park, Michigan, and of the clubhouses of baseball. But as the tape began to turn, I could see Bob Welch crystalize from jock to sensitive young man collaborating on his twenty-three years' worth of autobiography. His face softens, his speech slows down, his eyes stop darting, and his sentences elongate into paragraphs, into pages. He recalls the transition from being one of the smartest children in his grammar school into being just another cool athlete in junior high. We talk about alcohol and sports, and the ethos of the clubhouse, and the people and the programs that have treated him for alcoholism.

I told Bob he had to be responsible for every word, every thought in his autobiography. I told him I would write it, but that it had to start with his thoughts and end with him reading every word, editing every sentence. It had to be his book, not mine, or I would have failed him and myself.

Yet this book became partially my book in a way I could never have predicted. To know more about Bob Welch, I asked permission to spend a few days at The Meadows in Arizona, where Bob had received treatment. I thought I was going to observe the process, to be sympathetic as I usually am, perhaps even to help someone else with a problem. But I was told bluntly that there are no observers, only participants, at the group therapy meetings at The Meadows. On the first morning I was there, several counselors challenged me not to hold back, but to share myself.

I spent five days at The Meadows, an entire family week, becoming part of the alcoholics and drug addicts and their families. I saw how The Meadows treats addiction as a disease of the feelings, how people hide behind addiction to escape from themselves, from feelings they cannot handle. Sometime in the middle of that highly emotional week, I made a decision that I had much in common with the patients at The Meadows—and with Bob Welch. I realized I had often used my work, my busy-ness, to keep from reaching my own feelings and discovering people around me. The week at The Meadows stopped being a week for Bob Welch and became a week for George Vecsey.

When that week was over, I was much better prepared to understand Bob. He came down to The Meadows and sat in on my graduation from the family program. When it was over, we hugged, as The Meadows people do, and I told him, "Now I understand what happened here. Now you can tell me more. There can't be any bullshit at all." And we went on from there.

The rest of this book belongs to Bob Welch. I used my experiences to get closer to him, to tell his story. His story is the interesting one because he is the alcoholic and the athlete, but both of us will be disappointed if people see this as just another ghostwritten celebrity autobiography.

I have written over a hundred books by now, and this is the first book I have written that gives answers, that could save a life. Bob Welch's story tells anybody with an alcohol problem that there are ways to keep from dying of alcoholism. I admire Bob Welch for providing the example, and I am proud to have written this book.

GEORGE VECSEY
Port Washington, New York
September 1981

Chapter One

In the Shower

I was sober, and it was the saddest I had ever felt in my life. My tears mingled with the warm spray from the shower, and I slumped against the wall of the shower, and I cried and cried and cried.

I thought about other showers I had taken—the laughter in the clubhouse when five or six Dodgers were washing off after a game, the insults, the lies, the good times. Even when I'd give up a home run in the ninth inning to lose a ball game, when I'd feel angry at myself for letting my team down, I could always look ahead to better days. In this shower, I was down. I had never been so far down.

I thought about the showers I had taken with Mary Ellen, giggling and kissing and getting soap and water in our mouths, and washing each other's backs. That made me cry more, because Mary Ellen seemed so far away at this moment. I had never been so alone, so naked, so empty.

As sad as this shower was, I didn't want it to end, because there was nothing ahead for me, nothing I wanted to do. I had reached the bottom. If I stayed in the shower all day, all night, I wouldn't have to face where I was, or what I was. At least it was warm and private in that shower stall. Outside it was cold and frightening.

I couldn't believe this was happening to me. I was a pitcher for the Los Angeles Dodgers who once in a while drank too many beers. I was twenty-three years old, the kid who had struck out Reggie Jackson to win a World Series game, and when I walked near the stands, women would call to me, and Mary Ellen was always waiting for me back home. I had it pretty good.

There were times when I'd tell jokes, seem happy-go-lucky, the life of the party. I'd try to entertain, be more at ease with people, make people laugh. But what it was, I usually had a buzz on.

That's a phrase I use a lot—getting a buzz on. People ask me what it means, how it feels, and the best I can say is "clumsy, woozy, good." At first, I'd laugh my ass off, until I couldn't talk anymore. I was funny at first unless I was drinking whiskey and then the results would be a lot more serious. The first beer was all I ever needed. If I had time for twenty, I'd drink twenty and get all fucked up.

That's another phrase I use a lot for the stage that comes after getting a buzz on. It means being truly drunk, sloppy. When I'd get fucked up, I'd have an "I don't give a shit" attitude.

I didn't drink all the time, but usually when I did, problems would happen, including wrecking my car or starting a fight or passing out. One night on the beach I had overturned my Bronco, damn near killing myself and two buddies. I knew all this about me, but I had always said I would take care of it soon. I kept promising myself, but what the hell, I was young. You're supposed to have a good time when you're young.

As the shower poured all over me—I'd been in there half an hour by now—I thought about how I had arrived at this place, The Meadows, the day before. I was way out in the desert in Arizona, feeling lost, with people telling me I was an alcoholic. I didn't believe I had that problem because I had always thought of alcoholics as Skid Row bums. I wasn't a Skid Row bum. I was Bob Welch the baseball player —a Dodger. I didn't belong at this place.

I was enraged. I didn't know it was going to be like this when I arrived the day before. They put you in one of those zoot suits, those pajamas, man, you feel like you're sick. You stay in those pajamas until you're a good boy, maybe three or four days. But if down the line you're a bad boy, they put you back in the pajamas again. That's horseshit. I could have sat around in my jeans and it wouldn't have made any difference. At The Meadows, they want you to feel like you're sick.

Everybody's walking around and the old pros at The Meadows, they look at you like, "What's your problem, young boy?" I remember the first guy who asked me, I told him, "None of your damn business." A lot of the guys with three or four days left, they mark off the time like they were in prison—big shots, they're gonna show you how the program works. They knew I was a baseball player so they'd snicker a little. "Man, they got you in the right place." I felt everybody was staring at me. I could even imagine their eyes on me in the private shower.

The longer I stayed under the spray of water, the more I could formulate my plan. I was going to dry off, get dressed, sneak out the back, and hitch a ride into Phoenix. From there I could wire Mary Ellen for some money to get back to Detroit. And at the airport, I could talk somebody into buying me a couple of beers and a few shots to forget about this place.

How did I get here? I felt a pulse of anger toward the sons-of-bitches who sent me here. Early in January the Dodgers had called me in Detroit and said they wanted to see me about something. I think I knew what it was about, but I got on the plane to L.A., got me a buzz on the way out. When I arrived in L.A., a guy named John Newton, who's a consultant to the Dodgers, told me I was an alcoholic. I didn't believe him but the way he put it, I was going to screw up my baseball career—my whole life, even—if I didn't stop drinking now. Not six months, not a year, but now. So then I decided to get on a plane and fly to Phoenix, to this treatment center.

One thing I have learned about being an alcoholic is that we are the greatest bullshitters in the world. It's part of our personality. John is an alcoholic, too, but I have to say he never bullshit me about The Meadows. I mean he never promised me any winter vacation. I couldn't say he lied to me. He told me they'd dry me out, teach me about alcoholism, and put me in groups where I'd be confronted about my drinking.

What he couldn't have prepared me for was my guts feeling like they were carrying a hundred pounds of sand. He never told me I'd be standing in the shower crying like a baby, afraid that I'd never go back to Mary Ellen, never go back to Dodger Stadium, never go back to laughing and cussing, never go back to being a picture on a baseball card. He never told me I'd feel lost and forgotten in a grubby little room which I was sharing with an alcoholic who had the shakes and snored in his sleep.

I remembered how John Newton turned me over to Pat Mellody, the director of The Meadows, a small, quiet guy who hadn't seemed very friendly as he drove out of Phoenix into the rolling hills. I remember how I took notice of the landmarks as if I were Hansel dropping bread crumbs in case I wanted to split. On the way to The Meadows we had stopped for tacos, and a couple of people were having beers, so I said, "Maybe I should have one before I go there," but Pat didn't smile at my little joke and of course I didn't have a coldie.

When we pulled up to The Meadows I thought what a dinky place, just a little old dude ranch on a hill, surrounded by mountains. It was nothing compared to the hotels where the Dodgers stay. I thought how I had arrived at those hotels with the Dodgers, and there'd be all sorts of people clamoring around: the autograph hounds, the fans, the groupies, the bellhops fighting to do favors for me. I looked around and nobody rushed over for my autograph. As Pat opened his car trunk and put my suitcase on the pavement, I noticed a few people lounging on chairs, and some others walking around. Everyone was curiously checking out the new arrival. But in my mind I wasn't just another drunk. I was Bob Welch of the Dodgers, No. 35 in your program, right-handed pitcher, the kid who struck out Reggie Jackson in the 1978 World Series. But if I had been honest about it, I was also the kid who got so smashed in the last week of the '79 season that they had to throw me into a cold shower to keep me from tearing down the clubhouse and starting a riot on the field. That was me, too.

Nervous and arrogant at the same time, I looked around to see if anyone was going to help me with my suitcase. Pat Mellody eyed me with a fishy look that said, "Carry your own bag. There are no stars at The Meadows, just people diseased with addiction who want to recover."

I checked in at the office, signed some papers, and started casing the joint like I always do, looking for ways I could get out, seeing if there were any good-looking women, wondering who was staring at me. They put me in this room with a wino in the detoxification section, near the nursing station, and they said our door had to be open at all times.

Then they sprung the real news on me, telling me that for the first few days they would regard me as medically ill and I'd have to wear pajamas and a robe to all meetings. I was really angry. In the Dodger clubhouse you walk around naked with reporters standing around taking notes, even a few women these days, but that's a clubhouse, home away from home. I didn't want to wear pajamas and bathrobe in the middle of the day around a bunch of strangers. I could feel myself getting real angry when the nurse bought in these blue pajamas. I was thrilled when they didn't fit me. The nurse said I could wear my jogging suit until they came up with new pajamas. That was a small victory. My only victory.

All dolled up in my jogging suit, I put on some cologne and sauntered forth to further my investigation of the joint. I avoided all those alcoholics. I avoided the counselors' eyes. My counselor was a woman named Lynn Brennan, a soft and gentle-looking lady, around forty years old with piercing green eyes. I felt like those eyes could see right through me, and I didn't want any part of that. "I really want to help you," she said, "but the only way is if you help yourself. I can be really tough. I can really be bitchy at times." I was looking for a safe harbor and I tried my luck at the nursing station. I figured nurses would be more sympathetic than counselors. Maybe I could bullshit them, do my cute-little-boy act, flash my pale-blue eyes on them. Man, I know how women feel when I flash my eyes on them.

"I have a few beers, but I'm not an alcoholic," I told them. "I can stop whenever I want. I'm just here to make the Dodgers happy—so I can start the season again."

They stared at me and nodded. It wasn't until much later that I would learn how often they had heard that story. But I think I knew down in my guts that they knew. Everybody knew. The winos knew. The teen-age drug addicts with their bruises and scars knew. The puffy-faced housewives knew. All the patients knew that Bob Welch was an alcoholic. I wasn't ready to admit it but deep down inside I knew my career as a Dodger was in jeopardy, and if my career was in jeopardy, what would the people back in Hazel Park think of me? What would my parents think about their baby, Bobby, screwing up? What if I blew it? What if I couldn't beat this stuff?

If I was an alcoholic—and I wasn't sure—I felt like this place had been waiting for me all my life, waiting for me to screw up. I had been practicing getting screwed up, wrecking cars, picking fights, messing up my life.

The shower was still pouring all over me, my eyes were pouring tears, and I felt my body shaking with sobs deep in my stomach. The shower was warm but my legs were cold. I turned the hot water as high as it would go. I wasn't going to leave this shower until I knew: How was I going to get out of here?

Chapter Two

•••••••••••••••••••••••••••

Mary Ellen

◆◆

The thing that bothered me most as I cried in the shower was that they wouldn't let me call Mary Ellen. I wanted to hear Mary's voice, wanted to tell her I'd be back someday, in better shape, not the way I'd been the past year. But when I asked Lynn, my counselor, for permission to use the telephone, she told me no. Just flat-out no. I wasn't at The Meadows to call my girlfriend, I was there to save my life.

I remembered John Newton telling me that The Meadows would be the toughest challenge of my life, even tougher than pitching to Reggie Jackson in the World Series. But right now, Reggie Jackson was a long way off. I was scared, lonely, and I wanted a reassuring voice to remind me who I was. I wanted Mary Ellen.

The last time I had spoken to Mary was on the telephone from Los Angeles, right after my four-hour conversation with John Newton. I was in my hotel room at the Biltmore and I told her, "Mary, I just committed myself," like I had signed myself into a loony bin.

"Committed yourself to what?" Mary had asked. She thought I had committed myself to not drinking, like the New Year's resolutions and all the other promises I had made and broken.

"I committed myself to a drug and alcohol rehabilitation center in Arizona, so I can stop drinking."

Mary's first instinct was to protect me and she had said, "You don't have an alcohol problem. You just drink too much."

Maybe I was trying to get sympathy and denial from Mary to reinforce that I was different, that I wasn't like those other people with their red, wrinkled faces, their shakes from years of drinking, their puffing on three cigarettes at the same time, the look of an alcoholic all over them. I guess I wanted to pull the old "that's not me" routine on Mary, I wanted to be reinforced. But I had just finished four hours with John Newton, the world's greatest talker, and I was full of the spirit.

"I'm telling you, Mary, this guy gave me a test, twenty questions, and I scored eight out of twenty. This guy says I'm an alcoholic."

Then Mary said, "Well, it's good you're going for treatment, because there will be psychologists there and you'll find out a lot about yourself." It was very important that Mary had given me support over the phone, that Mary thought I could get help at The Meadows.

Now that I look back, Mary was not aware I was that sick, that alcoholism is a disease. Most people don't want to realize that. When Mary finally joined me for family week, people kept saying that one of the key factors in our relationship was that Mary was the motherly type and I liked to be mothered. There were reasons I was sick and maybe there was even a reason why Mary didn't mind if I was an alcoholic. The counselors would later suggest that Mary and I had been searching for each other before we even met. But standing in the shower, crying my eyes out, I only knew that I missed Mary, that she was my girl, that I would feel better if she could be with me.

Sometimes I feel like I've known Mary all my life. We're just a couple of kids from Hazel Park, who had the same friends and the same way of doing things.

Everybody knows how much I love Mary Ellen. I'm comfortable with her, I don't have to put on any false airs when I'm around her. She knows me and I know her.

We're not married, and I can't claim I have any immediate plans in that direction. There are times I think my family is throwing hints that I should get it over with and marry Mary Ellen and have a few kids, but I don't think I'm ready for that yet. In some ways I'm in my middle twenties, but in other ways I've been sober only since January of 1980, and my sober personality is just forming. I've heard Ryne Duren, the former Yankee pitcher, describe how he had to go through adolescence at the age of thirty-nine, when he confronted his alcoholism. I guess I'm ahead of the game, doing it in my twenties.

Mary is just out of college, working at her first job. I give her a lot of freedom and she gives me a lot of freedom. She's got things she's going through, she's got to do things for herself. She wants to work. I was so happy when she got a job and came home with a big smile on her face. I could tell she felt good about herself.

Who knows what either of us is going to be like in another year or two?

Mary is slender, dark-haired, with an expressive face that lights up when she's happy and pouts when she's upset. She's the fifth of six kids in a close family. Living with me in California, she misses her family, especially the weeks before Christmas, when she starts looking out the window as if she expects a snowstorm to come whipping in off the Pacific Ocean. It's about that time I know she's dreaming about being home in Hazel Park making Christmas cookies with the snow up to her ass.

Mary and I grew up about six blocks apart, but we never met until my senior year in high school. She was a sophomore in my chemistry class, giggling with her four girlfriends and taking up time in class, and knocking over stuff in the laboratory. I was a jock, sitting in the back of the room, thinking more about the basketball game than chemistry. Depending on whether I had gone out for a few beers at lunch or not, I was either very subdued or boisterous. Alcohol made the difference.

I was reading in the newspaper the other day that one third of high-school kids in America are problem drinkers, which they defined as being drunk six times a year, or having experienced "negative consequences of drinking with friends, family, school, the police, or while driving." Negative consequences—that was me. By the time I was a senior in high school and meeting Mary Ellen, I had been drunk a lot.

The main reason I drank was to get drunk. I loved getting drunk, but I also drank because I was shy. Scared, really. Scared of girls. By the time I went to high school I had discovered that if I had a few beers, I wouldn't be so awed of girls, who had such different bodies and acted so different from boys. I didn't lose my virginity until I was in twelth grade, which is late in life, the way things are going these days.

I met Mary Ellen at a party or a dance or something and started flirting with her. When I went away to Eastern Michigan University, I used to come home and visit her. We got it together from that, even when she went to college over in Kalamazoo, at Western Michigan University.

It's no secret that when I went away to play baseball in the Dodger organization, there would be other girls. There's nothing in this book that Mary doesn't already know about—not since The Meadows.

Whenever school was out, Mary would join me—San Antonio, Albuquerque, Los Angeles. We'd live together the way young couples do these days.

I never much thought about the way we acted together; just did what came naturally. The Hazel Park way of acting is to give a lot of verbal abuse, like among all the guys at the Rainbow Bar. I think it carries over into the way men relate to women. I would tease Mary because she was not particularly buxom. It was a way of getting a jab into her. I would tease her about her cooking also. Anything that made her smaller would make me feel better. But I didn't realize that as I stood under the shower and cried. That realization was still ahead of me.

I never tried to hide my drinking from Mary Ellen. I never felt the need to. She had grown up around drinking. There are probably a few people in her family who drink a lot, just as there are in a lot of families. She takes a glass sometimes, but two glasses and she'll fall asleep. In a lot of alcoholic relationships, one person will try to persuade the other into drinking more, but I don't think it had gotten to that state. Mary never abused alcohol, at least around me. I didn't care if she drank with me or not. The way I figured it, there was more for me if she didn't.

Standing in the shower, I couldn't remember all the bad deals I had pulled on Mary when I was drunk—that would come out later, and I would be amazed at some of the things I'd done. But even then, I could remember a few things:

• The times we'd go over to a neighbor's house and we'd have shots of whiskey. Whiskey makes me mean, man, and I'd have about fifteen shots if I got started at all. There were a couple of times when I made her look like an ass in front of other people. I would say things like, "What the fuck are you doing here? I don't give a fuck about you, anyway. I can get rid of you and find somebody else."

I knew I did it, but I don't know why. It was just my way of abusing her verbally, taking her apart like that. It was as if I were talking to myself.

• I never hit Mary or anything, but if I had continued to drink, I can see that later on down the line I might have hauled off and belted her. One time in a cabin in North Michigan, I was drinking shots and lost my temper really fast. I just got mad at her for no reason. I pushed her onto the bed and started ranting, "I don't need you," and then I fell asleep on the couch. She was miserable the whole night and the next day she told me what I had done. I didn't believe her, but that shows the state of blackouts I was getting to.

• During some of the incidents, I might not even have registered 1.1 or 0.9 on the blowgun, which measures how much alcohol is in your body. One beer or twenty, I'd be in trouble. One time I was supposed to pick up Mary to go to her cabin up north. I went to the barber to get a haircut, and coming back, I had one beer. This lady pulled out of her driveway and I hit her in the right corner. I couldn't see her. (I have a fetish for the right corner, which will be more apparent later in the book.) I really popped her, so I called up Mary and I said, "I've been in a wreck," and she said, "You didn't have a wreck, you just don't want to go up north."

Long after Mary joined me at The Meadows, I asked her what she thought about all the drinking I did. She said, "I just took it for granted. I thought it was what all guys do." She had no concept of alcoholism, or that I might be an alcoholic. A lot of people are like that. They see somebody drinking and they say, "Well, that's the way it is." They don't know how destructive it is, or how unnecessary.

A lot of people had been throwing hints to me and Mary Ellen about my drinking, but it wasn't until I went to The Meadows that I could help myself. Standing in the shower was the lowest point of my life. I wanted reassurance that I'd be all right, which was why I wanted to call Mary. Deep down inside, maybe I knew I wasn't all right and the only way I'd get better was to take care of myself one day at a time. Like the sign I had seen the first day I came to The Meadows: "Let Tomorrow Take Care of Itself."

I felt energy stirring in me. I felt like my body could move again. It was like after losing a game, when you know you've screwed up, and you want to bounce back. I'm very competitive, I always have been. I do everything hard: pitch hard; love hard; drink hard. I never started anything in my life that I didn't want to finish, whatever it was, a ball game or a bottle of booze. I'm bullheaded in some ways. Alcoholics tend to have strong feelings because we're sensitive people, so sensitive we try to hide from ourselves. I knew what I'd think of myself if I snuck out of The Meadows and hitched back to Phoenix. I could see the mental headlines, just as if I'd given up a game-winning home run:

WELCH QUITS.
PITCHER THUMBS RIDE FROM THE MEADOWS.
Stops for Beer at First Bar.
All Fucked Up.

I didn't like those kinds of headlines. I don't like losing.

I reached for the faucet and turned the water off. I felt like a damn prune, all wrinkled from forty-five minutes of hot water. My eyes stung from the crying and my chest ached from the sobbing. Deep down inside me, although I couldn't put it into words just yet, I knew I was different. I knew I was an alcoholic. I didn't know how I was going to do it, or what these people would do with me, but I was going to stick it out. I wanted to win.

Chapter Three

‹•••••••••••••••••••›

A Tradition of Drinking

‹•••›

I don't know when I became an alcoholic, not even after thirty-six big days and nights at The Meadows. I do know I was an alcoholic when I went to The Meadows. My second night at The Meadows, right after my long shower, I listened to the symptoms of an alcoholic and it made sense to me. I said, "Shoot, that's what I am," so I got up at the AA meeting and said, "I'm Bob, I'm an alcoholic." But how did I get there? How does anybody?

I go back home and my mom takes out the family albums. There's a picture of me striking out Reggie Jackson, a picture of me afterward, big smile on my face. I wasn't drunk when I struck out Reggie. I was stone sober for that man. I didn't even get drunk afterward. Went out and had a couple of belts with my family and rushed home to pack for the trip to New York. But I was already an alcoholic.

I sure as hell was an alcoholic the time in 1979 I chugged a bottle of wine in fifteen minutes and got drunk on the team bus giggling and crying, drunk as a skunk. I was an alcoholic when I gave Mary Ellen a hard time, and I was probably already an alcoholic on that college all-star tour to Japan when I stood on the edge of the hotel roof and started tightrope walking.

I know Rod Dedeaux of the University of Southern California, our head coach on that Japan trip, told me I was acting "just like an alcoholic," which was the first time I had ever been called that. In the best of worlds, I would have thanked him for the insight and maybe done something about it. As it was, it scared me for a second and then I forgot about it.

The one thing I know from being at The Meadows is that I can't blame baseball for my being an alcoholic. I've noticed that since Darrell Porter and Lou Johnson and I and some of the other guys went to The Meadows, there have been a lot of stories saying alcoholism and baseball go hand in hand. I don't think you'll hear any of us saying that.

If I went around blaming baseball for my being an alcoholic, could writers blame the tensions of a deadline? Could assembly-line workers blame the tedium of the assembly line? Could mothers blame the responsibility of raising children and keeping house? Can 10 percent of the population stand around and blame their occupations, when alcoholics reach into every possible job and income level in this country?

Like most alcoholics, I wouldn't mind having an excuse for my drinking. But I guarantee you, if you walked into an AA meeting and asked people if I am an alcoholic because of major-league baseball, they would say, "No way." Alcoholics are great people for denial, excuses. Bullshitting, really. They're good at it because they've worked at it for a long time: telling lies about where they've been. Part of the business of alcoholics is covering up. I'm not saying alcoholics are born liars. They develop the skill because they're alcoholics.

I see now where I used to need alcohol at every point in my life. It's like Bo Belinsky said when he was everybody's favorite playboy with the California Angels: "I drank when I lost and I celebrated when I won." I reacted the same way. The booze helped soften the losing and helped heighten the winning, but the main thing was, I couldn't face reality. The reality was too intense, so I would use a chemical to give me the mood I wanted. Alcohol is a chemical, a drug. When you're an alcoholic, you are addicted to a drug, is what it is.

Baseball is no different from other occupations, other ways of life, but I will say this: Baseball makes it easy for the alcoholic to move right along. There's beer just for snapping your fingers in the clubhouse, there're all kinds of parties, and you're on the road a hundred nights a year. You walk through a hotel lobby, and people are standing in line to buy you a drink. It's easy to say yes, if you're inclined to say yes in the first place.

Does baseball have more alcoholics then the 10 percent in the rest of the population? I couldn't say. Don Newcombe, the old Dodger pitching star, who kept tabs on me while I was drinking, thinks alcoholics might be 12 to 15 percent of ballplayers, maybe more. Ryne Duren, who is now an alcoholism counselor, says 35 percent of ballplayers have a drinking problem, including some of the guys you see on those amusing beer commercials. Some alcoholism doctors say no occupation has a higher percentage. It's hard for me to say. I know a lot of ballplayers who drink, including one or two who are going to lose their families, their livelihood, maybe even their lives if they don't do something about it. I haven't gotten around to grabbing anybody by the shirt and saying, "Look, alcoholism is a nasty disease. You've basically got three choices: Quit, go insane, or die." But if they're afraid they're going to die, they know where I am. Maybe people will listen to me more than they would to other people, because I was the first player to go through The Meadows.

I don't mean just ballplayers listen to me. I mean people, people in my neighborhood, high-school kids. I was in high school just a few years ago. If some doctor or teacher had gotten up in front of class and said, "Alcohol is dangerous," we would have laughed in his face. If it was lunchtime, chances are we already would have been flying on beer or pot or reds—pills to bring you down. But if a ballplayer, somebody near my age, had warned me, maybe I would have listened. I hope young people listen to me.

But where did it start? I look at my family photographs, and I see a regular little kid, well-dressed, well-fed, usually in the company of my mother and my father, or my sister, Diane, or my brother, Donnie. A good family, you can tell from looking at us. My father, Rubert, ran a lathe in an aviation factory for over thirty years. My mother, Lou-Nell, was always around when I was growing up.

When I was little, I was one of the brighter kids in the class, on the honor roll, doing artwork, starting to get attention for athletics. A little nervous, but a good kid. And a future alcoholic.

At The Meadows, they have a saying: "Nobody goes out and thinks up ways for screwing up their kids." I mean, there's no handbook for turning your pupil or your star athlete, your brother or your sister, into an alcoholic. They say there's no blame involved. It just happens sometimes. After I came out of my lengthy shower and started paying attention to what they were saying, I could see where I had my patterns of not showing my feelings even when I was younger. But compared to some of the environments I heard about at The Meadows, mine was pretty good.

Of course, the Welches are a drinking family. Everybody knows that when we get together, we like to drink and have a good time. I'm not pointing a finger at my family, because there are families like us on every block in town.

We didn't sit around and get bombed every day. No Skid Row bums. Drinking was associated with weekends and holidays and family gatherings, good times and bad times. At Christmastime we'd have parties at my uncle's house, and like my uncle says, "Well, hell, Bob, you thought it was the right thing to do growing up—to go out and get drunk." When Welches get together, we have a lot of fun. We love each other but there is a lot of drinking around.

I remember my father would drink sometimes on Saturday, and when he came home, Donnie or Diane or I would open a can of soup for him—that can opener was a challenge to us. We would have trouble opening the can, but once the can was open, he would heat the soup himself. It was always Campbell's chicken noodle soup. No other kind would do. It was like a little ritual sometimes on Saturday, but I never remember my father doing anything really bad. He'd finish the week and get a few drinks, just like a lot of other working people.

On my mother's side, there was drinking, too. All her brothers drank except for one, Teddy, the baby in the family. Maybe from seeing all his brothers drink, he didn't drink much at all.

I remember a couple of years ago at Thanksgiving time, my Uncle Charles was killed. He was driving his truck and some of those flammable chemicals exploded on him. He hung on for five weeks before he died, and when he died my mother and I drove down to Paducah, Kentucky, for the funeral, and I know that every night I was down there, I got as drunk as a skunk, partying with my Uncle Charles's daughters. Go out every night and get drunk.

I went to pick up my Uncle Jiggs in St. Louis and I was so drunk I drove eighty-five to ninety miles per hour all the way to Paducah. Just flew along, lucky not to get killed. None of the Welches could ever drink whiskey and control themselves. They'd do some crazy stuff, which is the way I got when I went over the line.

We never really talked about the drinking except in a joking way.

We're a fun family. My Uncle Bud says, "Hell, you think you got a drinking problem, I've spilled more than you'll ever drink."

My mom never drank too much and she's been very cautious about alcohol ever since The Meadows. She's been going to meetings of Al-Anon because she wants to be able to deal with drinking better. She says her life has been very simple compared to other people dealing with alcoholics in their families. She has met women whose husbands beat them up or wouldn't work, and my father has never done anything like that. But she feels bad that her son turned out to be an alcoholic, and she says Al-Anon is helping her understand more about herself. Like all mothers, she gets to feel guilty about her role, but I try to assure her that as far as I'm concerned she is a loving mother, and always has been.

My mom is dark-haired, a combination of Irish and Cherokee, like lots of people from Kentucky. I've read some books that say the Irish and the American Indians have a low tolerance for alcohol. My father's mostly Irish, too, so maybe that has something to do with my own weakness.

My mom has always been around for me when I needed her—when I was a little kid, and later when I was at The Meadows. I think she's had a lot of hard times in her life, and I'm sure she'd have liked to have more things. But I know that when I was a little kid and I asked for five dollars for a bat or a ball or whatever, she always found the money. And a lot of love besides. She knows more about hard times than any of my generation can know.

My mom came up to Michigan in 1942 because she was in a family of nine kids, and couldn't find anything to do back in Paducah. She came up and lived with an aunt and worked at U.S. Rubber and got to like life up North. She was telling us recently how she arrived at night, just a teen-aged girl from Paducah, and she saw the bright lights on Michigan Avenue, and she said, "Why, this is just like New York City," what she imagined a big city would be like, should be like. So she always wanted to stay in Detroit.

A lot of people were moving to Detroit in the Depression and during World War II, particularly poor whites and blacks from the South, looking for work in the factories, just like my mom. The whites seemed to find neighborhoods where they had lots in common. I bet most of the people in Hazel Park and Ferndale have southern roots. We're always talking how it's a red-necked neighborhood, that's the word we use. It's part of Detroit like in the song that Bobby Bare recorded, "Detroit City."

There are a lot of people who came to Detroit to make the cars, "but by night they make the bars." Lots of them still think of themselves as southern, and they want to go back down to Kentucky or Tennessee or wherever. Growing up around Detroit, I'm definitely from Detroit, but I'd say my roots are southern. My dad is definitely a southern man, a kind of quiet, very proud man, with certain ways of behaving and thinking he wouldn't change. Even while I'm writing this book, he's contemplating a move to Paducah, so he can go fishing and live a more peaceful life.

There was a time when my father couldn't wait to get out of the South. He grew up around Newport, Arkansas, and picked a lot of cotton when he was a kid. He came North in 1939 "looking for a better life," as he puts it. He came to Detroit and lived with his older brother, Ross, who later passed away. My father washed dishes at first, waited on tables, and then got a job in a tool-and-dye company. Except for the time out for the Army, he's been working in Detroit ever since.

Detroit is a factory city; everybody is aware of the motor industry. I think people talk more about cars there than anywhere else in the country. How can you help it? You drive along the highways and you see production signs—computerized up-to-date totals of how many cars have been produced that year at that factory.

It's been bad news the past couple of years—9 million cars in 1978, down to 6.2 million in 1980.

People make remarks that Hazel Park has a large per-capita membership in the Ku Klux Klan, but I don't know too much about that. I used to be one of two white players on an otherwise all-black team when I was a kid, and maybe some of my drinking buddies at the Rainbow Bar wouldn't care too much for that, but nobody hassles me about it, because they know I've got a lot of black friends. We've got a black family on our block, down from my uncle, but it's basically white and southern.

Ever since I was a little kid, those factories have been part of my life. I used to go to one with my cousin Dougie or my Uncle Ray, or go with my father to his plant, the Smith-Morris Company, a division of McDonnell Douglas, the airplane makers. I'd go visit my father, see everybody standing in their spot, putting in their time, punching a time clock. My father would carry a lunch pail to work, the same black one, for forty years I bet.

I was proud of my father going to work, didn't think badly of a factory, but now that I look back, my father was anxious for us to stay out of the factories. My father and my uncles always told us, "Bust your ass. Don't hang around. Get an education." My Uncle Bud had lost a couple of fingers at the hammer shop and he'd hold up his hand and say, "Don't get stuck in a factory, kid. You've got a good chance to make something of yourself."

This experience influenced me more than seeing the men in the family take a few beers on the weekend. I got the feeling I was expected to improve myself, to do better. There were expectations, ideals, goals. At The Meadows I realized just how confused I was about really making it out to California and playing ball. But growing up, it was, "Get an education. Get a job. Play ball. Get a scholarship." Not to push me. Just to make me want to excel.

There were times when the factory seemed like a good thing. I can remember going to college and seeing guys from my neighborhood making eight to ten dollars an hour in the factories, and driving new cars they bought at a discount. Meantime, I was mowing the baseball field at Eastern Michigan University to keep my scholarship. At the time I had to wonder if I was in the right business. Later I got to the Dodgers and the same guys were laid off by the auto makers and they were pumping gas for $3.50 an hour because they couldn't get a job in the trades. They had to hustle their ass for a buck. My father was lucky he didn't have to shift like that because he was in the airplane end of it. But I remember when my buddy, Bryan Carley, who played ball with me at Hazel Park, switched jobs. I was glad he got out of the automobile business.

It's gotten so bad that families are looking to leave the Detroit area. People who moved up from Kentucky and Tennessee during the Depression are now looking to go South again during the Second Depression, Detroit's Depression.

I saw an article recently that one bookstore in Dearborn sold 925 Sunday newspapers from Houston, 500 from Dallas, and 150 from San Antonio in one week, mostly to people looking for jobs. People would keep the help-wanted section and throw away the rest of the paper. One Sunday the *Houston Chronicle* had 112 pages of jobs, the *Detroit News* had 18. Texas, that's all people talk about in Detroit.

Go to Texas and get a job. And I was already out in California, living good.

I can see now where I was always comparing myself to my father, to my family, to my buddies. I can see where it was a hangup with me. Alcoholics have strong feelings, and they can't deal with them.

When I got to the majors I'd been sleeping on the beach out in California or lying around the sauna or pitching for the Dodgers or meeting girls and meantime I knew my buddies were hustling to make ends meet, freezing their asses off back in Detroit. I'd come back and want to let them know I was the same person I had always been.

It's a tough neighborhood, Hazel Park. People were raised to be tough. They're great competitors in sports, and they're the same way in life: chasing women, fighting in bars, drinking beer, playing pool. I'd go home from college or from baseball and there'd always be a card game, or just sitting around the Rainbow Bar, you'd be trading insults, good old verbal abuse. We'd be hollering and cussing up a storm. I'd go in there and they'd say to me, "Hey, when are you going to win twenty games?" and then I'd kick in the extra five dollars to buy a pizza because I figured most of them were unemployed. Or I'd buy a round of beer for the same reason. And drink some of those beers just to show I was one of the guys. I loved the beer anyway, but now it was a way to belong. I was on my way.

Chapter Four

◆◆◆◆◆◆◆◆◆◆◆◆◆◆◆◆◆◆◆◆

Addicted to Sports

◆◆

One thing was as popular as drinking back where I grew up, and that was sports. People drank and people watched sports. They really went together, when I think about it. The snow would be several feet deep in Michigan and you'd turn on the television on a Sunday afternoon and you'd watch a couple of football games and on every timeout they'd show a commercial of a bunch of former athletes hanging around in a bar, getting a buzz on, and trading insults and jokes and maybe even threats of violence.

The women didn't compete in sports when I was growing up, but they learned how important sports were to a man. They knew that on Monday night the guys would head down to the Rainbow and eat hamburgers and drink beers and watch Howard and Giff and Dandy Don. On Sunday afternoon you'd eat your lunch off a folding tray in front of a television set, with maybe a card of football games alongside you, so you could see how your bets were turning out.

The kids played sports because it was fun. As long as I can remember, I loved going outside and playing any kind of sport. We had a basket in the driveway, and we'd go out and play in the coldest weather, snow falling, we didn't stop. My older brother, Donnie, and my cousins Lloyd and Dougie would play daylight to dark. I was always playing with the older guys.

I went back to the Rainbow Bar one time after I was already with the Dodgers and this guy Mackey, who used to play with my brother, said, "I remember when you were the last one picked, Welch." I was always the kid, little Bobby, but I was able to hold my own with the bigger guys almost right away.

Sometimes I'd tag along with my brother, usually teasing him with my smart mouth. He and his friends would chase after me but nobody could catch me, I was so fast. "The Heckler," that's what they called me, I razzed them so much.

At The Meadows they tried to suggest I was pushed into sports by my parents, but I don't buy that. Nobody had to tell me playing sports was fun. We'd play whiffleball in the driveway, or we'd walk a few hundred yards to Martin Road Park, right behind the house, where we'd play hockey all winter on this frozen rink. It would get so cold I'd come home shivering and just fall in the doorway and say, "Mom, hurry up, take off my clothes, I'm so cold." I'd get warmed up and go out and get 'em again.

My parents never pushed me into sports, the way a lot of kids' parents do. I've seen it. The father standing on the sidelines yelling at the kid to play better, the mother getting in arguments because the coach won't play her son. Sure, my father liked to watch me play. Sure, my mother drove me to some games when I wanted better competition with black kids in the Detroit ghetto rather than in the suburbs. But it was always my idea. I wanted to be the ballplayer.

Even now, my parents are modest southern people who don't know how to lean on anybody. There are times when my parents come to see me play near Detroit, and my mother will write to the home team in Chicago or Pittsburgh and buy tickets rather than bug me for them.

I always wanted to make my parents proud of me. I'd tell Mary Ellen, "I just want my parents to see me play major-league baseball. Let them enjoy it, too." Heck, I was able to do better than that. I was able to bring them to a World Series game I helped save.

In high school I didn't even want my parents showing up for games. I don't know why. I just didn't feel as comfortable playing in front of them, but in college they started driving to Ypsilanti, and it was no problem.

But while I'd say they didn't push me, I would also say sports made me different, set me aside from everybody else. They brought this up over and over again at The Meadows, that I had always felt liked because I was an athlete. My whole personality was based on being a star. I'm not trying to puff myself up, but it was true. Even when I was a kid in the neighborhood, people would watch me play ball and they'd make comments.

Maybe it was only a game, but if I played better than the next guy, I'd get more attention. "Boy, you must really love basketball to be playing out here in the cold," or you'd hear remarks like, "Bobby sure has a good arm," or "Bobby can really scrap with those bigger boys." It wasn't even a matter of getting a swelled head, of being a show-off. It was feeling that maybe people liked me only because I could throw a ball hard. Of course, I never thought about it in those days. It didn't enter my mind until I was a twenty-three-year-old alcoholic at The Meadows.

I must have confused signals even when I was a little kid because my parents can remember when I'd come home and not communicate with people. They'd say, "How was the game?" and I'd say, "Oh, it was all right," and I'd wolf down my supper and go to my room. Later on they'd find out from somebody else that I'd gotten a couple of hits or scored a lot of points or whatever. We realized later that we didn't communicate very well in our family, just like a lot of families. I'd be holding in my feelings about myself, and maybe other people were holding in their feelings, too.

I started playing organized basketball at the age of eight, with my cousin Lloyd as the coach, and we won the league championship. My parents hung up pictures of our championship team around the house.

My father was always working at a steady job, and my mother was home when I was little. Every time I'd get hurt—my brother, Donnie, calls me "Big Foot" because I was clumsy around the house— my mom was there, or when Mom got a part-time job making floral arrangements, my sister, Diane, was around.

Diane is wonderful. We're really close. She was ten years old when I was born and she's been like an extra parent to me. She'd push me in the stroller when I was a baby or she'd try to take me to church or the drag races or just be around for me. When I was four or five years old, I remember helping dry and put away dishes. I was so short, I had to stand on a chair. One time I slipped and broke a glass, cutting myself. I was bleeding pretty bad and my mom was real upset. I didn't want my mom to take me to the hospital, but I let Diane take me. I always thought Diane liked that responsibility, but when I went to The Meadows, they gave us a lecture on families that showed how kids fit into certain roles. One of the roles is Little Mother; there are Little Fathers, too, but girls are more apt than boys to take on parental responsibility.

Diane and I have talked about that, whether she had too much responsibility and not enough childhood. I think after she was married and had a couple of kids, she realized my parents had never stressed a college education for her, but they always talked about it to Donnie and me. At The Meadows they suggested my family acted as if boys were more important than girls.

I love her kids, Erik and Jill. To me, it's like having my own family. I don't know when or if I'll ever have kids but I love being around other people's kids. I love picking out presents for Erik and Jill at the Dodger gift shop (I shouldn't admit it, but I get 50 percent off). I love going home and playing with them in the yard. One time Diane went out and saw me playing catch in the yard with my shoes off, running around in my socks. She called me "a little boy in a great big body." Now it's like a family nickname. When I announced I was an alcoholic, one thing I really worried about was her kids. I understand a couple of kids at school made remarks like, "Hey, I hear your uncle's a drunk." But they said, "No, he's an alcoholic." I want them to know about the dangers of drinking, but I don't want them to suffer because of my illness.

My brother, Donnie, is seven years older than me. Donnie was always smart but like a lot of boys he would get into fights at school. He's always been very outspoken. I don't know if he's suffered because of all the fuss over me as an athlete, but I guess there had to be some problems in that direction. I think there was some competition between us, but other times he'd let me get away with stuff, cheat in games, and I'd get mad if he'd give me an extra chance.

Being the baby in the family, I think I got a little less scolding than the two others. My mother says she was afraid she had been too tough on Donnie, and so she didn't want to be tough on me. Did that let me into a shell when I was a kid? I think Mom worries about that now, but she's also the one who gave me the most feedback at The Meadows and has continued with her Al-Anon attendance.

I started out being good in school. By the time I was with the

Dodgers, one sportswriter would describe me as a "man-child" who stared at his shoes and couldn't answer a simple question. Another sportswriter has said that I was the most spaced-out athlete he had met on the Dodgers. I wasn't that way as a kid. Teachers liked me, did special things for me. One teacher took a couple of us to New York City and Washington, gave me a love for travel at an early age.

When I was younger, I was one of the better students in my classes. In Mom's scrapbook about me there is a class newspaper from elementary school. At the end of the year they listed some of the "Memorable Moments": I was one of three kids who were neither late nor absent all year. I was on the honor roll twice, one time less than the three best students. I was one of five kids who received an A on every spelling test, 270 words plus spelling correctly every state and state capital.

At the same time, people wrote about "Carole and Bobby's romantic fights every morning at 11:15" and "Bobby's singing while he works" and "Bobby's silly laughter." I was a live wire, sounds to me.

At Webb Junior High, I won the sportsmanship award for physical education, and my coach, Charles Kirkland, the first black teacher I had, a terrific man, took me to the award dinner.

With my nervous energy I'd have to be finished before anybody else was done. I could read fast, I could read well out loud, I could get my math done. Kevin Smith and I would always be racing to see who could get done quicker. Plaster of Paris, whatever it was, I did good work and I did it fast. Even in junior high, I did good work, but when I got to high school, it just shifted down a notch. My A's and B's went to mostly B's and C's.

By the time I got to college, I was thinking about being a baseball player. It was my whole identity. I liked parts of school, and I liked to contribute, and if there were too many people talking, I might say to myself, "All right, all right, I'll talk, maybe I'll get a good grade." But I can remember by the time I was in high school and college, I was afraid what I would say would be wrong. I was afraid that I would sound like a jerk and embarrass myself.

I'd be shaking and nervous and hope that they wouldn't call on me. Then somebody else would give the answer and I'd say to myself, "Hell, I knew that, why did I let it slide?" That's one thing I'm learning now—be assertive. Don't swallow what you feel, what you know. Be in touch. But damn, it took me years to do that. If I feel somebody is screwing me on a business deal, I can call up and ask very specific questions, get right to the point. But when I was drinking, I'd just go out and get wrecked, and my anger would come out after the second or third beer—in the wrong way, to the wrong people.

The assertiveness was always there. I wanted to compete, wanted to win, but the only way I could do it was in sports. If we were playing one-on-one and I knew I could beat the guy, I wouldn't want to beat him so bad, or he wouldn't want to play anymore. So I'd keep it close, then beat him with the last basket or something. I can remember Kenny Wilson and I getting in fights, and how I'd always want to rub it in, keep it close. I was as assertive as hell on the court, and in class and at home I'd be swallowing my feelings, trying to look blank.

I was lucky I had the outlet of being an athlete. By the time most people were in high school or working their first job in the factory, they had become fans. They were getting their kicks rooting for the Tigers, the Lions, the Pistons, the Red Wings, the University of Michigan, Michigan State. Detroit is one of those old industrial cities, the weather just terrible enough that people spend a large part of the year indoors rooting for other people. They become good fans, really knowledgeable fans, letting out their aggressions on the athletes.

I was more of a participant, even as a kid. We might go to a Red Wing hockey game, and my friends would stand around the dressing-room door afterward trying to get autographs. I'd go with them, but it didn't mean that much to me. I was full of energy, wanted to do something.

I wanted to be a basketball player like Bill Russell, the center for the Boston Celtics, a great defensive player. That sounds weird because by the time I got to Hazel Park High School, I played defense only at the threat of death. I loved shooting the ball. I learned at an early age you don't get your name in the paper for setting picks for someone else. My coach, John Magiera, used to shout at us, "You guys play a bye-bye defense, you just wave at your man." And I'd laugh and fire up a shot. I was an all-league player as a senior in high school and then I realized that there were nine million brothers—black guys—who could jump and shoot better than me. I loved hoops, but it wasn't my best sport. Baseball was.

It was also the sport I loved to watch. I was a Tiger fan when I was growing up. We'd go into Tiger Stadium, one of the last of the old-time stadiums, painted dark green, with spark-plug ads in the outfield, fans tearing out seats and throwing 'em at the enemy right fielder. Welcome to Detroit. Let's give a Motor City welcome to Reggie Jackson.

The Tigers were a tough team, lots of old guys, professionals. I loved all of them—Dick McAuliffe, Al Kaline, Earl Wilson, Norman Cash, Willie Norton, Jim Northrup. The Tigers were a bitch. I saw Denny McLain's first game after he got suspended for gambling, and I saw Al Kaline make his debut at first base, but my favorite Tiger was Mickey Lolich, a fat left-hander who rode his motorcycle to work and was the hero of the 1968 World Series when I was eleven years old. I'd picture myself like Mickey Lolich, on the mound in Tiger Stadium, firing the ball past Curt Flood and Lou Brock in that World Series.

Years later I wanted so badly to pitch for the Tigers. The Dodgers? California? It was another world, man. I wanted to pitch for the Tigers, my hometown team, and those sons-of-bitches wouldn't even draft me because I had a sore arm as a junior in college. They said there were six hundred healthy prospects and they didn't need one who wasn't healthy. So now my dream has changed. Now I want to pitch for the Dodgers in a World Series against the Tigers.

Mickey Lolich, he put the idea in my head. I wanted to play in the major leagues, I was willing to work for it. That was my life. Get into the majors, everything would be all right. I always wanted to play at the toughest level, to prepare myself. One year my buddy Bryan Carley and I were playing in the local Hazel Park League and we heard about tryouts in Detroit, in some metro league, where they play good baseball. We said, "Wow, let's go down there and try out." We went out for the Little Caesar's Pizza in the Mickey Mantle League, a bunch of white hotshots, and we knew we could make their team. They said, "Get the hell out of here, we don't have room for you." We said, "All right, we'll find another team and we'll kick your ass in."

We heard of this other team in downtown Detroit and we met this black guy, Cootsie Brown, who asked, "Do you want to play on a good team?" and we said, "Yes," so he said, "I'll tell you what, you go to this high school at noon on Sunday and we'll put you on a team."

You've got to understand this was Detroit around 1972, a few years after the riots, with the National Guard riding the streets and whole neighborhoods on fire, and relationships between blacks and whites pretty bad. It wasn't hard to hear all kinds of racist shit back in

Hazel Park and I'm sure you'd hear the opposite in the ghetto. I'm sure people in Hazel Park would have said it was dangerous to go play in this area but we wanted to play in that league so Bryan and I drove down on Sunday in his beat-up old 1965 Cadillac.

We looked around and we were the only white people in sight. Black players and black spectators and these two kids from the suburbs. But this guy who must have weighed four hundred pounds, Ron Thompson, he heard about us from Cootsie and he took us and told his team, "All right, we've got these two new guys," and the next game I pitched and Bryan played second base. Right away we clicked with those guys, the West Side Cubs from the Kronk League, part of the Police Athletic League.

We won our league and went into a playoff, and wouldn't you know it, we went up against those bastards from Little Caesar's Pizza on their home field. Seven brothers and me and Bryan, and we whipped their asses. To this day I know playing on the West Side Cubs was one of the best things that ever happened to me. It really helped my relations with black people to the point where black guys would be among my best friends in the minor leagues and with the Dodgers.

Sometimes the West Side Cubs would come by and pick me up, a car full of blacks driving down my street. I made some good friends out of that, a guy like James Johnson. I remember after the 1978 World Series he came by with his wife and baby and stayed a couple of hours, just talking over the old days with the West Side Cubs.

Playing with the West Side Cubs and guys like Dusty Baker on the Dodgers is as good an experience as you could have in life. And to tell you the truth, being a major-league ballplayer, competing against the best, is about as good as anything you could do with your life, while you're young and have the ability. Still, I have to ask myself what sports did for my inner self.

At The Meadows I was told that I had been put on a pedestal by people. Some people in my group told me I was worried about my health, about my continued ability to play ball, that if my arm went bad, I wouldn't be the same person. My parents had never seen it that way, but now my mom asks, "Did Bob think if he wasn't good enough, if he didn't perform, if he didn't entertain, maybe people wouldn't like him?" I had never thought about it before, but my mom is probably right.

Chapter Five

❖❖❖❖❖❖❖❖❖❖❖❖❖❖❖❖❖❖

The Fragile Athlete

❖❖❖

Even before I identified as an athlete, I was getting hurt. I think it was the same hyperactivity that made me drink hard. Alcoholics never do anything halfway; they'd drink up the ocean if it had ethyl alcohol in it. I'm the same way with drinking or pitching—I can't do anything halfway. In the spring of 1981 I decided just to go out and heave the ball at the start of spring training, so much that I hurt my elbow. I couldn't break into it slowly.

My first recorded injury was long before I became a pitcher. Hell, I was only in kindergarten. My second day. I told my mom, "Don't come meeting me after school because I want to walk home with the other kids. I'm a big boy now." To prove I was a big boy, I tried to bail out of a swing in a park, just like a paratrooper. I broke my arm.

As soon as that healed, I was wrestling with one of my cousins and fell off a stoop, fractured my collarbone. I took it easy for a few weeks until that was better, then I climbed up on some building material in the park and somehow cut my head open. Ten stitches. Another time I caught my foot in a guy's bicycle and got twisted around, fell off, and broke my thumb. I was around eight years old by then.

These were trivial compared to my sickness when I was ten or eleven. We went down to Brownsville, Texas, where my mom's brother was living. We crossed the border into Mexico and on the way back we sneaked a parrot across the border.

We carried the parrot back to Paducah with us, where we left it. I didn't feel well in the car on the way back home to Michigan but I didn't complain because my parents had bought tickets for a Tiger game.

I still remember going to that game feeling so hot and watching Tommy John pitching for the White Sox. Years later TJ would be my teammate on the Dodgers, a friendly, positive guy, and I would tell him how much I enjoyed that game. TJ didn't enjoy that game at all because when Dick McAuliffe thought TJ was throwing at him he wrestled TJ to the ground and broke his collarbone. I loved the fight, but my mom kept saying to me, "Bobby, you've got a fever, don't you think you ought to go home?" and I'd say, "No. I want to watch the game."

The next day they took me to the doctor, who said I had a temperature of 104 degrees and my eyes looked kind of yellow. He said, "Take him home and give him this medicine," but I was still sick the next day and the doctor put me in the hospital, particularly after he heard about the parrot. The fever was up and my knees were swelling and they gave me a spinal tap and transferred me to Children's Hospital. They said something about "parrot fever." My mom says I looked like a skeleton lying there in the hospital, and I guess I felt like one.

I remember a doctor being in my room and telling my parents, "I can't promise you anything because I can't pinpoint anything." The fever would go down, but then it would shoot up again.

I was scared. I remember one time I woke up and there were seven doctors standing around, looking at me. I heard them talking about liver damage and I got it in my mind that they were going to remove my liver, which I did not take as a positive sign. I was scared but I didn't ask any questions. I mentioned it to my mother, and she got assurances they weren't going to take out my liver, since there was no such thing as a liver transplant.

Years later at The Meadows, people asked me if I had thought I was going to die. I can't say I did. I can just remember this black period in my life, when something was going on that was threatening me. They suggested maybe I had put the fear of death so far back in my subconscious that I did not even know about it, and maybe I used alcohol to hide from my fears. It's quite possible.

After thirty-nine days in that hospital, they put tubes in my ears to try to drain an ear infection. The fever came down immediately, and I was out of the hospital on the forty-second day, but I still had to wear the drainage tubes in my ears for nearly a year. They wouldn't let me play football in the fall, and I played basketball with tubes in my ears.

I still had the tubes in my ears when I played baseball at the end of the summer. My mom still recalls her terror of seeing me misjudge a fly ball and get conked on the head and fall down. But my head wasn't injured, just my pride.

Maybe I was preoccupied with injuries. In Mom's scrapbook about me is this little story I wrote in my school newspaper in grammar school. I had forgotten all about it but it reminded me I had been pretty good at writing when I was a kid!

The Little Boy Who Couldn't
by Bobby Welch

There was a little boy who couldn't see. He was a very smart boy who could play all sports very well.

It all started one day when he was walking across the street. His father hit him and he was blinded by a piece of glass that flew into his eye.

After the accident, he got a seeing eye dog. Then he went to a special school for blind people. He learned to read words by feeling them.

Many doctors operated on his eye. Finally the doctor got the piece of glass out of his eye, and he could see again.

When I got to junior high, I had to have a physical examination in order to play sports. The doctor was checking out my groin, and he told me I had only one testicle. I was as surprised as he was, but the only thing that bothered me was that I could not play sports until I checked it out with my family and my doctor.

I went home and told my mom what had happened and she said I had an operation when I was younger because one of the testicles had not descended properly. I didn't even remember it being done. I don't think I was upset by this, and I had my mom write a note to the school that said I had permission to play sports.

I don't think I ever worried about the operation except to wonder whether I could have children, but I know at least one former teammate who had the same thing, and he's got a couple of kids.

I found out more than ten years later at The Meadows that my mother had been feeling guilty because she hadn't told me about the operation, and she was afraid she had contributed to my drinking. To me it was not important, unless it was part of a general feeling that my health was always in danger.

My injuries continued into junior high. I was the quarterback on the football team until I tore up my knee and had to be taken to Beaumont Hospital. By that time, I had been there so many times, they had my records waiting for me when I arrived. My mom remembers me saying, "They won't let me play football anymore," and they didn't.

I stayed free of injuries for six whole years, until I was a sophomore at Eastern Michigan University. Coach Ron Oestrike told us to lay off basketball between baseball seasons, but I got into a heavy one-on-one in the gym and tore up my knee a few days before Christmas. They put me in Beyer Hospital, where Dr. Waldomar Roeser performed a great operation that probably saved my career. I'll never forget they had me in the children's wing for some damn reason, and the Brownies came up to sing Christmas carols, accompanied by Santa Claus. They left me some presents—a Yo-Yo and jacks and a ball and some comic books—and I was afraid my college teammates would come in and see me with the stuff.

Maybe the injuries and illnesses bothered me more than I know, gave me some fear of death. I know I really got bombed when my mom's brother died in the truck accident, and when Ron Oestrike's father died, I got wasted and was sitting in the last row of the service, just laughing my head off.

A couple of teammates and I got so hysterical from drinking and from being at the funeral home that we couldn't even stay at the service. We went laughing and stumbling into the night, wandered into a shopping mall, tripping over curbs, really messed up. I decided to tackle a store mannequin and I did—knocked it right over. Then I decided I was going to fight a German shepherd but I fell off a fence and got thirteen stitches in my head, which was probably less than what the German shepherd would have done to me.

Still drunk, I went to a girl's house, where she was going to fix some spaghetti for me. I was looking for a place to sit down, and I chose the stove. By the time I realized it was hot, I had burned my ass. To this day you can see the marks, or so I'm told. Was all that craziness triggered off by sitting at a funeral service for my coach's father, or were there deeper fears about illness and death from my past?

My mom still thinks I was more troubled than I let myself know. She remembers my response when I was a teenager and she urged me to become a doctor.

"Mom, I don't want any part of it, not after what I've been through," I told her. Because I couldn't talk about my feelings very easily, maybe I did have a deeper sense of having been injured too often. For me, drinking was a way to forget.

Chapter Six

Learning to Drink

It was inevitable that I would drink, growing up in Hazel Park. It was always there, wherever I went—family occasions, in the neighborhood, at school. Some people didn't like it, but everybody tried it, and I liked it.

The first drink I can remember in my life was when my sister Diane married Paul Karlovetz when I was around ten years old. I can remember my cousin Dougie and I grabbing hold of a couple of glasses of Seven-and-Seven and chugging them down.

The first time I got drunk was when I was around fifteen or sixteen and we were on our way to a football game. My friends Charlie Trulove, Steve Scott, and Bryan Carley and I went to this party store—that's what they call a liquor-and-food store in Michigan—and bought a bottle for each of us. The guy had to know we were nowhere near the legal age but he didn't care. He later lost his license for selling to minors.

My choice was a bottle of Mogen David blackberry wine. No idea why I chose that. I liked the taste and just kept chugging it down until it was almost gone, hanging out in Longfellow school yard. I just figured, "This is it, now it's my turn," like it was some initiation into a fraternity, coming of age in Hazel Park. I think I felt a little sick and acted a little crazy but I held it down. Bryan wasn't so lucky. We were cutting through the park and he got sick all over his shoes.

After that, I just kept drinking with the other kids. I don't recall ever asking myself whether I wanted to stop. I just kept drinking. Plus, I was good at it. I was a good drinker. I could guzzle down a lot of beer, more than most guys.

Looking back, I must have gotten a reputation early. I can remember a guy in my neighborhood, Craig, saying to me, "Aw, Welch, you'll never play baseball, drinking will end your career." I was probably in high school or college at the time. I wonder what he saw in me that he could make a statement like that. I must have been acting up with a few beers in me, which only got worse as time went on.

In high school I felt part of two different societies. I loved playing sports, but I never went strutting around the halls in my basketball jacket. Like a lot of schools, there was a division between the jocks and the rockers. I had buddies on both sides, and I didn't want to alienate my rocker friends by dressing like a jock with one of those team jackets.

Drinking made everything easier. It was a wonder drug. Science in action. I would get a buzz on and I would stop being afraid of girls. When I was starting in high school I was afraid to talk to them. I was shy. The girls liked me, but I was scared of them. The way they looked, the way they acted. But with a couple of beers in me, it was all right. In the tenth grade, the eleventh grade, after a few beers, I'd feel part of the crowd.

I remember going to a Sadie Hawkins Day dance and getting high, and I didn't worry about having skinny legs or being unable to express myself. I wasn't afraid to say hello.

There was a girl in one of my classes who really liked me. She had a car and we'd go to lunch to a place called the Shanty and have ourselves eight-nine-ten beers. I was the life of the party. We'd go for a ride in her car, then I'd go back to school and fall asleep in class.

When I was in the twelfth grade, I finally lost my virginity. Another girl who had already graduated used to come around and throw a few hints at me. I finally got up the courage to say, "Well, I might as well go for it." She had her own apartment, and it was pretty easy. I got worried when she started throwing hints about getting married, and I said, "Whoa, I'm planning on going to college." I didn't see her after that, but I was more interested in girls and comfortable with them.

That's when I began talking to Mary Ellen, who was in my chemistry class. Mary also was a cheerleader at the junior-varsity games, and I got to see her at the gym. One of our first dates was at Tiger Stadium. I was drinking a beer every inning and yelling at the players, verbal abuse. Mary added to the festivities by jumping up and kicking over the containers of beer where I'd left them on the floor. She didn't mean it, she just got excited, but now she jokes, "Bob, I was trying to tell you something."

Of course, it wasn't always beer. There were plenty of drugs going around at Hazel Park, just about anything you wanted. They had gotten popular in the sixties as a way to expand your mind, but we didn't care about consciousness-expanding. We just wanted to get wasted. Not to think at all. Alcohol was much more acceptable to the grown-ups because it was their way of getting smashed and it was legal. They'd see kids with a fifth of whiskey, that was all right, but if they saw a kid with a joint they'd have a fit.

I made a lot of money one winter, giving a guy some money and he'd sell the marijuana and give me some of the money back. A business investment, pure and simple. I was always scared when it came to drugs, even though I did smoke pot and tried a few reds, three for a buck. For two dollars you could have some reds and some beers. You could get by and get high.

I liked depressants and I liked the feeling of getting drunk. Pot made me jump around, want to eat, want to go to sleep. Our crowd didn't have cocaine in those days, but nowadays people are snorting cocaine, not only in California, but everywhere. I tried it before I got straightened out and it was relatively the same thing as pot. I couldn't see buying something and running it up your nose. Didn't make any sense to me. But beer? You could sit in a bar all night and drink and tell stories and laugh your ass off.

The drinking began to intrude on my other activities. When I was a senior in high school I went out drinking on a Friday afternoon when we had a basketball game that night. We had a good team that year, won a lot of games, and I was one of the cocaptains, but that didn't stop me from putting down fourteen beers at the Cozy Lounge in the afternoon. Usually I took a nap and my mom fixed a steak before a game, but this time I fell asleep on the bathroom floor, just wiped out.

My mother called in and said, "Are you going to eat that steak?" but I just threw my uniform in the bag and went over to the high school and fell asleep in the parking lot. One of my friends parked near me during the junior-varsity game and saw me asleep in the car and woke me up, or I'd probably still be asleep there today.

I went inside and told the coach I had the flu. In the locker room I put on my uniform backward about four times until I got it right. I went out there during warm-ups and I was so drunk, I tried a lay-up and couldn't hit the backboard. I made a quick right, ran down the stairs into the locker room, took off my clothes, and jumped in the shower to try to sober up halfway decent.

I'm sure my coach, John Magiera, knew I was drunk. He didn't start me, although I was one of the high scorers on the team. With about thirty seconds left, he put me in the game, to embarrass me, I'm sure. I stumbled around out there without getting killed and when the game was over we all had a laugh in the locker room about it. It was a big joke with some of the guys: Get a load of Welch. I was hysterical, I thought I was so funny, not realizing what an idiot I was.

When I came out of the locker room, my cousin Dougie was waiting. It was the first time he had come to see me play, and what did he get? Thirty seconds of me weaving from side to side. Later my brother Donnie and my cousin Lloyd told me what an asshole I was, asking how I could go to a ball game drunk.

"Aw, I was protesting," I told them. "I'm protesting because one of my teammates was kicked off the team this week."

That was a lie, of course. One of my teammates had been kicked off the team, but I doubt that I cared. I just wanted to get drunk.

What was there in my personality that led me to screw up before a basketball game? I can see where I was nervous, always anxious about something. By the time I was in high school I was a nail-biter, always chewing my nails.

I was so nervous I couldn't take uppers. When I got into baseball, I once tried a greenie, a pill that gives you energy, which was the last thing I needed. I couldn't get the ball anywhere near the plate and never tried that again.

I didn't want to be up. I wanted to be down, to hide from the feelings I had, fear of not being liked, being nervous. And whenever I had a good time, I gave credit to the alcohol and the drugs, not to my friends or myself or to life.

Now that I do a lot of speaking about my alcoholism, I tell kids not to associate all good times with drugs and alcohol. In Hazel Park and I'm sure in all towns people associate good times with alcohol. I hope some kids will listen to me, because they can see what happened to me, how I almost blew my chance to play baseball because the drinking caught up with me. People will listen more to the story of someone who's been there. If they think it's just a lecture, they'll tell you to screw off.

That's why I'm careful not to lecture my friends about drinking. They knew me the way I was. I don't have to tell them. When Eastern Michigan University invited me to be roasted at a charity dinner, Bud Yanus, who now pitches in the Montreal farm system, told people: "Bob's definition of a social occasion was when the sun went down and the moon came up." Bud also told people that I had two favorite kinds of beer: "warm beer and cold beer." With testimony like that, I don't have to enhance my legend as one of Hazel Park's all-star drunks. They know.

All the time Mary Ellen and I went out for dinner, I always thought it was the bottle of wine that made the dinner enjoyable. If it was, our relationship wasn't worth anything in the first place. When we first started dating, we'd order a bottle of wine with dinner and I'd drink three quarters of it. I thought I was having a great time, but I can't remember the taste of the food, or whether we talked about anything, or whether I really cared what she was thinking. What I really cared about was draining that glass as fast as possible and finding excuses to "refresh" her glass, which meant I had the right to fill mine to the top again. These are lessons a drinker learns early—how to get more for yourself, how to get messed up faster. I was a bright boy; I learned my lessons well.

Now that I'm sober, I can finally see what it looks like to be drunk. I never could see it when I was in the state. I go into a restaurant and I can spot a drunk a few tables away. Hell, I can hear him.

Like the night I went to Gibby's Restaurant in Montreal, right in the Old Quarter—snails, rack of lamb, sautéed mushrooms on the side, fresh bread, real espresso, and the waitress doesn't try to make us feel guilty when we don't order any wine. Just a perfect night on the town with my acquired taste for quality. I'm sitting there with George Vecsey and his son, David, and we're talking baseball while the noise from the next table is getting louder and louder.

I look over and there's this good old drunk, talking too loud, singing, spilling water, making faces, just being obnoxious. It's somebody else's birthday and he's ruining the party for all of them—his wife and two other couples. The women are nudging the men as if to say, "Just ignore him," and his wife is embarrassed, and deep down below his goofy smile you can see a malicious glint that shows how much he's enjoying his act. Whassamatter, can't a guy have a good time? This is probably a successful man but he cannot handle alcohol. The man cannot afford to drink.

When the dinner is over, the five other people walk to the coatroom but he belts down the last one. Can't let good wine go to waste. As the man weaves unsteadily between tables, David bets he will fall into somebody's soup. Instead, he discovers some buddies and starts telling them jokes with no punch lines, his baggy pants hanging over his shoes. Finally, his wife comes back and drags him away by the elbow. At our table, I silently offer a prayer: Dear God, let somebody else drive home.

I go back to Hazel Park now and I realize I've changed a lot in the past year. A lot of my buddies, I can see where their priority is to go out and get a buzz. Work during the day, get screwed up at night. It's a continuous cycle. My priorities have changed in some ways, but I still like to go back and hang out with them.

Did you ever go into a bar when you were the only one not drinking? You realize everyone's shouting at twice the normal conversational tone, because their senses are not quite right. But when I go back, I'm still friends with all the guys who came along with me. I was in the Rainbow last winter and my buddy Black Jack told me, "You know, you old son-of-a-bitch, you ain't changed a bit."

What could I say? I told him, "Black Jack, man, I'm the same as ever. I just stopped drinking." You can't fake it when you go to the Rainbow. They give you some verbal abuse to see if you still can take it. It feels like you fit back into the old puzzle again. You just slip back. Except that I see it with different eyes now.

There're a few guys who have beaten it, at least for now. There's even a bartender at the Rainbow who stopped drinking the last time I was in there. Cecil the bartender. I remember Cecil kicked me and Bryan and Terry Druckenmiller out of there one time a few years ago, after we drank a bottle of Southern Comfort on the drive from Ypsilanti to Hazel Park. We started fighting, making a mess, and Cecil called the cops and got us kicked out, but he used to drink in those days, too.

Now Cecil says he took a five-day alcoholism program and stopped drinking. That's got to be rough, being a bartender and knowing all your old drinking buddies are right across the bar from you. If everybody stopped drinking, the man would lose his livelihood, but some people can have a few drinks and be all right. Cecil knows the schedules of some of the AA meetings and he told me a good one I could go to last winter. A few of our buddies at the bar heard us talking and started making comments.

"Hell, I'm going to go, too," one of my buddies said. I didn't pressure him, just told him to give me a ring on Sunday. I wouldn't pressure him because I wouldn't want him to turn around and push a joint or a beer at me. I don't want to tell him to stop unless he decides he's got a problem.

That's one of the biggest problems an alcoholic has when he stops drinking. Do you become a strict prohibitionist? I know a couple of people I want to see stop, a few in Hazel Park and a few in baseball, because frankly they're killing themselves.

Everybody's aware of the nondrinker at the Rainbow. Cecil was closing up the joint the other night, around 2:00 A.M., and a couple of guys were loaded and they claimed Cecil was throwing hints about them stopping altogether. At closing time one of them yelled, "Well, Cecil, this is the last one I'm having—tonight." Everybody laughed.

Cecil and I didn't think it was too funny because we know when somebody is nervous about drinking, makes too many jokes about his own drinking, that's a pretty good sign he's worried about it, deep inside. I was like that when I was drinking. Denial. People would make a remark and I would bristle.

I've gotten to a point where I just don't want to be around if everybody is really drunk. After closing time at the Rainbow, the last time I was in town, I went over to somebody's house and they were telling stories about going to a hooker joint, and who could stay sober, and who couldn't, and they were playing cards, but to me it sounded like a bunch of guys getting drunker. So I went home. Sober. It took me a long time to be able to do that, and I almost lost everything before it happened.

At the Rainbow I see a lot of guys like myself—guys who had the same athletic ability, maybe even more, but they got involved with drugs and drinking and hanging around. Maybe they were as good as they were ever going to get in high school, and just couldn't go any farther, or maybe it was the chemicals. I was lucky, but it took me a long time to cope with wondering why I had been fortunate enough to make it. I didn't realize how much success bothered me until many years later.

Chapter Seven

Majoring in Baseball

The only thing that made me different from anybody else was my right arm, and I had nothing to do with that. I could throw the ball hard, and it kept me out of the factories.

At Hazel Park High School, Coach Chuck Mikulas used my arm at shortstop until I made four errors one day. Coach still likes to tell how "Bob Welch once broke up two double plays in one game—on defense." But the way it happened was, at our field the sun goes down at a fierce angle in the springtime and when you bend down at shortstop the sun glares right in your eyes. So I bobbled four balls in one game, big deal. Next day I was at second base for the remainder of the season and the following year I was finally switched to pitcher, and I pitched us to the state runners-up in the Class A tournament.

I knew there were scouts at our games. Those guys in the alpaca sweaters who brought their own folding chairs and stopwatches and notebooks, were not exactly relatives of the right fielder. Because of rules protecting amateur athletes, the scouts couldn't talk to us directly, but I thought they were interested, and I got it in my mind to be the next Mickey Lolich.

I kept waiting for the Tigers to draft me but the Chicago Cubs did me the honor of drafting me on the fourteenth round of the annual major-league draft. Some guy offered me five thousand dollars to sign with the Cubs, but hell, I could have cleared five grand selling marijuana in the neighborhood. Guys from my town were getting factory jobs at eight and ten dollars an hour, enough to keep you high sometimes, but I never really saw myself working in a factory. In all the leagues I had joined, I had never seen anybody with a fast ball as good as mine, so I told the Cubs to give the five thousand dollars to the needy, and I decided to go to college.

Not many of my friends went on to college. Our parents hadn't gone to college, and maybe it wasn't stressed in a lot of homes around Hazel Park, and a lot of kids couldn't afford college at all. Somebody's older brother would be working at Ford or Chrysler and come around with a new car and good jeans and tickets for a rock concert, and other guys would say, "Who needs college?" But my parents had been talking up college, and it was sort of understood I would give it a try.

More than a few colleges tried to recruit me, but the school that really cared about me was Eastern Michigan University in Ypsilanti, about an hour's drive from Detroit. The two baseball coaches, Ron Oestrike and Roger Coryell, would come around to games and manage teams in summer leagues and run clinics and camps in the off-season—always looking for prospects. Oestrike (or Oak, as a lot of people call him) likes to come off as good old country boy from Flat Rock, but he knows how to keep his baseball program solvent. He raises money by getting the beer concession at rock concerts in Ypsilanti, and using his players as the labor force, which I never minded a bit.

Oestrike attracted me by showing he was upgrading his program. He had won the 1970 National Association of Intercollegiate Athletics tournament—with Roger Coryell pitching the deciding game—but now he was aiming for the National Collegiate Athletic Association tournament . . . . going big time. He had two-week southern swings lined up every spring, so you could try to stay even with the southern schools. I looked at the schedule and saw such baseball powerhouses as Texas and Arizona and California, and I signed on the dotted line.

In the summer before college I pitched for Adray Photo, an amateur team composed of athletes for Eastern Michigan University. I attracted more attention, striking out twenty-two batters in the final game of the state tournament and going on to the All-American Amateur Baseball Association tournament in Johnstown, Pennsylvania. I began to realize I'd be worth more money in the next pro baseball draft. And I also knew that if I started at Eastern Michigan, I'd be committing myself to three years of college before I could again be eligible for the draft. However, if I went to a junior college, I could be drafted the following spring.

Late in August, just before college started, Pat Sheridan, who coached another team in the Adray league, talked me into attending Ranger Junior College in Ranger, Texas. He told me a lot of baseball scouts sent their prospects there for a year. I was easily swayed at the moment and I called up Ron Oestrike the day before school began and said I was going to Ranger. Oestrike shouted over the telephone, "Are you shitting me or what?" But he regained his cool and warned me, "Look the place over and whatever you do, don't attend any classes until you're certain. If you attend a class and then leave you'll lose your eligibility for a year. And call me collect if you have any problems."

Oak must have seen photographs of Ranger, Texas. I got off the plane and it was like an outpost from some cowboy movie, really out in the boondocks, a few barracks that passed for dormitories. If it hadn't been for the baseball diamond, you could have shot a movie about the Alamo there. I took one look and said, "I've got to get out of here." I went back to the airport and called Oak collect and said, "Hey, man, I messed up," and went back to Michigan. I think I was in Texas for three hours.

I liked college ball right away. They had a good fall program, working on fundamentals. Roger Coryell worked on my motion by playing catch barehanded. I couldn't throw hard, but I'd get in a groove. Oak was a hard loser, too. One time we lost a doubleheader at Western Michigan University, when Oak really wanted to beat those guys. He made us run a few miles in the pouring rain the next day, but I could handle it. I spent most of the day getting my body in shape, and a few hours at night pouring all kinds of garbage into it. Explain it to me. We also went fishing behind the baseball stadium at Ypsilanti, along the banks of the Huron River.

I wasn't as much into education as I should have been. In small classes with only five or six students in them, if you cut class, they would know quite easily, so I would go. But in some of the lecture classes with two hundred or more people, they wouldn't know the difference. On tests, I'd sit near somebody and watch them marking up their IBM sheet, and I'd do all right.

One professor I liked was Sally McCracken, who taught Interpersonal Communications. She taught a lot of things that would be stressed when I wound up at The Meadows a few years later. She was like Lynn Brennan, my counselor, talking about picking up on key words people use, how your body indicates your feelings, nonverbal communications. I liked the speech and psychology courses more than I ever knew at the time and they prepared me for the biggest thirty-six days of my life. But at the time I was mostly interested in baseball.

In my freshman year, 1975, I was made a starting pitcher and was named to the all-league team along with our other pitcher, Bob Owchinko, who later went to the major leagues. We had a good shot to reach the College World Series for the first time in Eastern Michigan history, but first we had to win the Mid-East regional tournament against the University of Michigan. For anybody growing up in Michigan, the University of Michigan and Michigan State are the two powerhouses, particularly in sports. If you go to Eastern and some of the other state schools, you hear little digs from your friends. You come to resent Michigan and Michigan State and hope that someday you'll have your chance to knock them off.

I got my chance in the regional, after saving two games in relief because Oak needed help. I started the final game against Michigan and blew them down until the rains came down just before the final inning. We had to wait until the next day, and my arm would not permit me to pitch again. Chink did the honors for the final inning, and later I was named Most Valuable Player of the tournament. Then we played in the College World Series in Omaha but I was blasted in my first start and we finished only fifth.

My second year in college looked bad in December. Oak had told the baseball team players not to indulge in basketball games during the winter, so we wouldn't tear up our baseball muscles, but I couldn't stay away, tearing up my cartilage and ligaments. I called Oak on the telephone to tell him about the knee. He was used to strange telephone calls from me ever since my escapade to Ranger Junior College.

I went back to school with a cast on in January, and attended a few classes, but most of the time I just got bombed up in my dormitory.

Every night was party night. I didn't know what else to do. I started rehabilitating the knee with Mike Strickland, the trainer, hoping to get back by the middle of the season. I got myself in good shape faster than I expected, and went out West for the first trip. I talked my way into a start against Arizona State, which is usually the best team in the country. I lasted five innings and we upset them.

My knee healed, and I began to have a super year. Bob Owchinko was our ace, and he'd draw the other team's best pitcher in the first game of a doubleheader, while I'd sit around waiting to start the second game. Then I'd just go in there and fire the ball. I pitched a perfect game against the University of Detroit and a no-hitter against Central Michigan and lost only a couple of games all year. The scouts were having to work extra duty because of me.

The first time I attracted any national attention was when Roger Angell of *The New Yorker* wrote a long article about scouting after spending time with Ray Scarborough, a scout for the California Angels. In the August 16, 1976, issue of *The New Yorker*, Angell described how he and Scarborough had gone to a Bowling Green-Eastern Michigan doubleheader in which Owchinko held on for a 5–4 victory in the first game. Scarborough said: "He's got a chance to make a pretty good pitcher."

Then Angell wrote:

> The second game began, and after Bob Welch had thrown about six pitches Ray Scarborough exclaimed, "There's a good-looking body! He's got these boys overmatched already."
>
> Welch, a right-hander, looked even taller and stronger than Bob Owchinko, and he threw with a kind of explosive elegance. There was something commanding about him.
>
> "See out there?" Ray said. "See him cocking his wrist like that behind his back? That could strain your elbow. It could hurt him. He's cutting the ball a little—turning his hand—which takes off some velocity. If he did it a little more, it would be a slider. I wish he'd turn loose—he's got a real good arm."
>
> Welch fired two fast balls, fanning the batter.
>
> "There!" Ray said. "I like that! He comes off that mound like he means business." He stood up, smiling with pleasure. "I believe I'll be making a trip back here a year from now. Maybe we'd better go quick, before I get dissatisfied with the whole 1976 draft."

I was happy at Eastern Michigan, felt I was getting somewhere as a ballplayer. Oak says I never gave him any trouble around the field, and it was true. Even when we weren't playing games, I'd be out there working out, just bullshitting with the guys, because baseball was really my whole life.

When I wasn't playing ball, I was drinking. I had a reputation for drinking even as a sophomore. Oak says they used to call me "The Magician" because I'd arrive at the practice field from nineteen different directions.

I caused him some problems on a trip to Texas, though. They take the game seriously down there, drawing four or five thousand people into the beautiful University of Texas stadium at Austin. They knew I was a hotshot and they got on my ass just like major-league fans do. We played our games and that night we were staying in a hotel. Oak warned us that if he caught us out that night, he'd kick us off the team. But I went out anyway with two other guys. We were crossing the highway to meet some women, but there was a fence in the middle of the highway. We started climbing over but this policeman came along and spotted us. He asked us what we were doing and we told him—hell, we were all drunk anyway—"We're baseball players." He said, "I bet your coach would love to hear about this." I remember one guy saying, "You're probably a father yourself. How would you like it if a policeman arrested your son for having a good time?" The cop turned us in and Oak had to get us a few hours later.

Coach didn't kick us off the team, though. I'd have been surprised if he had. He held a team meeting and warned us not to do it again. Hell, I was the best pitcher on the team and the other two guys were regulars. I didn't do it to cause him any trouble, to challenge him. I didn't want to get caught. I just did it.

We qualified for the College World Series again and this time we finished second to Arizona. After the tournament, I got a couple of beers in me and traded my socks to a lady in the hotel kitchen in exchange for a fish, a big trout with its head and tail still attached. I figured the season was over and I wasn't going to need my socks for a while but there was no telling what I might do with a fish.

I was wandering around the hotel with this fish and I spotted Ron Hassey, the catcher for Arizona, who's now with the Cleveland Indians. I got on this big glass elevator with Hassey and I said to him, "Hey, Ron, great game, no hard feelings, you were sure a lucky fish." And I reached out to shake hands with him. Not knowing me, he extended his hand and I gave him the fish. Put it right in his hand. He wasn't too happy about it.

That summer I was chosen to play for a college all-star team in a series in Japan—the opportunity of a lifetime. I wish I could say I remember a lot about Japan, but the truth of the matter is, I was so drunk most of the time that I remember very little. I pitched around ten innings in twenty-one games because we had so many pitchers. Mostly we just sat around, which was dangerous for me in those days.

One day they let me start a game with around twenty thousand people in the stands. I had a no-hitter going into the fifth inning, when I gave up a homer. We were ahead, 9–1, and they removed me after that inning to give somebody else a chance, but I got mad and made an idiot out of myself.

I went back to the hotel and stole about five or six cases of beer and brought them up to my room. I threw 'em in the tub and drank more than a few and went up to the roof and started firing bottles off the roof at the cars. Then I started "tightrope walking" on the ledge of the roof, which was about twelve inches wide—not nearly wide enough for a guy with a bunch of beers inside him.

Later that night I switched to an inside sport, kicking down hotel doors. Did a pretty good job on one and had to pay fifty dollars in damages. While I was on my rampage, one of the coaches, Larry Cochell of Oral Roberts University, caught up with me and told me to behave, but I just cussed him up and down. Or so they said. The next morning I did not remember a thing. Everything I have just described was told me by other people, a sure indication I was already suffering alcoholic blackouts.

That all happened on our last day in Japan. We flew to Los Angeles and stayed for a day at the University of Southern California. Rod Dedeaux, the famous baseball coach at that school, who had been our head coach on the Japan trip, took me aside and said:

"You've got as much talent as any pitcher I've ever had, but there's one thing you've got to do. You've got to stop drinking. You act just like an alcoholic when you've had a drink."

That was the first time anybody had ever used that word to me. I had always thought alcoholics were shriveled-up old guys who live in cheap hotels on Skid Row, or just sleep in the streets. Those words stopped me short for a while: "just like an alcoholic." Dedeaux was telling me that the problem went deeper, more than just having a couple of beers. He could see that my personality changed when I drank, that I abandoned all pretenses at being civilized. He could see there was a troubled human being inside that crazy kid heaving bottles off a building. He had enough guts to confront me about it, not just throw subtle signals the way other people had done, but he didn't have enough of a hold on me.

The way I learned at The Meadows, the way to stop an alcoholic is to gather his closest associates and family and everybody lists the things that he's done while drunk, to show he is a totally different person when drunk. This is what my family and Rick and Robin Sutcliffe would do to me in 1980. Rod Dedeaux cared about me, he really tried to help me, and so did Larry Cochell, but they just didn't have enough time or control to do more about it.

After the Japan trip, I flew to a summer league in Grand Junction, Colorado, and tried to follow the advice of Dedeaux. He had really impressed me. I discovered that the word had gotten around about my drinking episodes in Japan because my coach in Colorado, Sam Suplizio, asked me what I'd done and I said, "I just raised a little hell." I tried to cut down in Colorado for a couple of weeks but then I got to know people and began to try to outdrink them all. Still I had a good summer playing for Suplizio, who had been a promising Yankee farmhand about the same time as Mickey Mantle. I had been picked for another all-star trip, this time to Korea, but when I got out to California, I realized my ribs were aching from pitching since March. I tried to pitch two innings but my ribs hurt so bad I couldn't breathe. I told the coaches I wanted the United States to be represented by somebody healthy, and I went home to see my family and Mary.

I got home and could hardly wait to get messed up again. Some of the guys from Eastern Michigan University took a tour of Stroh's Brewery in Detroit, which for most people would be a pleasant tourist attraction, to see how beer is made and sip a glass of brew. For me, it was a chance to get as drunk as a skunk, mouthing off to people from the brewery. We topped off the day by going to a Tiger game, where I had a few more beers.

I had always enjoyed heckling people—my brother or ballplayers —but I was no longer a little kid with a squeaky voice, I was a fully grown, six-foot, three-inch adult with a loud set of pipes and a green Eastern Michigan University jacket. We got good seats near home plate and, with a few beers in me, I started giving verbal abuse.

I was getting on Vern Ruhle, a young pitcher for the Tigers, convinced that I was a better pitcher than he was. Don't ever believe ballplayers who say they don't hear insults from the stands. We do. If you've ever sat near the field, you've probably seen a player snarl back at a fan who's been getting on him. I was too messed up to notice whether Vern Ruhle heard me or not.

By the time I came up to the major leagues in 1978, Ruhle was with the Houston Astros. (He developed into one of the best control pitchers in the National League in 1980, pitching the Astros to a Western Division title ahead of us.)

I had forgotten all about insulting Ruhle when I batted against him for the first time. He had perfect control all night, but—wham—the guy hit me right in the ribs with the first pitch. Knocked the wind right out of me.

It wasn't until I got to first base that I remembered having been a fan in Tiger Stadium a few years earlier. I have no idea if Ruhle really remembered me from Detroit and plunked me on purpose, but at the moment it crossed my mind.

This is a perfect example of how an alcoholic goes around making enemies. I fully believe that I would have gotten myself killed if I had gone on drinking. I would have insulted the wrong person at the wrong time, and my ass would have been dead.

In Alcoholics Anonymous, the sixth step toward recovery is apologizing to other people for what you've done. This has its practical side, particularly for an alcoholic who probably made enemies he doesn't know about. So to Ron Oestrike, Roger Coryell, Rod Dedeaux, Larry Cochell—if I ever hurt you in any way, I apologize.

Chapter Eight

◆◆◆◆◆◆◆◆◆◆◆◆◆◆◆◆◆◆◆◆◆◆◆

Going West

◆◆

My career almost ended before it began. There was one pitch when I felt my elbow explode, and I thought I might never pitch again. This is the frightening thing about being a pitcher—worse than any other sports position, really.

In football, somebody can tackle you the wrong way and your knee falls apart. In basketball, you come down the wrong way on your ankle and you're out for the season. But in pitching, you throw the ball the way you've done it a million times before and one time the pain rips through your arm. I'm sure other pitchers always have this in the back of their minds. I know I do.

The pain came on our southern swing in my junior year. I knew it was going to be my last year in college because I was eligible to be drafted and I was eager to turn professional. I could always get the degree later. I felt great all winter throwing in our field house. In March we took off by bus from Ypsilanti to Missouri, to Texas, playing games in warmer weather each day, good to feel alive again.

We got into Austin, where the fans remembered me from the years before and started getting on my case. I enjoyed that part of it. I pitched four or five innings on a cold, windy day—not throwing well at all. Then I threw one more pitch, an overhand curve ball, and my damn elbow just went—aaaagh!

Oak came out and asked what was the matter and I said, "My damn elbow hurts." He suggested I throw one more pitch, which I did, a fast ball, a scary, painful thing, I'll never forget it. It was as if somebody had stuck an ice pick into my elbow.

I went to the dressing room, packed my elbow in ice, and accompanied the team to Arkansas, hoping the elbow would improve. But it didn't. Oak said, "Let's get you back on a plane to Michigan," so I went home and rested while the team worked its way North.

I could see my entire career disappearing as I waited for the club to come North. When Oak got back, I had to tell him it wasn't any better. He was in a pretty rough spot. He was trying to build Eastern into one of the country's best baseball schools, Bob Owchinko had already signed with the San Diego Padres, and now I was saying I couldn't pitch.

A lot of college coaches probably would have told me to take some shots and give it the best I had. I'm sure Oak was tempted. A lot of people on campus might have thought I was faking it, but Oak seemed to agree I was in pain. I remember one time he said to me, "We could put you out there. You're better at three quarters than anybody else we have." But he never urged me to pitch.

One day I was warming up on the sidelines ready to go into a game against Ohio University. I decided I was going to try it, but Oak came over and looked at me and went with another pitcher. I continued to warm up, and a few pitches later the elbow hurt again. Our doctor told me, "Don't throw any more for a while." I was very scared at the time.

After that Oak had me take treatment and work out on my own. The man never made me feel guilty, or tried to pressure me into pitching, and I owe my career to him.

Some scouts lost interest in me, while others would walk away from the game if I was warming up in the bullpen. They wanted to see if my fast ball still had any hum. One guy came around more than most: Dale McReynolds, a tall, white-haired guy, a former schoolteacher, very straight, very intense, from the Los Angeles Dodgers. He always tried to be around when I was testing my arm. The man was willing to get off his ass and check me out, and by the time May rolled around, he had to like what he was seeing. My fast ball was starting to pop again.

I liked throwing the ball hard, knowing the scouts were watching, but I also got the feeling of being on inspection, like a horse or something. Scouts would put their heads together and discuss my muscles, my elbow, my form, my mind, like racehorse owners deciding whether to breed me or send me to the damn glue factory. At the time, I just accepted it as the way the world works. Years later at The Meadows I would realize how I felt less than human when scouts did everything but put their fingers in my mouth to see if I had strong teeth.

I knew the baseball teams drafted amateur players in June, and I realized I needed some advice about what to do. Bob Owchinko had signed his contract a year earlier with the help of Robert L. Fenton of Detroit, a lawyer who has major clients in sports, show business, and the auto industry. I contacted Bob Fenton but he reminded me that if he seemed to be representing me, I would lose my amateur standing. Under college rules, if you are represented by an agent, you are already a professional. The only thing Fenton could do was advise my father to send out letters to some clubs, saying I was interested in signing. It's all right for your father to do that, but not an agent.

One of the clubs my father contacted was the Los Angeles Dodgers, partially because they had impressed us with their scout, Dale McReynolds. To this day, Mac says other scouts will come up to him and say, "How much did you pay Welch to get him to sit out his junior year?" They are suggesting that Mac and I cooked up a deal in which I would claim I had a sore elbow so other clubs would not draft me. Mac says a few scouts even think my college coach was part of the deal. He says he and Ron Oestrike always joke about the fancy car Oestrike was supposed to receive for hiding me. It's funny on one level, but also insulting to honest people like McReynolds and Oestrike. And me, too.

What these other scouts don't take into consideration is that Mac and Ben Wade, the head of the Dodgers' scouting department, were smart enough to follow me out to the bullpen and see that my arm was coming back. I had no deal with the Dodgers and really didn't know or care anything about them. They were just another team—with good scouts.

On the day of the draft, I went out for a bicycle ride. On the way back I bought a candy bar—a Nestlé's $100,000 bar, hoping it would bring me luck. I got back to the dorm and my roommate, Chuck Gillum, shouted at me, "Hey, man, you're going West." I asked him what he meant and he told me, "You just got drafted by the Dodgers." I had seen a few games on national television and knew they played in this beautiful stadium in Southern California, and they had a third-base coach-turned-manager named Tom Lasorda who was always saying he has blue Dodger blood in his veins. But I was too busy playing ball in Michigan to have much image of a Los Angeles team in the other league.

Dale McReynolds came to Hazel Park and said I should go out to California and let the Dodgers take a look at me before they could make me an offer. I knew I was going to sign, so I asked Bob Fenton to accompany me and my father to Los Angeles. We flew to California, first class, on the Dodgers, and checked into a fancy hotel in Beverly Hills.

I was very impressed with the way that the Dodgers were putting me up. I looked around my hotel room and saw piles of thick towels with my initials on them. Even the damn cocktail napkins had my initials on them.

Man, I thought to myself, the Dodgers must really think I'm a great prospect if they have my personal monogram put on everything. I still felt that way as we left the hotel to go to the ball park and I glanced back at the fancy sign that said: BEVERLY WILSHIRE.

The first stop was at the office of Dr. Frank Jobe, one of the most famous sports doctors in the country, who was supposed to check my elbow. He seemed more concerned with my knee injury from my sophomore year. But he decided I was fully recovered in both places. He sent me to Dodger Stadium.

I had no real image of Dodger Stadium except from the game or two I had seen on television. In Detroit, Tiger Stadium is a dingy old dark-green ball park, on a downtown corner. Been there a million years, surrounded by parking lots and bars, kind of a Skid Row with pennants flapping in the breeze.

Dodger Stadium was like a castle. We breezed over a freeway—a highway surrounded by lush plants—and then started climbing this mountain road.

As the car climbed, you got glimpses of a ball park up there, like one of those hilltop castles in Europe that could withstand any attack. I remember somebody telling me how it used to be a wilderness, Chavez Ravine, where an old hermit woman kept goats, until the O'Malley family built the stadium for the 1962 season.

The parking lots are all terraced along the hillside, and you enter the park from the top, looking down. I think my father and I both were impressed with the beautiful pastel seats—light blues and oranges, everything so clean, nothing like Tiger Stadium. You had the feeling that if you dropped a hamburger in the corridor, you could pick it off the floor and eat it.

We walked to the Dodger office, passing a gift shop with all kinds of T-shirts and caps. In the office we were met by Al Campanis, the Dodger general manager, an Old World gentleman in a suit and tie, who told me to go to the clubhouse to get ready for my tryout.

We took the elevator downstairs and the clubhouse man, Nobe Kawano, who's been with the club forever, showed me to a locker. There was a creamy white home uniform with the red and blue Dodger trim on it. I can't remember the number they gave me, but the shirt did not have my name on it. I looked around and could see the Dodgers starting to arrive for the night game. I could recognize Don Sutton, Tommy John, Davey Lopes, but nobody said anything to me.

I got dressed and was directed to the bullpen out behind left field, where Campanis and Ben Wade introduced me to Mark Cresse, their young bullpen coach, who was going to catch me. I started loosening up, just tossing the ball to Cresse, and I could feel my entire body coming together after the first few pitches. I was throwing fast balls and sliders and I knew I had some real nasty shit. The ball started popping into Cresse's glove and I couldn't wait to get it back again. All the pain from the spring had gone. Ron Oestrike had allowed me to recuperate. I still could throw.

I looked around me and I could see some of the Dodgers drifting over. I heard one player say, "Get a load of this kid."

I was firing the ball and actually wishing I could get into a game, just go out there and pitch that night. Campanis turned to my lawyer and said, "I've seen enough. Let's sign him," and that was it. The show was over for the night.

Before he left, Campanis told me, "We'd like you to stay away from throwing the slider. We want you to throw the overhand curve."

I nodded in agreement, but when I got to the clubhouse, Don

Sutton came over and told me I looked good and said, "Listen, I don't care what anybody says. You know what got you here. You've got to be your own pitcher."

I've always remembered that advice, probably the best I've ever gotten. Sutton was great, from that first meeting. He never looked at me as a rival, even though I was a right-handed pitcher more than ten years younger than him. He always stuck up for me, taught me a lot of things, like how to pitch when you don't have your best stuff. I know I miss him, now that he's taken that big contract from Houston.

I finished changing and caught up with Bob Fenton, who told me they had worked out a bonus of fifty-five thousand dollars. That was fair. I signed the contract and the Dodgers told me I would go to San Antonio, their second-highest farm team, in the Texas League. After playing for Oak at Eastern Michigan, I would never have to go through the rookie leagues like a lot of young guys. That's what college baseball can do for you, if you go to the right school. I got three years of education and moved right into double-A ball with a fifty-five-thousand-dollar bonus. It seemed like more than I could have dreamed. All I had to do was produce.

We went back to the hotel and ordered up some whiskey and some beers, all on the Dodgers. I was with my father and Fenton, and my brother came up from San Bernardino and a buddy from Hazel Park, Leo Lafler, came up from Laguna Beach. We just sat around and toasted my career with the Dodgers. As I recall, it was one of those rare times when I knew when to stop drinking. Had a few pops and went to sleep.

I got to San Antonio and it was the first time I had ever lived that far from home. I didn't have a car. I didn't have an apartment at first but stayed in some hotel until I got settled. I felt really alone until I got friendly with some of the black guys on the club, like Marvin Webb and Cleo Smith, who seemed to have more time for fun, I guess because they were single. A lot of the white guys were more distant, probably because they were married.

Plus I got the feeling that a lot of the guys didn't like the idea of me jumping in there, being the No. 1 draft choice. We were all competing for the major leagues, really. There was less feeling of team than I had ever noticed in baseball. In college, some of us were prospects and some were not, but we played together as a team. In the minors, you figured maybe one or two guys would make it, and you wanted to be one of them. As it turned out, Jeff Leonard went to the Astros in a trade, and Joe Beckwith, Ted Power and I wound up with the Dodgers, and nobody else really did it.

I had a slow start, really, just learning to get my curve over. They were letting my arm get stronger and would take me out after five innings or so.

Dale McReynolds says he checked up on me after I reported to San Antonio. He says the manager told him, "Geez, I can't understand this kid. I say something and he just gives me the fisheye, the blank stare. What's going on in his mind?" McReynolds says he assured the guy that I was a hard worker and something of a free spirit, loosey-goosey. But really, what I was doing was hiding myself. I was getting drunk to cover up all the time when I couldn't be on the pitching mound.

The best two weeks of the summer happened when Mary Ellen came to San Antonio while we had a long home stand. This was really the first time we had ever lived together for more than a few days at a time. I had known Mary over three years, going back to chemistry class at Hazel Park High School, and our relationship had been growing all the time.

One thing I had found out about Mary: She was definitely not like some of the girls who had thrown open propositions to me back in high school. It took us a year to get to know each other before we even began necking—her decision, her values, I should add. After that, she might come up to Eastern for a weekend or we might borrow her parents' cabin up in the woods for a weekend or something. By the time I signed in pro baseball, I knew she was going to be special to me. She had high standards in every way: the way she took care of herself, the way she insisted on a college degree, even the way she wanted me to act. She was always sweet, always positive.

It was a big event when she arranged to come down to San Antonio the summer of 1977 after finishing her freshman year at Western Michigan University in Kalamazoo. I didn't have a car, so we spent the two weeks just hanging around the motel apartment—in the room, out in the sun, eating meals, taking walks, going to the ball park. She'd tell me stories about her classes, how she was going to have a career when she got out of school. We'd talk about our families, about all the people back in Hazel Park. Sometimes Mary would sing pop songs to me in her cute little high-pitched voice. On that two-week home stand, for the first time, I began telling Mary Ellen Wilson that I loved her.

Living with somebody, even for two weeks, was an adventure. It still is. No matter how much you love somebody, your personalities are bound to be different. I'm restless, introverted, don't need a lot of conversation or affection. I found out quickly that Mary likes me to show her affection and love. Mary says I only got out of control a couple of times from drinking. I did most of my drinking away from her.

We had two good weeks getting to know each other better, and then my team went on the road and Mary went back to Michigan. I finished the season with a very sub-par 4–5 record, but the Dodgers thought enough of me to send me to a winter league in Tempe, Arizona, where I was named to the all-star team. I also won a long-distance race for pitchers. I've always been proud of being in shape, and I had bet I could beat all the pitchers, which I did. We celebrated with a few beers, and I remember they had to carry me up to my room. My reputation was getting established quickly in the Dodger organization.

I spent the winter working out with the basketball team at Hazel Park—and getting drunk. I was a professional baseball player now. I had some money in the bank. I was going to play the part.

I pulled a real beauty on New Year's Eve. Mary Ellen and I had plans to go out for dinner at a fancy restaurant, then go to a party. I couldn't wait for the main event, however, but pulled the alcoholic's trick of getting a buzz on somewhere else, so I could have a head start. Alcoholics will do that, just as they will volunteer to fix drinks for everybody else, so they can sneak a belt or two while they're working.

Before I picked up Mary Ellen, I decided to say Happy New Year to Jim Penzabene, a good friend of mine who used to go out with Mary's sister. It just happened that Bean was working New Year's Eve at Scotty's, the party store he owns. I felt sorry for the poor guy because he had to work on New Year's Eve, so to drown his sorrows, I belted down a bottle of wine from his store. Actually Bean tells me I belted down two bottles, but I remember only the first.

By the time I picked up Mary, I was drunk. We got to Sixteen Mile Road and I pulled over and let Mary drive. When we got to the restaurant, at a motel, my cousin Dougie said, "You're already loaded."

We got to a table and I was doing the honors, pouring the wine, and I remember spilling a glass of wine on Mary Ellen's lap and talking smart to Dougie's wife, Pat. The people at the next table asked me to move because they thought I was going to spill wine on them, too, and to serve them right, the woman at the next table wound up spilling a bottle anyway. I was screwing up everybody.

We finished dinner and I was so drunk I couldn't walk. We got to the other party and I went into the john and passed out on the toilet seat. Just fell asleep for an hour and a half. Mary went looking for me and saw a Welch was registered at the motel so she knocked at the door but it wasn't me. By that time I was outside in the parking lot, temperature below freezing, throwing up. Pat took a picture of me just before that, staring at the camera, leering, making an ugly face. It's really ugly.

I should get that picture blown up into a poster and look at it whenever I get the urge to drink. The picture is ugly—ugly and sad. Makes me curdle at the stomach to know I was ugly like that. Alcoholism is an ugly disease, and I just could not control it. It is quite apparent in that picture that I was a human being totally out of control, getting worse all the time. I undoubtedly consoled myself by saying I hadn't hit bottom—yet.

In Alcoholics Anonymous, they call this the "Yet Syndrome." It means an alcoholic says to himself: "I haven't ruined my health yet, I haven't lost my job yet, I'm not on Skid Row yet." As long as you can convince yourself you haven't lost it all, you can continue to drink, which is just what I was doing.

I was certainly jeopardizing my relationship with Mary. She didn't understand my outbursts, my insulting her. She tried to deal with it by keeping her dignity, by respecting me, by loving me, by not bad-mouthing me in front of other people. It never got to the point where she threatened to leave me and, in fact, she walked out on me only one time, one Christmas, when I got so smashed and started yelling at her. She just silently walked out and went over to my house and talked about it with my mom.

Mary always felt I would outgrow it, would behave better the next time, because our love was growing deeper. That winter of 1977–8 was beautiful, even in the sad days before spring training. I didn't want to be away from Mary for months at a time anymore. I went up to Kalamazoo for the last few days and we stayed in her room, laughing, loving, crying.

The last night we must have stayed up all night. I asked her to sing every song she knew, "Where Have All the Flowers Gone?" pretty pop songs, in that little sweet voice of hers. Next morning I put my stuff in my backpack, like any other twenty-one-year-old, and walked her to the bus stop. She got on the bus to go to class and I started trudging through the Michigan snow toward the train station. She told me later that she was crying in the bus and I damn well know my eyes nearly froze from all my tears. I still felt sad as I headed to my first spring training.

Chapter Nine

◆◆◆◆◆◆◆◆◆◆◆◆◆◆◆◆◆◆◆◆◆◆◆◆

My First Alcoholic

◆◆

In the spring of 1978 I went to Florida with the Dodgers for the first time. I had heard about their camp in Vero Beach but I did not believe the stories until I got there. It was like a paradise—great dining room, comfortable dormitories, beautiful ball field and training rooms, three practice fields, a whole row of batting cages. There was a swimming pool, four tennis courts, and a theater with a different movie every night.

The biggest luxury to me was the golf—one eighteen-hole course called Dodger Pines and another nine-hole course, surrounding the complex. Before they started playing exhibitions in the second week of March, you'd finish your work at noon and play eighteen holes of golf in the afternoon. And everywhere you went, the smell of oranges from a forty-five-acre citrus grove. If that's not paradise, tell me what is.

People told me the Dodgers had taken over the land in 1948 when the government didn't need a naval air station there anymore. Walter O'Malley, the owner of the Dodgers, built the only privately owned baseball training camp in the country, more luxurious than a lot of private clubs I've visited. It was an earlier version of the Dodgers' buying the goat pasture in Los Angeles and turning it into Dodger Stadium—goat droppings into pure gold.

The free time of spring training was not all good because I would find ways to get bombed. People came down to visit the players and would invite me to go out drinking. Sometimes I would drink all evening. Sometimes I would start in the afternoon.

In their thoroughness, the Dodgers even had a lecture on the dangers of alcohol. They assembled a bunch of the younger players in a locker room one morning, and in walks this huge guy named Don Newcombe—about six-foot-four and weighing about two-twenty, with a big nose and chin that seemed to stick about a foot in front of him. A very pugnacious man. You could tell just from the way he strode into the room, like one of those Roman centurions in a Charlton Heston movie.

I had heard Newcombe's name around camp. I knew he had some kind of front-office job with the Dodgers—director of community relations—and that he had been one of the best pitchers in baseball about twenty-five years earlier, for the Brooklyn Dodgers. Later I found out he was also one of the best-hitting pitchers, who was used as a pinch-hitter between starts.

I have since heard Don Newcombe speak a number of times, so his speeches tend to blend together in my mind, but I still remember that morning in Vero Beach when he announced that he is an alcoholic who had ruined his playing career through drinking. He also told us he worked for the federal government, sharing his experiences on the dangers of alcoholism.

I was not thinking about myself in the slightest when Newcombe began his talk. As I recall, he said his earliest memories were about growing up in a "drinking family" in New Jersey, where his father was a chauffeur for a wealthy family.

"My father drank beer during the week and whiskey on weekends," Newcombe said. "He gave me home-brewed beer when I was eight years old. They all drank something. Many's the time I saw my father couldn't go to work on Mondays because of what he drank on the weekends. But I thought that was how it was."

That part of his talk did not touch me at all because I had never seen my father miss a day of work because of drinking. I was not relating to Newcombe's speech in the slightest.

Newcombe told how he had gained a hope that blacks like himself could play in the major leagues when Jackie Robinson was the star rookie for the Dodgers in 1947, and how he and Roy Campanella, the great catcher who is now confined to a wheelchair because of an auto accident, helped the Dodgers win the 1949 pennant.

"I don't think I was an alcoholic in those days," Newcombe said. "I only drank a beer or two on the night before I pitched. But after a game I would drink six cans of beer in the clubhouse just to get liquid back in my system. Then my father and I would drink a couple of six-packs on the drive back to New Jersey, and we would drink at night at home."

He described how his marriage fell apart and how he moved out to Los Angeles with the Dodgers in 1958, but was drinking so much that the Dodgers traded him to Cincinnati that spring. He fell in love with Billie, who is now his wife, but nearly killed them both by driving his car into the opposing lane when she criticized his drinking.

Later he told her he did not remember swerving the car, and she thought he was lying. Newcombe told us how alcoholics often suffer blackouts and don't remember what they did. I thought that was very interesting. Of course, I didn't think it applied to me.

Newcombe told how he stumbled around with Cleveland in 1960, slipped to the minor leagues in 1961, and finished his career in Japan in 1962, antagonizing the Japanese with his drinking habits. I never even made the connection with my own drunken episode in Japan, when Rod Dedeaux told me I acted "just like an alcoholic."

Newcombe summed up his baseball career for us:

"In 1956 I was the best pitcher in baseball. Four years later I was out of the major leagues. It must have been the drinking. When you're young, you can handle it, but the older you get, the more it bothers you.

"I could make excuses. I could say it was the pressures, the criticism in the papers, being one of the first blacks in baseball, but the truth is: I am an alcoholic. I have a weakness with alcohol, and I let it drag me down."

Newcombe told how he could not hold a job after baseball and how Billie Newcombe, a religious woman, had threatened to leave him. One time he picked up a knife while he was drinking and another time he almost drowned his son in a swimming pool.

"To this day, I don't know why she didn't throw scalding water on me while I was passed out one of those times," Newcombe said. "I wouldn't have blamed her if she did, the way I treated that woman."

Finally, he recalled, his wife began packing to take the children to a safer place, but Newcombe got down on his knees and placed his hand on the head of his oldest son, Donald, Jr., and make an oath he would never drink again.

"In my mind, if I ever drank again it would endanger the life of my son," Newcombe said. "My wife told me: 'Well, you've done everything else. You might as well try one more time.' But this time I meant it. If I had to choose between alcohol and Billie, I chose Billie."

Newcombe said he had stopped drinking on his own, without any help from Alcoholics Anonymous or other groups. He said at first he tried substituting ice cream for alcohol and ballooned up to three hundred pounds. He added that it took him three years of not drinking to accept the fact that he was actually an alcoholic, rather than just somebody who drank too much.

From my vantage point today, I think it is safer and easier to get support and understanding from a place like The Meadows and a group like Alcoholics Anonymous rather than to try to stop on sheer willpower, the way Newcombe did. As I recall from his talk at Vero Beach, he did give the other side to it.

"I'm not saying my way is the best way," Newcombe said. "Maybe it was my professional training as an athlete. I always had pride in running hard in practice. Maybe my pride was still there. I'm not putting down any group. People need fortification any way they can get it. But a man still has to do it himself. God upstairs cannot make you stop if you don't want to. The important thing is to realize you've got to do it yourself."

Newcombe told us that as ballplayers we would be traveling a lot, staying up late at night in hotels with plenty of temptations to drink. He told us we would be tempted to drink to relax, to laugh, to feel we were more manly. But he told us over and over again that he was happier in every way now that he didn't drink.

He told us that part of his job with the Dodgers was to help anybody with a drinking problem. I didn't think he was addressing me, but I was impressed in a distant way when he told how people will discuss diseases like cancer or diabetes more openly than alcoholism, which is true. People die of alcoholism but their doctors and families cover up by giving another cause of death. I also think that was the first time I heard Newcombe say that alcoholics comprise 10 percent of the population and that he personally believes ballplayers have a much higher rate than that. Ten percent. That would have meant three or four guys sitting around in uniform in our clubhouse were alcoholics. I wondered who the poor bastards were.

He told us he would be glad to talk to anybody with a problem, and could recommend programs or groups that would help. He said he had gotten to know a lot about Alcoholics Anonymous, and how the meetings were open to anybody. He said our anonymity would always be respected if we came to him, and urged us not to wait until our careers ended prematurely, the way his had done.

"I destroyed my baseball career and nearly ruined my family and my life," he said. "Don't let that happen to you. If you've got a problem, admit to yourself: 'I'm sick. I'm a drunk. I'm an alcoholic. I'm a sick person and want to get well.' You'll always be an alcoholic, you'll never be totally cured, but you'll find ways to make it lay dormant. You'll learn that the only thing that keeps you from being drunk is not taking that first drink.

"In baseball, there's a lot of drinking, but people don't want to face it. As long as you don't embarrass the club, they may not notice your drinking. I had friends who died young because nobody cared about them drinking. The Dodgers care. I care. You can come to me."

I remember feeling sorry for Don Newcombe that day. The poor guy, it must be tough being an alcoholic, I thought. The guys in the clubhouse were impressed with his powerful, articulate manner, but when he offered his room number at the hotel in case anybody wanted to call him, I doubt anybody did. I didn't need to talk to the man. It was his problem, his disease, not mine.

I was so impressed with Newcombe's talk that a night or two later I went out to a bar after dinner and got loaded. Coming back with another young ballplayer—I'd better not give his name because he's still in the organization—we stole a golf cart from the Dodger golf course and we wheeled out to a liquor store to buy some beer.

We sucked up those beers as fast as we could and I volunteered to drive us home.

Coming back, we had to cross one of those bridges over a drainage ditch, which must have been twenty or thirty feet down, and not much water in it. There may have been not much of a moon that night and the bridge is narrow enough that a sober person would have to be careful—but I was totally smashed. I had no business on that cart at that hour in my condition. I figured I could just blast right over the bridge, but I must have been going at a bad angle because I hit the railing and the golf cart toppled over.

For some reason, the Man Upstairs must have been watching over me because the cart did not topple over the railing, but just kind of hung there. We jumped out of the cart, leaving our extra beer bottles behind, and ran through the golf course to our rooms.

That same night they found the cart and started asking a lot of questions. My buddy and I were safely back in the dorm, but they checked out a bunch of other players and narrowed down the suspects. The coaches had a pretty good idea who had done it, and questioned me carefully the next day, but with true alcoholic cunning I lied like a bandit and said, "Why is everybody always blaming me for shit like this?" I was so indignant, they dropped the questioning, and I figured, well I've put it over on them again.

Chapter Ten

◆◆◆◆◆◆◆◆◆◆◆◆◆◆◆◆◆◆◆◆◆◆◆◆

The Promised Land

◆◆

Maybe the reason I loved spring training was because I was pitching so well. I even got to pitch against the Yankees for two innings after I struck out three of them, and somebody said they clocked my fast ball at ninety-three miles per hour. Al Campanis said after the game that my fast ball "puts him in the Tom Seaver category." I think I was loose because I knew I was ahead of schedule. The Dodgers wanted me to open up in their triple-A minor-league team at Albuquerque and I was making it difficult for them. One day I picked up the paper and saw Al Campanis quoted as saying, "If I had any guts, I'd put Bob Welch on the big club but I've got rubber legs." I laughed when I read that. He said when I came up to the Dodgers, "it wouldn't be to sit. He'd be in the rotation," as a starter. Personally I thought I was ready.

I got to meet Tom Lasorda, the manager, and listen to his stories about the Great Dodger in the Sky. I would get messed up on occasion and give them my famous stare. I think Lasorda was a little hesitant about breaking the bad news to me about Albuquerque because he was uncharacteristically silent one day.

"Bob, we've got to send you out," he finally said. "Don't be mad."

"Hell, I ain't mad."

"You're not?"

"Hell, no. I'll be back."

I went to Albuquerque and pitched opening day and won four of my first five decisions. The competition at the triple-A level seemed even stronger than the year before, at San Antonio. All the guys and their wives knew they were only one step away from the major leagues, from Dodger Stadium and big money and California, and they wanted to get there first.

One of the best pitchers at Albuquerque was Rick Sutcliffe, a tall, cocky, red-headed guy who had been drafted No. 1 by the Dodgers a couple of years ahead of me, right out of high school. I had met him in Arizona in the instructional league, but now we were starting back-to-back, knowing the Dodgers were already loaded with good pitchers.

There is a certain aura about being the No. 1 draft choice. Obviously, you know you have a lot going for you, and the club wants you to succeed, but you're not sure about the other guy. You're competing; it's that simple. Guys would talk about Sutcliffe behind his back, say what a jerk he was. I personally didn't think that was called for—I liked him and his wife, Robin—but everybody was in a clique, rooting for so-and-so. I could feel people talking about me, too, and my way to deal with it was to do my best on the field.

When he and Robin came to The Meadows to be with me, Rick admitted that he hadn't known me very well those first few years. He said he always thought I had a lot of confidence but now that he looked back on it, I was actually showing my insecurity. He says he heard gossip in the clubhouse about how I got carried away when I was drinking, but it didn't affect him that much because we weren't roommates or particularly close.

I was pretty much of a loner at Albuquerque, just waiting for Mary to finish her semester at school. Late in April, she and my sister Diane drove my new truck, a Bronco, to New Mexico, and Mary stayed out with me when Diane went back. I was figuring on being in Albuquerque most of the 1978 season, even after I had a good start, winning five and losing only one.

In June, the general manager of the Albuquerque team started paying attention to me. One day I was sitting in the stands, keeping a chart of our pitcher, and he sat next to me and asked, "Do you have an agent?" He was trying to act casual, but I thought, "You just blew it, buddy, because you wouldn't be asking me those questions unless something was going on." Also, I knew Charlie Metro, a scout for the Dodgers, was following us, and I figured I might be the reason.

I told the guy, "Yeah, I've got a guy who helps me with my contracts."

The guy from Albuquerque said, "The Dodgers want to make a move, but they're not sure if they want you or somebody else." I figured that was bullshit, too, but I just let the man talk. He said, "Why don't you come down to the office?" and he told me the Dodgers were eager to sign me for three years. I could sense what was happening. This guy was going to try to get me to sign a cheap contract to tie me up to the Dodgers for three years so he would be a big hero in their eyes. He was trying to scare me that the Dodgers might never call me up if I didn't agree to their terms.

He mentioned figures like $25,000 or $30,000 or $35,000 for three years, something absurd like that. He was trying to snooker me, like a card player, be a big hero with the big club, and didn't give a shit about me. I called up Bob Fenton and said, "Bob, they're trying to screw me," and asked him to take care of it.

Damn, I'm an alcoholic but I'm not stupid. I could read in the papers how players were jumping from one club to another because guys like Catfish Hunter and Andy Messersmith had been able to get out of contracts. I didn't want to get stuck with a low salary for three years. But Bob Fenton worked it out with Al Campanis, the Dodgers' vice president, where I would sign for the minimum contract for 1978—a whopping $20,000—and then negotiate a new contract. As it turned out, I would jump to $47,500 and $77,500 the next two years, and the Dodgers seemed happy about it. It was just a game; you've got to go through that stuff every time. I thought I had laughed it off, but I found out later the negotiating had bothered me more than I was willing to admit.

After Fenton worked out my contract, the Dodgers admitted they wanted me to join the big club. I got the news on June 18 and I asked if I could drive my Bronco out to Los Angeles, but they said no, they wanted my ass out there right away. I jumped on a plane, and Mary drove up the next day, all through the desert by herself, and we stayed with my brother until we found a place.

I remember the first time I walked into the Dodgers' clubhouse on June 19. I knew most of the guys, and I'd seen most of them a few months before, so it wasn't a big emotional moment. I saw my name over a locker and started unpacking, when I noticed they had given me No. 35. I didn't like the number at first, and I liked it even less when Don Sutton walked over and said, "This is a terrible number. Everybody who gets this number gets sent back to the minors right away. You'd better do something about this." Tommy John and Doug Rau, sitting on both sides of me, agreed with Sutton completely. I didn't have a prayer with No. 35. I just gave 'em my famous stare and put on the uniform.

I got adjusted the first night and Lasorda put me in a game the next night, June 20, with the Dodgers behind the Astros. The first batter was a skinny young guy named Mike Fischlin, who had just been called up himself. I didn't know if he could hit worth a damn, so I threw as hard as I could, and struck him out with three pitches. A few pitches later I threw a change-up to Bob Watson, and he smacked a double right up the alley. I found out later that he is very good at hitting the off-speed pitch. I had a lot to learn, but I just was happy to be in there.

The next night I pitched two more innings against the Astros. I struck out four and I became the winning pitcher as the Dodgers won in the eleventh inning, 5–4.

Three nights later, I came in against the Cincinnati Reds, who were supposed to be our closest competitors because the year before they had picked up Tom Seaver from the New York Mets—a guy I figured would never be traded. Some fans were saying Seaver gave the Reds a lock on the pennant, but I remembered the night I had my tryout, Reggie Smith, one of our veterans, sitting around the clubhouse saying, "We're still going to win," which they did.

I replaced Don Sutton in the eighth inning and gave up a base hit to Pete Rose, which didn't bother me a whole lot since he already had almost three thousand of them. I got the last four outs to save a victory. People were starting to get excited about me, and I was feeling pretty good, too.

The mound felt great, and home plate seemed to be fifty feet away instead of the sixty-five it had seemed to be the first night. I was getting the ball low and fast.

After that exposure to the Reds, Lasorda told me I was going to start against them in Cincinnati on July 2.

The Reds did not think I had great stuff that day because they hit the ball pretty hard, but right at somebody. Pete Rose hit a real shot, a one-bouncer to second base, and he was out at first base. He ran back into the dugout yelling stuff like, "Come on, we can hit him, this guy doesn't have anything," and people in the stands thought we were having an argument or something. Hell, I knew what Pete was doing. He was trying to get his team going, trying to start something, trying to get me nervous. I didn't say a word to him, just concentrated on pitching, and I shut them out for six innings before Lasorda called on the bullpen to wrap it up. In my first eleven and one third innings, I had no walks, no runs, and thirteen strikeouts.

I got my first taste of National League hardball in my next start in Philadelphia. The Phillies didn't like it when my fast ball moved inside, purely by accident, to Greg Luzinski and Mike Schmidt. Late in the game, I came up to bat and Tug McGraw threw a pitch inside to me and started yacking to our bench. We won, and I was undefeated in five decisions.

Just before the All-Star game, I let the Dodgers know it wasn't going to be all sweetness and light with me. I made a pick-off throw to first base and the ball sailed and skipped off Steve Garvey's glove, hitting him square in the chin. The blood was pouring down his face and he had to get twenty stitches. I was afraid it was my fault, but everybody assured me it was a freak accident.

That night a couple of my buddies, Bryan and Dave, were in Houston and we stayed up all night drinking Jack Daniel's and a bunch of beers. The Dodgers had a day game at one o'clock the next day but we didn't get done playing dice till around seven in the morning and I didn't show up at the ball park till about ten minutes to game time. My uniform was all packed and there was a piece of tape across my locker with the words, "Don't worry about it, Cy Young, you can come in any time you want to." Lasorda yelled at me and fined me for what I did, but I figured, "What the hell, I'm 5 and 0, they ain't gonna get rid of me." That's how an alcoholic thinks, right there. I sat on the bench all hung over, and there was Steve Garvey, twenty stitches in his chin, playing first base, knocking in a few runs, and I was falling asleep on the bench. At the time, though, the Dodgers thought it was funny. That's what Dusty Baker told me later. He said, "Guys were saying, 'Look what the rookie did.'"

I was enjoying playing for the Dodgers. The O'Malley family runs everything first class, including their own jet plane outfitted with only two seats on each side, so you can stretch out. With most airlines getting out of the charter business, a lot of ball clubs have to take scheduled flights now. Sometimes we'll hear the other team say, "Gee, this game better end soon, or we'll blow our flight." We never have to worry about that. Our plane is always waiting for us.

I quickly came to love playing in Dodger Stadium, even if it has one of the bumpiest infields in baseball. I love it around five o'clock on a clear day when you can see the San Gabriel Mountains out in the distance. I also love it around seven thirty-five when the game starts and there are forty thousand or more people cheering for the Dodgers.

People used to make fun of the Dodger fans for bringing their transistor radios to the ball park to let Vince Scully tell them what they were seeing. They're still not as rabid as Tiger fans but they cheer for you, make you feel at home—particularly if you're winning.

I learned that lesson early. They love you when you're going good. They loved Tom Lasorda when he won pennants his first two years as manager, and they loved him when he went on national television talking about the Big Dodger in the Sky. But when Lasorda didn't win the pennant the next two years, the fans got on his case.

The Dodger organization wants you to be loyal, but they also expect you to produce. If you don't, they'll get rid of you. They never give their manager more than a one-year contract. Walter Alston, who came before Lasorda, lasted twenty-three years that way, but I guess it can be tough on the nerves.

I certainly can't blame the stress of baseball for my alcoholism coming out. Lots of people have stress—housewives, doctors, laborers. The fact is I won my first five games and I was feeling no stress whatsoever about my pitching but I was starting to have trouble coping with daily life.

As soon as the Dodgers called me up, a lot of my friends started coming out from Michigan. Mary was with me for most of the summer in an apartment we had rented, and the guys would drop in, sleep on the floor, call me at all hours of the day and night, just like at home. The difference was that I was supposed to be preparing for work every evening, and I was letting my social life get in the way of my baseball life.

It was very difficult for me to say no to anybody. Each player gets a couple of free tickets to every home game, and you can get a few more by scrounging around and trading favors with other guys. But your friends think nothing of calling you up every day and saying, "Hey, you got your tickets covered?" If I had come home late from a game the night before and some friend called at eight in the morning and said, "Hey, can I come over?" it was hard to say no.

I didn't realize it at the time but I had this need to be liked by so many people. I felt bad if somebody was mad at me because I ran out of free tickets.

It was also hard to say no to a beer. A baseball player has a lot of leisure time, particularly a starting pitcher, who knows he will play only once every four or five days. Even though you have to be at the ball park, sometimes you get the feeling you're just killing time between assignments. You can drink away a whole weekend if you get in that frame of mind. I know a couple of guys who tried—myself included.

Because I'm so hyper, I get butterflies before I'm going to pitch. I think most athletes do. I've heard of basketball players and football players who throw up just before the combat begins. Now that I'm sober, I'm aware of all that tension flailing around inside me. On the day I'm pitching, I cannot sit around my house or my hotel room in seclusion. I've got to get to the ball park, talk to some people, take a few cuts in batting practice.

Being sober, I'm much more aware of feelings, and also more aware of the normal aches and pains that come from being an athlete. After a game I pitch, I can feel my arm, my legs, my insides, my adrenaline starting to slow down. I've got to adjust to that. When I was drinking, I never felt those things. I was totally oblivious. I wouldn't drink before coming to work, but my system was still working off yesterday's alcohol. It takes one hour to work off every ounce of alcohol. Sometimes I'd be working off last week's intake. I never knew when I was nervous or tired or aching or sick.

While I cannot blame baseball for alcoholism, I do think my business makes it easy to drink. Being single, having a few dollars in my pocket, being in the same town a couple of days in a row, it was inevitable that I'd be invited to party with somebody, or find a bar I liked. Lots of guys can handle this. I could not.

When I played at Albuquerque, Del Crandall, the manager, used to tell us: "If you want to have a beer, go drink somewhere else but the hotel bar, because I don't want to see your ugly faces." People tell me Casey Stengel had the same philosophy, that the hotel bar belonged to him and "his" writers, but I never heard Lasorda say anything like that.

I didn't drink around the club that much anyway. I liked going off by myself and finding nice bars where nobody knew me. I liked exploring strange cities. Some guys bitch about coming to New York, afraid they're going to get mugged or something, but I loved coming to New York. I would get out of the hotel and start walking, uptown, downtown, looking in windows, admiring the stylish New York women, doing some shopping, eating a little of this and a little of that. Every ethnic group in the world has a restaurant in New York.

I even love taking the subway in New York. Most of the guys are afraid to try it, so they'd rather sit in the team bus in rush hour when you're stuck in traffic. Me, I go out of our hotel, buy a token, catch the "RR" train to Queens Plaza. You walk across the platform, take the Flushing Express, and get off at Shea Stadium. I have never been mugged on the subway. (But I admit that I take the team bus back after night games.)

Even though I tried going off by myself in every city, I was always getting caught by one of the coaches. I'd stagger back into the hotel lobby and somebody would see me. If they said anything to me, I would tell them, "I'm a victim of circumstances"—my favorite line.

I cannot complain because there was beer in the clubhouse and a couple of bars in every hotel. An alcoholic can find a drink in the middle of Death Valley. I know I could.

I have nothing against alcohol being available for people who can use it right. For people who want to abuse it, that's their responsibility. It comes down to the individual to make a choice.

I've heard some alcoholics say they would do away with all alcohol, but let's be honest. You're not going to do it, and you shouldn't even try to take something away that relaxes so many people. I've heard people call alcohol a wonder drug, saying that if alcohol had been invented in the twentieth century, all the doctors and scientists would be calling it a modern miracle. I once heard a doctor say that a glass of wine relaxes you, makes you live longer. I remember thinking, "Damn, with all the wine in me, I'm going to live an extra twenty years." But actually it was the opposite. I was probably going to die young.

Even in my first couple of months in the major leagues, I was heading downhill. I can see now, I was going to be out of baseball by the time I was twenty-five or twenty-six. I might have bounced around from one club to another—one of those "problems" you always read about being traded—and I might have covered up, but I would have been out of baseball by now. I was crazy when I was drunk.

I almost killed myself that first summer in the majors. I had borrowed an apartment out by the beach. That's what I loved best about Southern California—being at the beach, hearing the waves. I fell in love with the Pacific Coast right away, the rugged-looking waves, the sand, even the oil wells along the shore. George Vecsey says the wells remind him of a prehistoric bird, a pterodactyl, with their sharp beaks bobbing up and down continuously. I don't even pay attention to them anymore. I love lying on the beach in the sunlight and enjoying the scenery as it bounces before my eyes.

I also loved driving my Bronco on the beach at night, which is how I nearly killed myself. It happened after a game when I took my two buddies for a spin on the beach after popping four or five beers. I wasn't drunk, or so I thought, but I had that good old alcoholic's courage—no fear at all. I was zipping along the edge of the water on the hard sand and decided to show them how fast I could turn that sucker 180 degrees, just like the stunt drivers in the movies.

Maybe I was capable of that when I was sober, but this time I overcompensated and turned that Bronco over, right onto the sand. Two of us were thrown clear, but my third buddy was trapped under the Bronco.

Even with some beers in me, I knew enough to be scared.

"Damn, I killed him," I thought.

We ran over and saw his leg was just pressed lightly into the sand. We scraped away some sand and pulled him out from under the Bronco and discovered he had only a slightly stretched neck and a cut near his eye. I had a bruised leg and my other buddy had a cut finger. I began getting the chills when I realized how close I had come to killing some people.

I was able to talk myself out of any troubles when the truck was towed away, but because I needed another car to get around, a couple of people found out the reason. Before long, about forty-eight people knew Welch had tipped over his Bronco at the beach, but most people thought I was just a flaky rookie. They didn't realize I was an alcoholic flirting with disaster.

Meanwhile, I was having a great summer on the mound. The Dodgers went into Candlestick Park in San Francisco having lost four straight games, and we lost two more to the Giants, putting ourselves four and a half games back, in third place.

The season was moving rapidly along, August 5 already, when Lasorda gave me a start on Saturday afternoon, in a nationally televised game. If the man had any doubts about how much I love to compete, he found out that afternoon. We took a 2–0 lead against Ed Halicki and the Giants going into the bottom of the ninth inning, but they got a little rally going. Jack Clark, who was a contender for the Most Valuable Player Award that year, had not started the game, but they sent him up to pinch-hit.

Lasorda came out to the mound to look me over. I could tell he was reading my face to see if I was scared or tired, but I was neither. He asked me, "Do you want Clark?"

I knew that if I said, "It's up to you, skip," if I showed any indecision at all, my ass was in the clubhouse. I just gave him my famous stare and said, "Yeah, I want him." I just wanted everybody to go away and let me get the guy.

But Lasorda wasn't satisfied. He asked, "How bad do you want him?" I went along with the game of Twenty Questions and I said, "Bad. I want him real bad." That seemed to satisfy Lasorda, and as soon as the coast was clear, I fired three strikes past Clark, got Heity Cruz on a fly ball, and ended the game. Some reporters would describe that as the biggest game of the year for us.

I'll never forget after the game, belting a few beers on an empty stomach and waiting for the reporters to come around. Tommy John, who has this weird sense of humor, dropped by my locker to tell the press that I had pitched to Clark "just like your namesake."

I didn't know what TJ was talking about, so he explained who my namesake was: "Just like Lawrence Welch. A-one, and a-two, and a-three." I thought that was so hilarious, I had another beer to toast the wit and wisdom of Tommy John. Then another beer to toast the good sense of Jack Clark to get it over with. Then another beer to toast Abner Doubleday for inventing this wonderful game.

By the time I had pounded my eighth beer, still on an empty stomach, the team bus had departed, leaving me stranded at Candlestick Park. However, Lasorda and a couple of coaches and players were on their way to some guy's boat for cocktails before going out to dinner. Somebody asked, "What are we going to do with Welch?" and they let me tag along with them to the guy's boat.

My performance as a guest was not as tasteful as my performance as a pitcher. I started pounding down whiskey, still on an empty stomach, and having a pleasant conversation with our hostess. I remember calling her a "mullion," which in clubhouse language means a very ugly woman. I was like that when I was drunk. Usually

I verbally abused people I love, but sometimes I would share the abuse with strangers, too.

When they got moving to the restaurant, they put me in the back of the van, where I fell asleep, Copenhagen dribbling down the side of my chin, a lovely sight for all. By the time they got from the marina to this Japanese restaurant, I was totally skunked, just out of it, so they assigned the team trainer to take me back to the hotel. He threw me on the bed, where I slept for about five hours. I woke up at eleven-thirty and was ready to start all over again. My roomie, Lance Rautzhan, a great guy, dissuaded me from any further celebrating for the night.

People were willing to put up with me because I was pitching the Dodgers toward first place. Four nights after my stunt in San Francisco, I beat Vida Blue of the Giants, 12–2, to pull us into a tie for first place, even though Clark hammered one out on me. Then I beat Philadelphia, 5–2, to put us in first place for the rest of the season.

I finally lost a couple of games, but in September I beat my old teammate from Eastern Michigan, Bob Owchinko of the San Diego Padres, 4–0, to clinch the Western Division title.

I celebrated in appropriate fashion. We had this party in the Stadium Club to celebrate the pennant, and everybody was being introduced. I was already drunk from the champagne in the locker room, and I felt the need to tell a joke in front of all those people. I am not exactly George Burns, the master of delivery.

My joke was about the Super Bowl of Africa, a football game involving all the animals of the jungle. Just in case you haven't heard it—I'll give you the short version now, I promise—it tells how all the damn gorillas and giraffes are playing in the Super Bowl. It boils down to the centipede saving the game by tripping up the rhinoceros on the five-yard line.

The rhinoceros says, "Where the hell were you the rest of the game?" and the punch line is, "I was in the dressing room putting on my shoes." Naturally, everybody goes "aaaagh!" when you get to the punch line. Only I never got to the punch line. I thought the joke was so good, I started stretching it, bringing in the leopards and the zebras, but I was so drunk I started giggling and swaying back and forth. Finally I just got tired of telling the story, and I sat down without telling the punch line. I don't think anybody cared. My brother Donnie was at the party and he told me he was embarrassed for me, but he never told me that until we got to The Meadows more than a year later.

I wasn't embarrassed. Hell, I had won seven games and lost four with a super earned-run average of 2.03. I had helped the Dodgers win the Western Division pennant and I wasn't embarrassed about anything, not even the next day when Burt Hooton called across the locker room, "Hey, Welch, here's another beer." People were regarding me as a drinker but it didn't bother me a bit.

Chapter Eleven

The Series

By now Reggie Jackson and I are locked into the memories of almost all baseball fans. If you mention my name to a fan, he or she might say, "Bob Welch . . . isn't he the one with the, ahem, drinking problem?" (I think it is strange how people stammer over the word "alcoholic." It's more acceptable to say "cancer" or "heart disease" than "alcoholism.")

An even larger percentage of fans would say: "Bob Welch . . . he's the guy who struck out Reggie Jackson in the 1978 World Series." I can see where I'm getting part of my notoriety from Reggie, because of his colorful personality, all his endorsements. We've become a sports memory, like Joe Louis and Max Schmeling, Army and Notre Dame, or Bobby Thomson hitting the home run off Ralph Branca in the 1951 playoff game.

I was awed by Jackson the first time I saw him. I was around fourteen years old when my parents took me to the 1971 All-Star game in Detroit. Reggie blasted one about nine million miles, an incredible shot. Tremendous power and great concentration. I remember it was as if Reggie were putting on a show. This was his time. He just wound up and murdered the ball.

I got my chance against Reggie seven years later, in the second game of the 1978 World Series. People seem to remember what they were doing while that game was on. I got one letter from a guy who said he and his wife were in bed when Reggie came up, with the television on but the sound turned down. The guy said he glanced up and saw Reggie fouling off a few pitches, so he and his wife stopped what they were doing to watch me pitch to Reggie. Had I known, I would have gotten it over faster.

As it was, it took seven minutes, which is a long time for one batter to stick with one pitcher. Seven minutes on national television, with Mr. October growling and spitting and flexing his muscles to try to shake me up.

To tell you the truth, I loved every moment of it. I am a performer, a competitor. I wasn't scared, I wasn't worried. I just wanted to get the man out and get the game over with. In case you're wondering, I was stone sober, too. I hadn't gotten around to drinking before a game, particularly a World Series game, although given time I would have.

We went into that second game leading the Series because of Davey Lopes's two homers in the first game. We were playing in front of 55,982 fans in our ball park after we had beaten the Phillies for the National League pennant. Everybody in Los Angeles was rooting for us to win our first World Championship since 1965. The Dodgers had lost the Series in 1966, 1974, and 1977, and some fans were getting impatient.

We went into the Series in a highly emotional state because Jim Gilliam, our coach and one of the most dependable players in Dodger history, had died a few days earlier. Jim had suffered a stroke and gone into a coma late in the season, but when he died, it stunned us. We buried him in the afternoon and went right to the ball park to play the game, wearing a black patch with his No. 19 on our sleeves.

I took it easy in the first game because there was talk that I was going to start the fourth game in New York, but in the second game they told me to stay in the bullpen in case I was needed. Burt Hooton went six innings and Terry Forster pitched us into the ninth inning with a 4–3 lead. Reggie Jackson had driven in all three Yankee runs with a double and a ground-out.

In the ninth, I was throwing nice and easy, loosening up my arm, just in case, when Bucky Dent got a single and Paul Blair walked with one out. That brought up Thurman Munson and then Reggie Jackson, the two best hitters on the Yankees. I was throwing the shit out of the ball, and they told me Lasorda wanted me.

I was glad, to tell you the truth. I guess I was nervous, but in a good way. Like, "Give me the ball, let's get it done." That's my hyperactive way, do everything in a hurry, whether it's drink, make love, or pitch a game. Do it.

I got to the mound and Davey Lopes told me, "Just throw your pitch," and Lasorda said, "Just throw strikes." I started warming up to Steve Yeager, trying to throw the ball through him, trying to knock him over, nothing subtle.

I threw a fast ball to Munson and he hit a line drive to right field but Reggie Smith was playing him in exactly the right spot. That made it two outs and runners on first and second, and there was Jackson. He's a big SOB with glasses and a wide-eyed glare. Very emotional. Lots of energy. I remembered what Lopes and Lasorda had said, just to throw my best heat.

Later, Tom Seaver, who was broadcasting the game, told me that if I had a little knowledge of Reggie, I might have gotten him out easier. He said I didn't take into mind that Reggie wanted to be a hero.

I had never met Reggie up to this point, had no feeling about him. But after talking to Seaver, I later realized that Reggie would not want to walk in this situation, that he had to be the hero. If I had thrown Reggie way outside once I got to a one-and-two count, Reggie would have gone for it even more than in a regular-season game. Reggie is always aware of the situation. Reggie knew even more than I did that this game was going all over the world, and that he had this nickname, "Mr. October," to uphold. Reggie's got one of the highest IQs in baseball—he has said so—and he always sees the total picture. But I didn't have any idea at the time. I just wanted to heave it past him.

Actually, I was stupid in another way. Everybody was watching Reggie intently, including Bucky Dent on second base. When the count got to three-and-two, I took a glance at Dent and said, "I can pick that sucker off." He was taking a running lead and I said, "I've got him dead to rights. All I have to do is wheel and deal." I really wanted to, but I was scared of screwing up. Suppose we didn't get the signal right, and I threw it into center field? I didn't want to disturb things the way they were. Besides, I figured I'd blow it past Reggie and we could all go home. Not that easy.

Warming up in the bullpen, I knew I had a good fast ball, but it seemed to get faster when I got to the mound. It was really popping. Yeager gave me signals to pitch Reggie up and in. The man is a good low-ball hitter, and we were aiming for this spot on the inside.

The reporters said the first pitch was thrown at 8:09 P.M. It was the start of a very long seven minutes.

The first pitch could have been the last. It was a fast ball, not in as far as it should have been, right down the pipe, too damn low, and he could have knocked it out of the ball park, but he missed.

The second pitch was a ball, under his chin, a little too far up and in, but it made Reggie spin to the dirt. I wasn't trying to knock him down or even to move him back. It just happened that way. I sure as hell wasn't trying to scare that man because I don't think Reggie Jackson scares. He got up, kicked the dirt out of his spikes, straightened his uniform, and dug back into the same trench he had occupied before my bomb. You do not scare Reggie Jackson.

The third pitch he could have murdered, too, but he got just a tip of it, and it fouled back to the screen. By this time the crowd was screaming and Reggie was trying to establish control of me. I knew he was gesturing a lot but I just reared back and threw the ball. I was thinking strikeout and he was thinking home run. Looking back, it would have been better to have him pop the ball 150 feet in the air, and let somebody catch it, but I wasn't thinking that at the time.

What was I thinking at the time? I would have to say I wasn't thinking much at all. Just following my instincts. If I start fooling around I lose my concentration. Concentration is not the same as thinking. It's almost the opposite.

Reggie fouled back the fourth pitch.

He fouled back the fifth pitch.

At one point I had to step off the pitcher's mound because the fans were really loud. But I wasn't looking around savoring the moment or any of that stuff. Just trying to concentrate. Up and in. Up and in.

The sixth pitch was a ball, too far inside.

The seventh pitch was a foul back.

The eighth pitch was high and outside, to make the count three balls and two strikes. Now the runners had to move on the pitch.

At eight-sixteen—a hell of a long time later—I threw my ninth pitch to Reggie Jackson, who swung and missed. I casually pumped my arm one time before my teammates came over and hugged me. All I knew was that I had saved a 4–3 Dodger victory. I didn't have time to watch Reggie's swing, but I've seen it dozens of times since. The force of his swing turned him into a human corkscrew, his left knee on the ground, and if you can read lips you know he's mad. He grabbed the bat by its thick end and stomped away from home plate, still cursing. I certainly didn't see Reggie storm into the Yankee dugout but I know that when the Yankees didn't scatter fast enough, he bumped into a couple, including his manager, Bob Lemon.

The next morning we would pick up the papers and see some of the reporters trying to make it seem that he and Lemon had been in a shoving match. Lemon was quoted as saying: "The guy was hyped up. The kid just struck him out to win a World Series game. Hell, I didn't expect him to walk into the dugout and set his bat and helmet down gently and say, 'Gee, fellows, I'm sorry I struck out.' Reggie was hot, and we should have gotten out of his way."

We were already celebrating in our clubhouse, with television crews and packs of reporters in front of every locker. I was exhausted, as if I had pitched eight or nine innings, and I couldn't think of anything to say. It had been like that all season, actually. The press thought I was vague and distant, and I guess I was. The only quotes they got out of me that night were:

"We've got quite a lot of veterans on this team and I get to watch them every day. They're poised in what they do. That helps me. I hope to learn a lot from them."

And, "Lasorda just gave me the ball and said to throw strikes. I just wanted to go after them and make them hit my pitch."

And, "The first pitch was his best chance. If he was going to hit, he would have hit that one."

I was not good with the press the way Tommy John and Don Sutton and Steve Garvey are because I didn't think I belonged. I'd only been with the Dodgers since the summer and frankly I didn't think I had the kind of personality they did. I was more scared in the interviews than during the game. I'd look at these reporters with their pads and pencils and know some of them wouldn't understand what I was trying to say anyway, or maybe they wouldn't care. Others would care, but I was afraid to be myself. I didn't know myself. Even striking out Reggie, I retreated behind my stare, the wall of a budding alcoholic.

Fortunately, a lot of other guys did the talking for me. I read the quotes the next day and they made me feel real good.

DAVEY LOPES: "He's the Ice Man. There's something about the guy that's hard to explain. When he was out there, I know he didn't hear the hollering. He's cold out there. I can't really explain it. He does things at his age that a lot of guys never do. Nothing fazes that man."

RICK MONDAY: "He's just an ordinary twenty-one-year-old with a hundred-mile-per-hour fast ball."

REGGIE SMITH: "If it wasn't for Bob, we wouldn't be where we are."

In the other clubhouse, it turned out, Reggie Jackson had cooled down quickly and paid me compliments:

"We were told he had a good curve and change-up, so when I was down one-and-two, I was half looking for another off-speed pitch.

"We knew he was a good pitcher. Give the guy credit. He beat me. I'm not proud. I admit it. The man beat me. He's a major-league baseball player and he can get in there with fifty million people watching and he beat me. Give him credit."

I dressed as fast as I could after the game because I knew my mother, father, brother, and his wife, and two of my uncles, Carl and Ted from Paducah, were all at the game. We went over to the Marriott Hotel and had two drinks, but I didn't have time to celebrate or get a buzz on, because I had to drive down to Seal Beach to pack. We had a plane ride at seven o'clock the next morning. The Series wasn't over, although we were hoping we could knock them off twice in New York. We were all high because we were whipping their butts. But the whole thing turned around when we got to the other coast.

Do I think it's because Mary Ellen flew from Kalamazoo to New York to take in the middle three games? In some of my more cruel moments I have suggested it.

The truth of the matter is, I blame Graig Nettles more than Mary. That man made some incredible stops in the third game to turn the whole series around, as Ron Guidry beat Don Sutton, 5–1, and we were starting to get annoyed at the cursing and the objects being thrown at us by the Yankee fans.

I got to see Reggie again in the fourth game. Lasorda brought me in to relieve in the eighth inning and we went into the tenth inning tied.

I struck out Mickey Rivers and got two strikes on Roy White but lost the man with a base on balls. Once again I managed to get Munson, this time on a pop-up, and that brought up Reggie. I threw a low ball, down near his ankles, and he reached down and whacked a single to right field, White stopping at second. I still figured I'd get out of it, but Lou Piniella hit a pitch around his forehead for a single to right center that ended the game. Now we were all even, and I was ticked off because everybody was playing up the battle of the relief pitchers, Goose Gossage and me, even though I was no relief pitcher, and he'd been around for years.

The next day I ran into Reggie in the outfield before the game. He came over and said hello and told me, "Nice pitching the other night." I said to him, "How the hell did you hit that pitch yesterday?" He admitted it was around the ankles.

They hammered us, 12–2, in the fifth game, to send us back home, with their fans yelling at us, helping their team any way they could. Mary was in the stands for those games and she said the fans weren't so terrible—just tough fans screaming their heads off.

We got home and I ran into the big guy again. Or rather, he ran into me. He came up in the seventh inning and blistered a two-run homer on a pitch that just went right down the middle. Stupid on my part.

We wound up losing four straight games to drop the Series.

I went home and somebody played the second game on a recording machine and I got nervous as hell just looking at it. I suppose Reggie went home and played the fourth and sixth games on his Reggie-vision. What the hell, he was entitled.

I spent many winter nights toasting the 1978 World Series. All winter long I could see myself walking Roy White after getting two strikes on him. I was searching for alcoholic excuses to go out and get drunk—and my pitching in the fourth and sixth games gave me more than enough reasons. Piniella's single? Have one on him. Jackson's homer? Have one on him. Losing four straight? Let's have a double. But I can't say I really drank because we lost. If we had won, I would have gotten drunk to celebrate. There was always a reason if you looked hard enough.

Chapter Twelve

•••••••••••••••••••••••••

Crying for Help

•••

When the season ended, I told myself I was no longer a kid trying to make the major leagues. I was a full-fledged big-leaguer. Even though the Dodgers sent me to Arizona to work on my curve ball with Ron Perranoski, who was then their minor-league pitching coach, I felt like an instant celebrity because of that second World Series game.

I was getting invitations from Michigan to be honored by both my hometowns: Ferndale, where our house is, and Hazel Park, where I went to high school, and where my favorite bars are. When I got back from Arizona late in November, Hazel Park had a day in my honor, and on December 7 Ferndale did the same. I spoke to businessmen's luncheons and visited schools and told the kids they could make it in the world if they worked hard. I was even introduced to the state legislature in Lansing by Representative Dana Wilson, Mary Ellen's brother.

I was enjoying being back home in Detroit, seeing all my buddies again. They all made a fuss over me, in the good old Hazel Park fashion. I'd go back to one of the bars and nobody would say, "Well, here's Welch. Boy, you were terrific on television striking out Reggie." Instead, they would say, "Welch, you asshole, we saw

Reggie hit a dinger off you in the sixth game. He really took you downtown." Those guys could really get on your case, but if you needed help, they'd be there.

I also started to get invited to a lot of banquets all over the country. I discovered people would pay me five hundred or a thousand dollars for going to a dinner and telling a few stories and signing autographs. I'd sit at a dais with other sportspeople like Willie Pep or Greg Luzinski or Sparky Anderson or whoever they invited. Plenty of drinks.

Now that I look back, I was too involved with speaking arrangements, and did not take care of myself as well as I should have. I didn't run hard during the off-season. I didn't take care of my body. I didn't do shit, really. I just lived off my one inning of glory in the World Series, flying around the country, going to banquets, celebrating more than was deserved, not concentrating on my priorities.

I can't say that anyone else nudged me along the path of alcoholism. I did it myself. Because of the way I am, I was susceptible to every drink, every party, every banquet that was offered to me. I didn't have the sense to say no. Offer me a sip of life and I'd swallow the ocean.

My buddies laugh at me, even today, cold sober. We were in San Francisco last season and I was so happy to be back in that city that I couldn't wait to get to Alioto's Restaurant at Fisherman's Wharf. I had to stop at a street vendor for a cup of crab cocktail with cocktail sauce, slurping it and spilling it on my sports jacket on the way up the restaurant stairs. Rick Sutcliffe laughed at me and said, "Look at you. You're a mess. Can't you wait to sit down at the table?" But that's the way I am. Got to do it all at once. If I'm hasty with a paper cup of crab cocktail, you should have seen me with a bottle of alcohol. Down the hatch, man.

I spent some time in California early in 1979 before joining the Dodgers in the Superteams competition in Hawaii. The weather wasn't great in Hawaii and I didn't do much to keep in shape except take part in the tug-of-war and some other contests. Mostly, I just drank for about ten days in Hawaii, got slow and lazy, just before spring training. Then Mary went back to Kalamazoo and I went to Vero Beach, in no shape whatsoever to prove I belonged in the major leagues.

I got to spring training assuming I had a job handed to me. I worked hard to get in shape, to undo the rust of drinking all winter, and with typical alcoholic frenzy I overdid my workouts. I didn't have enough sense to realize I would get thirty-five starts in the season, and that I had six weeks to prepare for them. Not me. Instead of working my arm into shape slowly, I tried to fire fast balls so I could win twenty games in April. For a few weeks, my fast ball was ahead of everybody in camp and I felt terrific. So I just kept heaving the fast ball instead of working on my curve ball and change-up, which they had been teaching me in Arizona. Just headstrong.

I got into a nasty little routine that spring. I'd run in the morning, work on my fast ball, throw to the catcher, and go play golf in the afternoon. Evenings were for drinking—sometimes afternoons, too. I remember one day right after the morning workout, I ran into the relative of one of my teammates. The relative had a camper parked in the Dodgertown parking lot and he invited me in for a quick sip. We must have killed a bottle of Jack Daniel's with beers for chasers before I staggered back to my room. To show you how stupid I was, I got messed up in the camper while my teammate—a pitcher—was staying away from his own relative.

After a couple of weeks of heaving the ball, inevitably I strained my arm and had to sit out eleven days. This gave me more time to party. Three of my buddies from Michigan—Bryan Carley, Dave Richardson, and Jeff McKinney—were down in Florida, and I went over to their motel to watch a boxing match on television one night. I guess I only had about five or six beers and we started playing cards and before I knew it, the time was after the twelve-o'clock curfew. I rushed back to Dodgertown and found a note on my door that said: "Bob, I was at your room at 12:52 A.M. but you were not here. Call me when you get in—Tom Lasorda."

I didn't bother to call him, but the next morning at practice I was running and he walked near me and said, "Hey, Bob, you know you're really a major part of this ball club. I want you to take better care of yourself." Deep down inside I really cursed the man. I was angry that he was talking to me at all. I tried to play the indignant act of pretending I hadn't done anything. I said, "I'm sick and tired of everybody picking on me," trying to be enough of a pain in the ass that they wouldn't lecture me anymore.

Lasorda said something about being a professional athlete, having to take care of myself. He told me not to stay out so late. He said there was nothing wrong in having a beer but I didn't have to stay out till the wee hours of the morning and get drunk. But the truth is, there *was* something wrong with my having a beer. I couldn't stop at one or two. I don't think anybody realized it at the time. This was the first time anybody had said anything directly to me about my drinking since Rod Dedeaux back in Japan.

I was still denying everything when the Dodgers were ready to go West to open the season. My arm wasn't ready, so they left me behind in Dodgertown, where I got drunk every night with some of the guys on the minor-league teams. One night I was drinking whiskey and I called my mother back in Michigan and started jabbering away.

I said, "Mom, I'm worried about Donnie. I think he drinks too much." My mom told me later at The Meadows that she could barely understand me, I was so badly stoned, but there I was babbling about Donnie. She admitted later that she was really worried about me. I must have been worried about myself, giving off a loud cry for help like that. A lot of alcoholics do this. They express concern over somebody else, but it's actually their own fears, their own feelings coming through. They're asking for help but they just don't know how to do it, and this is what I was doing.

What should people have done when I was acting like this in spring training? Probably, the Dodgers and my family should have confronted me with my behavior. Just pull me in a room and say, "This is what you have been doing." To confront alcoholics, you have to love them enough to hurt them, to cut through their defenses, their denial. I was putting up a wall, trying to frighten people away. But there are ways to break down those walls which I would later learn at The Meadows. You have to confront alcoholics directly. Hints are not enough. I turned away all their hints.

My arm finally came around and I went out West in time to open the season. We started the season slowly and I was doing well as a starter, but we were having trouble in the bullpen. I thought they might want to use me as a relief pitcher and one day on the plane coming back from Montreal, where we had lost a couple of games, I told Lasorda, "Don't be afraid to use me in the bullpen." I guess I meant it, but really I was saying it to be a hero.

We got to Los Angeles and Lasorda said they might take me up on my offer. At first I tried to back down, insisting they would have to renegotiate my contract, but then I agreed to follow up on my volunteering for the bullpen to see if I could help the team. My reasoning was so faulty, I began to blame Lasorda for putting me in the bullpen, when actually it was my own grandiosity that got me there. I began building up resentments toward Lasorda that would make me uncomfortable with him for many months and perhaps act out toward him in my alcoholic behavior. I think I wanted a scapegoat, and Tom Lasorda was the closest target.

It's normal for players to carry around resentments toward the manager for not using them the way they think they should be used. Most of us think we should be stars. Somebody told me how one old-time manager, maybe it was Casey Stengel, used to say his main job was to "separate the five guys who hate me from the five guys who aren't sure." I don't think I hated anybody but I was a developing alcoholic looking to use my boss as an excuse to get drunk. Pitching relief was as good an excuse as any.

Pitching relief is a different form of pitching. You have to be able to get warmed up in a hurry and go into a game with runners on base. There is no margin for error. I wasn't smart enough to handle it, although I had done some relieving in 1978. I didn't have the arm for it—or the head. When I didn't have my best stuff, I just didn't know how to get by with finesse. I'd just try to fire the ball, which usually is a mistake.

One day against St. Louis, after pitching two and two thirds innings the night before, I got bombed. My arm was hanging and the Cardinals just knocked my shit off the wall. Ted Simmons. They finally traded him out of the league in 1981 and I wanted to give a medal to the man who made the trade. It was too late to help me in 1979. He just murdered me. We went on to Pittsburgh and I gave up a game-winning home run to Bill Robinson and I said, "Hey, I can't handle this anymore. I've just got to rest my arm." I took off seventeen or eighteen days and my arm started to come around.

That home run to Robinson touched off one of my most unpleasant episodes—at least that I can remember. I was feeling terrible at losing the game as we flew to the next town. We had a day off and Rick Sutcliffe and I went out on the town early, drinking shooters, a combination of just about anything alcoholic. I must have had six or seven shooters and maybe a dozen beers and we were partying all evening, getting messed up. When we decided to go back to the hotel, we called a taxi, but the driver seemed to be as loaded as we were. He had just dropped some people off at the bar who were kicking his tires and making noise and so I decided to join in the fun and kick his tires, too. He said, "Come on, get in the cab." I took one look at the man and decided he was as bad off as we were and I said, "I ain't getting in this guy's cab. Take a hike, man." But he said, "Come on, get in the cab," something like that. I thought he was getting out of his cab so I reached out and smacked him across the cheek. I had a ring on my finger and he started to bleed, not a deep cut, but just enough to draw blood.

We got in another cab and he followed us across town to the hotel. We were entering the lobby at the same time as a hooker, and the cabbie was coming right behind her. The security guards moved in to stop the hooker and saw this cabbie with blood on his cheek and figured he was with her.

The guy kept protesting, but I put my ring in my pocket and told the guard, "I didn't hit that guy, get him out of here." The guard chased the driver but started asking us, "Who are you guys?" I told him, "We're with the Dodgers," and he said, "Do you think your manager would like to hear about this?" I told him he could do anything he wanted, but I was tired and going to sleep.

The guard must have said something because the next day Lasorda asked me, "What were you doing last night? Did you punch a taxicab driver?" I lied. I just lied. I said, "I was out partying last night, man, I didn't hit anybody. Why are people always blaming me for things like this?"

That was my tactic. When somebody would accuse me of something, I would become indignant, make up the wildest stories, anything to change the focus of the discussion. I think I actually believed most of my stories because like a lot of alcoholics I did not have a firm grip on reality. We are the best bullshitters in the world.

At the time, these escapades were just a blur. It wasn't until The Meadows that people began to detail my actions and I realized I could have hurt somebody or gotten myself deeply in trouble.

I could have been mugged, maybe even killed, because of my alcoholic habit of carrying around a lot of cash. One time we were in Cincinnati and I told Mary to fly down from Michigan to meet me. She didn't have extra money but I told her I would meet her at the hotel and pay the cabbie from the airport. I went out with one of the young players and got absolutely knocked-down slaughterhouse drunk and totally forgot Mary was arriving. I was wandering around an alley near a rib joint, flashing over three thousand dollars in cash, when one of the guys hustled me back to the hotel before somebody could roll me or knife me.

When I got to the hotel, Mary was waiting in the lobby. She had arrived by cab, couldn't pay the guy, and she was lucky she ran into Mark Cresse, our bullpen coach, who put out the money. But the hotel clerk wouldn't let her go up to my room until I arrived, so she had to wait in the lobby with her suitcase, and then I showed up, just totally wrecked. She was not too pleased with me at that moment, and things did not improve once we got upstairs.

Drink was giving me problems in another area. I had started drinking as a teenager because I was shy with girls. At first it gave me the nerve to talk to them, to put some moves on them, but in my first full year out in Los Angeles, I was drinking so much that it was actually messing up my love life. In all the literature in Alcoholics Anonymous, it says that drink will increase your appetite but diminish your performance, and that is certainly true for this man. There were times when I was convinced I was ready for one of the world's great moments—violins throbbing, cymbals crashing—but really it was more like a lonely kazoo going squeak. It was getting to the point where I'd come home blasted and just fall asleep in Mary's arms. The alcohol was starting to work on my system, affecting me physically as well as psychologically.

On the road? Let's put it this way: If I could get skunked in hotel bars or get in fights with cabbies, I could also get myself in situations with women. Not too long ago I was at an AA meeting and I heard a young guy describe how he woke up in bed with an old couple, a man and a woman, and couldn't remember how he got there or what happened. That never happened to me as far as I know, but it could have.

In my time I have fallen asleep in cars, on toilets, in corridors of hotels. I remember one time the assistant trainer of the Dodgers, Herbie Vike, found me asleep on a table in the corridor and woke me up, saying: "Hey, they sent me here to take care of you. Get your ass up."

I have fallen asleep in a cemetery, on floors, in a Japanese geisha house. I once fell asleep in a whorehouse with a handful of one-hundred-dollar bills. Fell asleep on the corner of Nine-Mile Road and John R. in Michigan.

Fell asleep under a girl's arm once, a coyote woman. You've never heard of a coyote woman? This is a woman you go to bed with at night and you wake up and your arm is underneath her head and you think to yourself, "God, I didn't go to bed with that, did I?"

She's so ugly you don't want to wake her up. You're like a coyote, caught in a trap.

I have fallen asleep in three countries—the United States, Canada and Japan—dozens of hotel rooms, and maybe even while stopped for a red light or two. The only place I never fell asleep was a bar. Too busy drinking.

My main reason for going out and getting drunk was not to meet women. I wanted to get drunk. Every alcoholic has to face that he or she just likes to get drunk. When you do, you wind up in situations you may not want.

I remember one time I was making a talk at one of those winter banquets where they give the speakers as many drinks as they want, which in my case was too many. I started coming out of my alcoholic buzz, not knowing where I was, and I was in an apartment with one woman and about half a dozen furry cats. I went into the bathroom and saw she used the tub for a litter box, and I damn near threw up right there. All I could think of was, "Get me out of here," but I was so drunk that I had to sleep on her couch until I could sober up.

When I got to The Meadows, months later, I realized this is a pattern for alcoholics, winding up in situations they didn't choose, which could be unpleasant or even dangerous to them.

Besides, in my sober life, I realize how much I love Mary Ellen, and call her almost every day. A good, honest relationship with Mary is important to me. It is also true that now that I am sober I am more selective about the people I meet—not for drinking, not for sex, but for conversation, for learning. I can stop and talk with somebody in the hotel lobby or in the street and not have this nagging feeling, geez, I'd better get about the business of getting smashed.

It wasn't that way in 1979. Everything was coming apart. I was angry at Lasorda for putting me in the bullpen and I was blaming him for the pain in my arm. The reporters started coming around and asking me how I felt about the bullpen. Most of them thought I was so screwed up they didn't expect any serious answers from me. Sometimes I'd say, "Hell, yes, I'd rather start but I'll do anything to help the team." If I was feeling resentful that day, I might fix my fishy stare at the reporters or even curse at them or turn away. I got annoyed when one reporter used a comment I had asked to be off the record, and the next day I grabbed him in the larynx and shoved him. The reporters must have had an idea I was drinking—

or maybe they blamed it on dope—but they never wrote anything about my behavior.

My teammates thought I was weird, too. Rick Sutcliffe had become a starting pitcher early in the year and I had been moved to the bullpen, a reversal of roles that maybe produced some kind of resentment in me. Rick was having a great year—he would win seventeen games, the best by a rookie pitcher that season—and we would become good friends, as much as possible with me. We hung out together at night, but I pretty much kept to myself at the ball park.

After Rick went down to The Meadows to spend a family week with me, he described my appearance in that disintegrating summer of 1979:

"You could see Bob in the clubhouse. Others would come in, bounce around, and say, 'Hello, how are you?' But Bob wasn't that type of person. He would come in silently, walk to his locker, start putting his clothes on, without acknowledging anybody was there. Lots of times to me, that indicated he was hiding something or he had an insecurity. Sometimes they work hand in hand.

"I thought maybe Bobby had been out drinking the night before or maybe he had wrecked his car. You never know with Bob, because he never lets you inside his mind. You never got to know Bob Welch. I think he was afraid that if you got to know Bob Welch, you wouldn't like him.

"If it could go unsaid, Bob wouldn't say it. He was the type of person you really couldn't carry on a conversation with. We called him 'Ork' and 'Mork' and 'Spaceman.' We had all kinds of names for him. He was constantly flying, buzzing around everywhere without sitting on one planet for any length of time. He was impossible to get to know.

"I don't see how a person can live like that. I need to talk to people. I need to talk to my wife, to my friends. But Bobby had nobody to confide in. Everybody liked Bob. He was fun-loving. He'd buy everybody a drink. If you had no money, he'd buy the drinks. I can see now that Bob was headed for big trouble, but then you just didn't know."

From my viewpoint, I can't remember what I actually felt about Rick, whether I resented his success or not. But I did try to drag him down.

I did things that I never realized until Rick and Robin told me about them at The Meadows. I definitely tried to get him to drink more. That's a favorite trick of alcoholics—to try to drag other people into the net. Rick told me at The Meadows that I was trying to bring him down to my level because he was having a good year and I was having a horseshit year. Subconsciously maybe that was so.

I remember working on Rick during the games, trying to get him to join me. There is a supply of beer in the clubhouse, along with soda and juice. We pay clubhouse dues so the clubhouse man will keep the room stocked with chewing tobacco, candy bars, gum, cigarettes, and food after every game. It's the same on the road. The visiting clubhouse man puts out a spread of roast beef and potato salad, and when you leave you tip him around ten dollars a game.

Having beer in the clubhouse was a perfect setup for an alcoholic. I would always slip a couple of cans inside my coat for the hotel room or the drive home from the ball park. By the end of 1979, I was stopping in a store near the house and buying the fixings for strawberry daiquiris, eventually making them so strong that Mary didn't want any, which left more for me.

I even started drinking during games. Midway through 1979, I was getting bored hanging around the bullpen or even the dugout, and I would prowl back to the clubhouse to see if I could make a hit on the beer supply. Our clubhouse man, Nobe Kawano, who knows almost everything that goes on, likes to tell me now: "I liked you better when you were drunk." I think he's joking.

Nobe couldn't be everywhere at once. If I would see him in the dugout, I'd slip into the clubhouse for a few beers. There's nothing illegal about going into the clubhouse during a game. Some guys take whirlpool baths or swing a bat or grab tobacco or whatever. I'd slip down to an extra room down the runway, where they keep the weight machines. That room was always empty during a game. I'd hide behind a locker and belt down the beers, then I'd go back to the bench.

After a while I wasn't watching the games at all, but was wondering how I could get more beer without getting caught. I also wanted to bring somebody else into the act. Spread the good news. I settled upon Rick Sutcliffe. One night at Dodger Stadium I plopped down next to Rick on the bench and whispered, "Hey Rick, let's go get a beer."

Rick looked at me sideways, his forehead wrinkled in puzzlement.

"Not during a game," he whispered back. "You're out of your mind."

"Nobody will see us," I said. "We can drink in the weight room."

"No way," Rick said.

Why, that ungrateful SOB. After all I had done for him. If Rick didn't want to join me in happy hour, I'd drink his share, too. I followed my familiar path to the weight room, where I proceeded to drink my beer, Rick Sutcliffe's, Bobby Castillo's, Don Sutton's, Tommy Lasorda's, Sandy Koufax's and even one for the immortal Dazzy Vance.

Chapter Thirteen

◆◆◆◆◆◆◆◆◆◆◆◆◆◆◆◆◆◆◆◆◆◆◆◆◆

People Were Watching

◆◆

I persuaded myself that nobody was noticing my drinking, but I also began to feel that everybody was spying on me. Delusions and paranoia at the same time. I'd convince myself that nobody knew I was sneaking off and getting drunk in the weight room, that nobody could see I was giggling and walking crooked toward the end of a game.

At the same time I started getting the creeps whenever Don Newcombe came around. I couldn't put it into words at the time but I was convinced Newk was spying on me. If I would see his big craggy face sticking through the door, usually with a cowboy hat or some other hat on him, I would turn the other way. It was like one of those spy movies where you hear footsteps and see the shadows but can't tell where they're coming from. Newk would walk through the clubhouse and say hello to somebody at the far end from me and I'd turn my back and stare into my locker.

Newk worked part-time for the Dodgers in a position called "community relations," which didn't have much to do with us in the clubhouse. I didn't know this at the time but he and another Dodger executive, Merritt Willey, a vice president for marketing, were helping Peter O'Malley form the Dodgers' company program for alcoholism. This was not yet public knowledge. For all I knew, Newk was visiting the clubhouse to line up a speaker for a Cub Scout supper in Canoga Park, but I had other suspicions.

Newk told me a year later that his first hint about my drinking came at a party given by Steve Yeager. Newk told me how I went up to Newk's wife and said: "Your husband thinks I drink too much, doesn't he?" To this day, I don't remember saying it. I don't even remember the party. But Newk says this kind of voluntary denial was a clear cry for help, an admission that I was an alcoholic.

"I wasn't going to let that boy go down the drain," Newcombe told people months later. "I know what happened to my career, and it wasn't going to happen to Bob Welch."

All I wanted to do was to avoid the man. It was like Rick Sutcliffe said at The Meadows: If I let people get to know me, I was afraid they wouldn't like me, so I kept my distance.

Other people were keeping tabs on me, too. Sometime during the summer I got a letter from Dale McReynolds, the scout who signed me. Most scouts don't have much to do with a player once he's signed, but McReynolds is a conscientious guy who still remembers the responsibilities he had toward young people when he taught school. Mac began hearing stories at staff meetings about my drinking and he cared enough about me to write a long and touching letter that said:

Dear Bob:

I'm home today for a rather rare appearance. The weather is brutal and dismal and I feel lower than a snake's belly for some reason. I should feel good; I got both our first-round drafts this week. . . .

This letter is a very personal one, Bob—a hard one for me to write. . . . My signing you in June, 1977, was without a doubt the greatest thing that ever happened to me in my twenty-five years of scouting. . . . I've logged well over a million miles in auto travel over these years and scouted perhaps 8,000 or more games. I've signed my share of players and have been able to get twelve or fourteen to the Majors. But no one like Bob Welch. . . . My signing you didn't make me one penny extra in money, Bob, but what it has done for me inside can in no way ever be measured in dollars.

Now, I feel badly, Bob. You owe me nothing—absolutely nothing. If anything, I always feel like I owe you. So what I say now is from my heart. I guess I love and respect you as I do my own son. I would do nothing in the world to ever hurt you or upset you. So read this slowly and try to digest what I'm trying to say.

The reports are coming back to me, Bob, that you're not coming close to taking proper care of yourself. That you're drinking much more than you should be. Cutting corners short. The word seems to come from all corners to me. People tell me now you could go downhill just as fast as you came uphill. I know that playing in LA, you're subject to a life style that is different, to say the least. When I first got this news about you, Bob, it hurt like hell. I have to admit, I broke out in a cold sweat. I felt weak and really "down." I sat in my chair and my shirt was soaked in a few minutes. It was somewhat like the time about fifteen years ago when my wife told me she was sick and in need of a serious operation. It scared hell out of me, to say the least.

Bobby—what can I say? I may even be out of bounds to even write to you about this. I sure as hell don't want to just preach at you. I'm told that our various club officials have tried very hard to slow you down and get you to shape up, but they say you pay little or no attention.

I read many stories and articles about you and they all bear down about that "space man" shit. Hell, you don't have to play any special role for all those dumb-ass writers, Bob. Inside, I think you have just about all the makings. You have the guts and super makeup. Space man, hell! You have the balls and courage and you have the pitching tools that can make you millions—and a super good life! All you have to do is just be the Bob Welch I think I signed and just take a little better care of the gifts God gave you.

I have no idea what you'd tell me if we could talk about this face on. You might even punch me out—or you might give me hell and tell me to mind my own damn business. I have no idea. If you do have a problem with your drinking, it can be curbed if you grit your teeth and work at it. In a way, I wish you'd come up with a super gal you might fall ass over heels in love with and then settle down with her. Somehow, as I look back on my case history, had I not met and married the little broad I've now spent thirty-six years with (as of Friday night, the Eighth of June), I'd have surely ended up being a tail-end, ticky-assed dump-truck driver. She's far too good for me, but God how she has helped me over the years!

I'm not what I'd call a deeply religious man, Bob. I mess up more than my share along the way, but I go to Church when I can and I've always found that I pray hard when I'm hurting and in need— and then I'm far too fast to forget once my prayers are answered!

Last night I prayed hard for you—for some answer as to how I might try to help you. This letter surely may not be the best answer but right now it's the only way I know. I'm selfish, Bob. I want you to make it and make it big in the years ahead. I want total happiness for both you and your family. . . . The price? Just a little common sense and some self-discipline. Like maybe getting seven–eight hours of sleep a night, eating a good diet, and not messing up your guts with drinking. Hell, Bob, there is seldom a day ever goes by that I won't have one or two drinks, but it stops right there. Twenty or more years back I made up my mind I wanted to be the best scout I could make myself be, and drinking was something I was going to make sure didn't hold me back.

I don't think you drink excessively because of the pressure. This thing of pressure was always something I thought you could handle about as well as any human being down here on planet earth! Maybe it's just restlessness. Dig into yourself and try to find out why you do some of the things you've done. For God's sake, don't just allow all that beautiful talent to dribble down the tube.

If you feel you'd really like to make some changes, then make them. Talk to older people who have been over the road a little and you may find some answers. Example: Dave Winfield.

Just go out and be a mean SOB on that hill. They say you've already lost a bit of the heat you had in the beginning. Other clubs say this, I'm told. So show the SOBs some heat they won't be likely to forget! You can, Bob. You damn well can. The price you need to pay isn't even all that high. Just some common sense and some care of your habits in your daily life.

I hope this will not set you out to kill me. Read it slowly and just try harder, Bob, to take care of yourself. You're an intelligent human being with a beautiful life ahead. For God's sake, Bob, don't sell yourself out for nothing when you're still in your early twenties. Like it or not, each night I'll say a prayer for you, asking God only that he guide you and give you the strength you so badly need. You may look at this and think I'm wacky now, but fifteen–twenty years from now you may well see me in a different light. Bless you and good luck!

> *Your friend,*
> DALE McREYNOLDS

Mac's letter definitely hit home. It made me stop and think. For at least ten minutes. Then I got ticked off, angry. I was mad at everybody for thinking I was a drunk, that I wasn't taking care of myself. I resented it at the time.

Things were not good between me and Mary. She had been worrying about my behavior since the time during the winter when I pushed her around in her family's cabin up North in Michigan. I told her to get the hell away from me, that I didn't need her. She had seen that other side of me, the violent side, and it scared her a little. She didn't know she was living with an alcoholic and she felt that if she was nice to me, and patient, I would see the errors of my ways.

It was hard for Mary and me to get our relationship going. There were times during the winter when we were together, when we knew it was going to end, and I would just get pissed off at her and say, "God damn it, Mary, just go." We always knew we would have to separate while she was in school and I was playing ball. It was hard to set myself up for a big love affair or something because I was going to leave, or she was going to leave.

Sometimes she'd call me on the telephone and she'd want to come right back out to California and I would say, "I know it's tough right now, you want to come back, but damn it, we're young, just don't worry about it, go to school." A couple of times I pushed her and said, "Hey, you need to go to school." But I knew she wanted to say, "Just send me a plane ticket, I want to come back," and she would start to cry. Each summer on her vacation from college, we would get together. In 1979 she was with me a couple of months, the longest we had lived together.

Mary started to get hints from other people in 1979. She had become friendly with Jean Ann Cresse, the wife of Mark Cresse, our bullpen coach. The two women began staying together while the Dodgers were on the road because neither of them likes to be alone. One night while we were out of town, Jean Ann told Mary, "People are afraid Bob is drinking himself out of the majors." Mary was stunned because she had not seen any of my worst drinking bouts, which were often on the road.

When the trip ended, Mary met me at the airport and on the way back to the house she told me what Jean Ann had said.

"I'm sick of all the big mouths getting on me," I said. "It's a lot of crap. I'm a victim of circumstances. People see me coming out of a bar and they assume I'm loaded. I don't have but one or two beers, and not even every night."

I got so indignant that Mary dropped the subject, which is just what an alcoholic plans in the back of his manipulative mind. Maybe I even believed I drank only a little bit, which was hardly the case. A couple of times I promised Mary I would stop but I'd go back in a week or two.

Dale McReynolds became concerned enough to call my brother, Donnie, and ask him to talk to me about my drinking. Donnie had moved out to California about three years earlier, but we didn't see each other that much. He was having his own problems with his job and his marriage but he found the time to invite me over to breakfast to talk something over.

"What does Donnie want?" Mary asked me.

"Oh, he's got some problem he wants me to help him with," I said, but secretly I think I knew what was coming.

At breakfast Donnie said, "Bob, people have been calling me, and telling me you're having a drinking problem. Why don't you quit for a while?"

I got mad and launched into my "victim of circumstances" speech, saying, "They wouldn't care if I drank a fifth of whiskey every day as long as I was winning. They're just getting on me because my arm is hurt."

Donnie didn't get very far with me. Nobody did. Alcoholics don't listen to "advice" or "suggestions." We need family and business confrontations. Threats about what we will lose if we don't seek help. My attorney, Bob Fenton, says guys like Rick Sutcliffe and Burt Hooton were passing hints to him in 1979—subtle little clues like, "Hey, Bob, you know Welchie is bending his elbow too much," and they were not talking about my pitching motion.

Fenton asked me about it, and I got angry and told him if he kept asking me about it he didn't have to be my agent, either.

Other players began to mention it to me. Davey Lopes had seen me drinking doubles in the hotel bar in Atlanta, and he and Dusty Baker had casually approached me in the trainer's room one night.

"We think you should check your priorities," Dusty said. "Make sure you're keeping yourself in good shape. You're too valuable to the club and to yourself to waste your talent."

They said it in a nice way and I assured them there was no problem. But the drinking wasn't helping my pitching. I had won four of my first five decisions before my arm started to hurt, but then I lost five straight decisions, including the game just before the All-Star break that dropped us to seventeen and a half games behind Houston. The season was turning into a disaster for me.

I took time off from throwing to rest my arm and yet I stayed with the team, going out to the ball park and running every night, but mostly it was running to sweat the alcohol out of me. I'd get upset over not pitching and get buzzed during the game, or after it. The next day I'd have to run the alcohol out of me again.

My reputation was catching up with me. Somebody saw me with a brown paper bag going up to my hotel room and passed the word up the line in the Dodger front office. When we got back to Los Angeles, Al Campanis called me in and made the first major intervention by the Dodger organization.

"Bob, we see you in bars, drinking quite heavily," Campanis said. "Somebody saw you leaving a bar with a brown paper bag and said it looked like you were carrying whiskey up to your room."

I blew my stack. I told him I was sick and tired of people telling me this. I said if I was pitching well they wouldn't be calling me in, which is probably true. Nobody would have noticed for a long time. Tom Lasorda was in the room and he said, "Bob, we care for you. We want to help you." But I didn't want to be helped.

Looking back, I can see how the Dodgers were trying to do their best with me at this stage. They knew enough to stage an intervention, but not a confrontation. There is a difference. The way they did it, they staged a general concern and brought up a few rumors and a few impressions. But that left me plenty of leeway to get mad and storm out.

Since going to The Meadows and reading some of the material, I know the way to handle an alcoholic is to get all the goods on him or her—specifics, like when and where and how and how much and with whom—and bring in enough family members, friends, and business associates who will make specific confrontations.

Also, the company has to be prepared to deliver an ultimatum: If your work doesn't improve to such-and-such a level, we will do such-and-such. Suppose the Dodgers had threatened to send me to the minor leagues or suspend me for health reasons? Would I have been more attentive? It's hard to say. A lot of companies and families are learning to confront alcoholics, and the Dodgers were getting to that stage, but it would take one more massive drinking bout by me to bring it to pass.

Chapter Fourteen

✦✕✕✕✕✕✕✕✕✕✕✕✕✕✕✕✕✕✕✕✕✕✕✕✦

Out of Control

✦◆◆✦

It all came to a head in San Francisco, my favorite city in the league. From the first time I visited the city, I felt as if I had discovered it myself, like Sir Francis Drake. I love the hills and the harbor and the food. Love going out and having a good time there.

I should have been in a good frame of mind going into San Francisco late in September because I had just combined with Joe Beckwith for a shutout earlier in the week, my first victory since May. But I was sulking about the season getting away from me, and I was out of control.

On Tuesday night, after our first game in San Francisco, I went to my favorite hangout—the Pierce Street Annex on Fillmore Street. I had discovered the place all by myself my first year in the majors. We stay at the Hilton downtown but I like some of the neighborhoods better. I hailed a taxi and told the guy I wanted a good local bar where you could hang out and listen to music. He took me to a section not too far from Fisherman's Wharf, to this bar with an open front and cartoons of some of the patrons hanging on the walls. Lots of guys, lots of pretty girls, lots of laughing and music. No sports motif at all. I don't think anybody cared about my being a ballplayer, although nowadays you might find a few of the guys in there

123

when the Dodgers are in town. Even though I'm sober now, I still make a beeline for the Annex when I'm in San Francisco, to visit my friend Gary Ferrari, a big, tall guy with a beard who is one of the owners.

I closed the Annex both the Tuesday and Wednesday nights after our games in September of 1979, and on Thursday I flopped back there around noon, pretty well messed up from the night before. I had a few drinks at the Annex and then I joined Gary Ferrari and Mickey Hatcher, one of my teammates, for lunch. I love the seafood in San Francisco, can't get enough of it. Sole, crab, shrimps, calamari, you name it, man, and put some cocktail sauce on it. Gary took us over to Alioto's on the Wharf, where he knows the owners. We hung around the bar for a while and I drank six Seven-and-Sevens while we waited for a table. Just belted them down like water, with a couple of beers for chasers. Then we sat down and ate lunch and I must have put away a bottle of wine. I would have stayed there forever but Hatcher reminded me we had to pack and put our luggage on the team bus to the ball park because we would leave for the airport right after the game.

I had only thirty minutes to pack and catch the team bus but there was something I had to do that was even more urgent. I needed a drink. I called room service and persuaded them to send up a bottle of wine right away. As soon as the waiter was out of my room, I chugged down that bottle like a kid drinking water from a canteen on a long hike. Just glugged it down. Somehow I put my clothes in a suitcase and checked out of my room and stumbled to the team bus, carrying my overnight bag.

The bus was crowded because we had brought up a lot of younger guys from the minor leagues, so there was not much room. I had to stand in the aisle, holding my bag, and I couldn't manage to place it in the overhead rack. I was laughing and I was crying—out of my mind.

One of my friends, Gerald Hannahs, did not want me to get caught by Tom Lasorda, who always sits in the front seat, so Gerald got up and gave me his seat. When we got to Candlestick Park, somebody ran into the clubhouse and alerted Rick Sutcliffe that I was in bad shape. Rick had become my closest friend (I guess you'd say he was my protector) on the team. I had pulled Rick into my army, as they say at The Meadows, and now I was really going to make him serve me. Rick has since supplied me with most of the details for this ugly moment in my life, because I do not remember them on my own.

According to Rick, I was slobbering tobacco juice all over my suit, weeping out of control and saying, "I'm drunk, I'm drunk," which anybody could tell from looking at me. He hustled me into the bathroom and got me some hot coffee and tried to pour it down me. Although most people think this is a good way to treat a drunk, it is not very effective. Alcohol is one drug, one chemical, for which there is no antidote. There is nothing you can take to alleviate the effect of the drug alcohol. You have to wait until it passes through your system, doing whatever it will to your brain cells, your liver, whatever.

Rick somehow managed to get me dressed and he shoved me into the locker room and told me to take a short nap while the rest of the guys were out taking practice. I guess I slept a few minutes and then woke up again. The trainer gave me some more coffee but that only made me more hyper. I decided to go out and take practice.

The visiting dressing room at Candlestick is down a long runway from the right-field corner. I stumbled down the runway and managed to push open the door and stagger onto the field. The Giants were taking batting practice and their guys were in the outfield shagging flies, but I decided to join them. I made one effort to catch a long fly but fell flat on my face. Couldn't take two steps. It was the way I had been in high school when I couldn't hit the backboards with a lay-up during warm-ups. People in the stands must have laughed. Rick says I just keeled over, as if I were shot.

I didn't care. I wandered toward home plate, where some of the Giants were standing around, waiting their turn to bat. Rick had followed me, afraid I would do something dangerous, and his instincts were correct. I saw some of the Giants looking quizzically at me as I lurched toward the batting cage. I decided that one of them, Terry Whitfield, was making fun of me, which was probably not the case. Nevertheless, I started cussing him out, in the worst language you can imagine.

Rick says Whitfield or anybody else would ordinarily start fighting at some of those words, but Whitfield apparently could tell I was not in my right mind. Rick says he shouted, "Terry, I'll explain later, don't think anything of it."

Whitfield did not go after me, although I understand I was challenging him to fight, shouting, "I want that man," like a regular

Muhammad Ali. You have to understand, I did not even know Terry Whitfield. Had nothing against the man. Rick slapped me across the face five times before he could shove me into left field, away from Whitfield and the rest of the Giants.

Rick walked me around left field, where some of the guys were loosening up. I must have been a sorry sight, because some of our pitchers started staring at me. Burt Hooton called over, "Hey, Bobby, what's up?" which was all I needed. I cursed at Hooton, who came over to investigate, but Rick told Hooton, "Just leave him alone," which got Hooton annoyed at Rick. A few months later at The Meadows, Rick said he was still angry at me for getting him caught between me and Hooton, a friend of ours.

At the end of practice, Rick took me back to the clubhouse, where Lasorda was looking for me. He's got a few people on his staff who are supposed to keep him informed, and somebody had done the job.

Lasorda told me he had to file a report to Al Campanis because too many people had seen me drunk. Lasorda chewed out my ass for not taking better care of myself, which just made me madder.

"You don't give a shit for me as a person," I yelled at Lasorda. "You let me go to the bullpen and I hurt my arm and now everybody's down on me because I had a horseshit season. You wouldn't care if I got drunk if I could pitch. You just throw me out there to win for the team."

I had volunteered for the bullpen, but now I was making Lasorda the scapegoat, turning it all around. Because he had no way of knowing I am an alcoholic, he was trying to be reasonable with me, stressing loyalty to Dodger Blue, urging me not to let my career go down the drain because of drinking. He kept saying he didn't want to hurt me but he had to tell Campanis because otherwise the front office would hear about it from some other source and get mad at him. In the meantime, Lasorda told me to stay in the clubhouse and sober up, which I did eventually.

The next afternoon, in Los Angeles, Al Campanis called me into his office, along with Lasorda and Red Adams, the pitching coach. Campanis said, "We've got information you're drinking on the plane. We warned you about bringing bottles in paper bags to your room"—which I never did—and he said he knew all the details of my drunken adventure in San Francisco the day before.

Lasorda said he was fining me five hundred dollars but that if I cut down on my drinking he would cut the fine in half by spring training. Campanis said, "I know what I would do if I were acting the way you are." His implication was that I should stop drinking altogether, that I just couldn't handle it.

The Dodgers also ordered me to see a liver specialist to determine if I had any malfunction or enlargement, since some people can ruin their health in a few months of drinking. The doctor did not find any damage but the Dodgers did implant in my mind the possibility of long-range physical harm from drinking. This scared me so much I got drunk during the final home games that weekend. Sneaked some more beers into the weight room.

By now everybody on the club knew about my behavior in San Francisco and were pretty much disgusted with me. Almost nobody talked to me that final weekend. I said to myself, "I'll show them," and I sneaked a few more beers and packed my gear and went home to Michigan, hardly saying good-bye to anybody.

When I got home, I could tell my parents were worried about me, too. They must have heard some of the stories, or maybe they just picked up on my actions. They didn't say much to me, however. I have come to realize this is a pattern in my family and in most families. Things go unsaid, even the most basic feelings. People think to themselves, "Well, they know how I feel." But it's much better to get it out, the way we later did at The Meadows.

My objective for that winter was to prove I did not have to get drunk all the time. I could tell that a lot of people were worried about me, and I wanted to stop. I worked out at Hamilton Place, a private club in Detroit, playing a lot of basketball. I even met a psychologist hanging around the club and thought about talking to him about my drinking. It hadn't dawned on me that I was an alcoholic, but I was beginning to realize I had some kind of problem. I could go a few weeks without taking a drink, and then I'd have a beer or two and go out and get loaded. I could not stop, once I started.

Late in October, Dale McReynolds invited me to have lunch with him at the Renaissance Center in Detroit. I think the Dodgers may have asked Mac to check up on me, and I agreed to have lunch because I really liked the man.

Mary and I drove into downtown Detroit, and over lunch Mac told me I was his No. 1 project for that winter. He said he was going to keep tabs on me, and he urged me to visit a hypnotist in Minneapolis who had worked with some other athletes' problems. I remember him saying, "Hell, it might even cure you of biting your nails."

I listened to Mac and agreed with everything he said, but I made that private reservation that I could drink in moderation. I was a little scared after fucking up in San Francisco and I wanted to stop for a while. Mac was telling me to cut down, but that wasn't enough for me.

In late November the Dodgers invited me to Toronto, where the baseball winter meetings were being held. Al Campanis asked me how I had done over Thanksgiving and I lied to him, saying I just had a glass of wine, when actually it was about forty beers, too. I was really trying, but there would always be a holiday or a family gathering I couldn't handle.

At Christmastime we visited my Aunt Lorraine and Uncle Art and I drank a whole fifth of C&C, got disgustingly drunk right in their house. I remember my father looking at me as if to say, "Son, there's a lot I'd like to tell you right now," but he didn't say it. I didn't give a damn, really. I was so badly drunk, yet I kept insisting I had to see my buddies at the Rainbow. I talked my father into driving out of his way to drop me off at the Rainbow, and later I passed out in Bryan's car and they just tossed me in the back doorway of my house.

Right after New Year's, Al Campanis called me again. He wanted to know how I had gotten through the holidays. Great, I told him. Just an occasional glass of wine with meals. He sounded skeptical on the phone and maybe a little unhappy I had been drinking at all. Maybe he knew more about my holiday drinking than I suspected. It's a possibility. The man did not discover Sandy Koufax and Roberto Clemente without having a few sources of information.

A few days later, Al's secretary, Marge, called me and said Al wanted to talk to me again. This time he said, "Bob, we'd like you to come to California and talk to somebody." I had just read an article in the *Sporting News* that the Dodgers had become the first club in sports to form an alcoholism program. I think I knew what they had in mind for me, but I really didn't ask. He said they had a plane reservation for me to come out and meet this person. I think they said he was a counselor.

I had been planning to go out to California toward the end of January because the Dodgers hold winter workouts in Dodger Stadium a month before spring training. It's a great time for baseball. While the rest of the country is freezing their ass off and watching pro basketball on television, the Dodgers get the jump on every other baseball team. You can tell it's time for baseball around the third week in

January, right after the Super Bowl, because there's a picture of Steve Garvey wearing Dodger Blue, taking his first cuts of the season. I was ready for that.

But was I ready for what the Dodgers had in mind? If the Dodgers were going to start a program about alcohol abuse, maybe they were going to use me as a speaker, since I took a drink once in a while. This was my line of reasoning, at least outwardly, but I think deep down inside I knew they were going to do something about me and I was glad. I was out of control, I knew I had a problem, but I didn't know what to do about it.

Mary didn't have any idea what was going on. I took her to the train station to go back to Kalamazoo and told her I was going out to Los Angeles to take care of some business. She had expected me to stay in Michigan for a few more weeks, and she was sad that I was leaving. Her face was full of tears as I put her on the train, but I couldn't tell her what the Dodgers planned. I really didn't know.

The next day I was flying to Los Angeles to meet this counselor. My friends, Jeff McKinney and Janet Falendysz, were going to drive me to the airport. We stopped for a package of eight little Millers to tide us over on the way to the airport. On the way out, I was giving them this bullshit story about how the Dodgers wanted me to work with youngsters who had alcohol-abuse problems. As I described my future in the alcohol-abuse field, I belted down five of those beers in half an hour. Then I got on the plane and drank as much as the stewardess would serve me. When I got to Los Angeles to begin my new career as a counselor to wayward youth, I was halfway smashed.

Chapter Fifteen

◆◆◆◆◆◆◆◆◆◆◆◆◆◆◆◆◆◆◆◆◆◆◆

A Game of Twenty Questions

◆◆

The Dodgers reserved a room for me in the Biltmore Hotel, one of those good old downtown hotels. I debated getting bombed that night, but kind of sensed what was coming in the morning, so I declined.

The next morning I was supposed to meet a man named John Newton, who works for Union Oil. We spotted each other in the lobby. He was wearing a business suit, with short hair, kind of thin and nervous, a persuasive talker. A salesman. He invited me to lunch at the special buffet—all you can eat for six dollars—at the Biltmore, and we talked about the Reggie Jackson game and the Dodgers.

After I had gone back for seconds, John Newton began talking about himself. He wanted me to know all about his life, nothing held back. He said he is an alcoholic who has been in jail five times for the things he did while drinking. This was the second time I had ever listened to an alcoholic's story, the first being Don Newcombe's history back in the spring.

Newton's story scared me, but I kept saying to myself, "This is his problem. He is an old drunk. It has nothing to do with me. I'm a young ballplayer. I'm different."

130

Nevertheless, I listened carefully as he told of his progression as an alcoholic since joining Union Oil thirty-four years earlier, and how he had used alcohol to cover up his ambitions and his frustrations.

"I always wanted to get ahead in the company," I remember Newton saying. "I started running a service station in Long Beach, then after a year I got the break I was waiting for—promoted to retail representative. This meant I could work in an office and drive a company car with a '76' decal on the side. It also gave me the privilege of using the company expense account, and I would take dealers to lunch.

"After a while I found myself entertaining the same two or three dealers all the time. Why? Because we all liked the same thing—a couple of martinis or more. Soon I stopped thinking about lunch and just drank in the middle of the day. We would sit around and tell each other the great things we were going to do when one of us got a toehold in the top management.

"I was very ambitious, Bob. That's one of the things people don't understand about alcoholics. They think alcoholics are shiftless bums, but we're very intense, very idealistic. We want things to be better for ourselves. For a long time I was able to drink and still do my job. This didn't mean I was bombed out of my skull all the time.

"When I came home late and drunk, I told my wife that drinking was a necessary part of the job, and the reason I had my job was that I could hold my liquor taking people to lunch. That was a lie. Sometimes I'd rush home and fix a pitcher of martinis before I kissed her hello. I wanted her to think that what she smelled on my breath was my first drink of the day. But she knew all along."

I sat and listened to the man and wondered a little if people detected when I was lying about my drinking. But I wasn't going to let on to this gruff, energetic man. I was going to sit and listen to his story and see if I could slide through this meeting.

Newton told me how he began doing promotional work at Dodger Stadium, buying drinks for people in the Stadium Club with his company credit card.

"One time after a game, I went to a bar downtown and then tried to drive home. I realized I was sleepy, so I pulled off to the side of the road, turned off the engine, and went to sleep. A few minutes later I woke up with a flashlight shining in my eyes. I told the officer I was just taking a nap and he told me I was parked in the fast lane of the Santa Ana Freeway. That's what drinking will do."

I thought about my car wrecks and my aggressive driving, cutting off people, flipping them the bird, falling asleep in my driveway. It was starting to sound familiar, but I wasn't going to tell him that. He continued:

"You can imagine what kind of father I was. When my children were playing Little League ball, I never had time to watch them play. I was too busy drinking. Of course, when they wanted to build a new Little League field, I could work a deal between the Dodgers and Union Oil and name the field after Vince Scully and get him down to dedicate it. To me, that was being a father—pulling a deal, getting a job done. But I was never around for my kids. I was an embarrassment to them, I suppose."

He told how he had been arrested for drinking, and went to Alcoholics Anonymous, only to fall off the wagon after ninety days. He said he saw the look of disgust on the face of his wife and children, and added: "Even my dog wouldn't come near me." But he said he had not taken a drink since then, St. Patrick's Day of 1968, after facing a simple truth from Alcoholics Anonymous.

"I told the company I could never promise them I would not take a drink. I wish I could, but in AA they teach you not to think about the future. They teach you to think one day at a time. That's what I've done.

"The weird thing, Bob, is that now I have everything I ever wanted. My family life is great. I've got a better job than I ever had. I work in the Medical Department at Union Oil, running a program that reaches all the alcoholics in our company. We run seminars for our executives to help them understand alcoholics. And we want to include family members in our program. A lot of workers have husbands or wives who drink at home. It's almost worse for women. They need to conceal it more. A housewife can't go to a bar the way a working somebody can who is working downtown, and call it a lunch break. So she has to lie more, hide bottles in closets, even in the water tank of the toilet. We're learning to help people who have a problem."

Newton reached into his attaché case and pulled out a thimble. He said, "I'm only one thimbleful of alcohol from being drunk. That's all it takes, because alcoholism is a progressive disease. I'd be more affected by one thimbleful now than on St. Patrick's Day of 1968, even though I haven't had a drop since."

The talk was making me nervous, so I tried to get off the hook by saying, "Yeah, man, but I don't drink whiskey. I mostly drink beer. I could cut back to just beer any time I wanted."

Newton reached into his attaché case and pulled out another prop. He was a regular traveling salesman with all his wares in his luggage. He held up a beer can and said: "All right, so you only drink beer. Do you know there is one shot of alcohol in every can of beer?" And with that he flourished a shot glass, looking like a Tupperware salesman pushing his forty-eight-piece set. With a gleam in his eye he asked me, "Do you ever drink a six-pack?"

"Once in a while," I lied.

"Well, that is the equivalent of six shots of whiskey," Newton said. "That would take six hours to get out of your bloodstream, and you would fail any drunk test the police could give you. Beer is just as bad, just as dangerous as whiskey."

We finished lunch and went up to my room. He still had not made any direct challenge to me, and I was wondering how this master salesman was going to approach the subject. When we got settled, he pulled out a yellow card, about the size of a postcard, with twenty questions printed on it.

ARE YOU AN ALCOHOLIC?

To answer this question ask yourself the following questions and answer them as honestly as you can.

If you have answered YES to any one of the questions, there is a definite warning that YOU MAY BE ALCOHOLIC.

If you have answered YES to any two, the chances are that you ARE AN ALCOHOLIC.

If you have answered YES to THREE OR MORE, YOU ARE DEFINITELY AN ALCOHOLIC.

"Bob, this test was devised by Johns Hopkins University to determine whether somebody is an alcoholic. I'd like you to mark yes or no to the questions," Newton said.

I took a pen and deliberated the answer to each question:

1. "Do you lose time from work due to drinking?" I marked yes, remembering how I didn't pitch the last week of 1979 because of my epic drunk in San Francisco.

2. "Is drinking making your home life unhappy?" Yes, thinking

about Mary worrying about my drinking, and how I acted at my family's Christmas party, and the worried look on my mother's face.

3. "Do you drink because you are shy with other people? I marked no. Looking back, there might have been more to it, but at the time I said no.

4. "Is drinking affecting your reputation?" I thought of the looks of disdain around the Dodger clubhouse after I got drunk in San Francisco. I could tell people thought I was a bad drunk. I marked yes.

5. "Have you ever felt remorse after drinking?" Yes, definitely. I just didn't know what to do about it.

6. "Have you gotten into financial difficulties as a result of drinking?" Not yet. I marked no.

7. "Do you turn to lower companions and inferior environment when drinking?" I marked no.

8. "Does your drinking make you careless of your family's welfare?" Since I wasn't married, and was making a good income, the answer, for the time being, was no.

9. "Has your ambition decreased since drinking?" Not my ambition, my performance. No.

10. "Do you crave a drink at a definite time daily?" No.

11. "Do you want a drink the next morning?" No. Not yet.

12. "Does drinking cause you to have difficulty sleeping?" No.

13. "Has your efficiency decreased since drinking?" I marked no.

14. "Is drinking jeopardizing your job or business?" A definite yes. I knew that.

15. "Do you drink to escape from worries or troubles?" I thought of my arm troubles and my resentments about the bullpen and marked yes.

16. "Do you drink alone?" Even if Al Campanis thought I did, I didn't. No.

17. "Have you ever had a complete loss of memory as a result of drinking?" I remembered Mary telling me how I shoved her around the cabin up in Michigan, and how I didn't believe her when she told me. I had to be honest. I marked yes.

18. "Has your physician ever treated you for drinking?" I realized the Dodgers had sent me to a liver specialist. I marked yes.

19. "Do you drink to build up your self-confidence?" I marked no.

20. "Have you ever been to a hospital or institution on account of drinking?" No. Not yet.

I handed over the card to John Newton. He scanned the results. Eight yes, twelve no.

"Bob, according to the Johns Hopkins test, if you answer yes to just one question there is a definite warning you may be an alcoholic. If you have answered yes to two, the chances are you are an alcoholic. If you have answered yes to three or more, you are definitely an alcoholic. Bob, you have answered yes to eight of these questions. In my mind, you are definitely an alcoholic."

He asked me about my answer to No. 17, about loss of memory, and I told him about Mary telling me how I shoved her and told her I didn't need her, and how I couldn't remember it.

"That is called a blackout," Newton said. "Alcoholics start having blackouts when they've been drinking for a while. You are progressing right along, Bob."

"Well, I can stop on my own," I said. "Any time I want."

"Bob, your answers indicate that you are powerless over alcoholism. You can't stop drinking on your own. People have been covering up for you, lying for you, denying for you, helping you get this far. This is the time to stop. This is the time to admit you are powerless."

"What do you want me to do?"

I expected he would ask me to attend some meetings or some lectures in Los Angeles while I prepared for the season. I had a shock coming to me.

"Bob, the Dodgers are setting up a program to combat alcoholism in their organization. Peter O'Malley, the owner of the Dodgers, is a board member of Union Oil and he has heard about our program. He has been talking to people like Merritt Willey and Don Newcombe, and he wants to get involved. My boss, Dr. Richard Call, has agreed to let me be a liaison to the Dodgers, and when I proposed a company program, some of the Dodger people asked, 'Does this apply to players? We have at least one player we suspect.' They mentioned your name. Bob, they're worried about you.

"We think it's best for you to enter an addiction treatment center called The Meadows, in Wickenburg, Arizona. It's about an hour outside Phoenix, a former dude ranch, and you'll stay five or six weeks. They'll give you medical and psychological treatment there, lectures on what alcohol does to your body, but mostly you'll be part of encounter groups among patients who examine why they drink. Toward the end of your time down there, you'll have your own family down to help you. But mostly, you'll have to do it on your own."

He mentioned that The Meadows had a pool and horseback riding but he added, "It ain't Disneyland, pal." He said the food would be basic and that most of my time would be spent in encounter groups, being prodded to open up about myself.

"If you don't tell them things at The Meadows, they'll find out anyway. You'll find out more about yourself if you talk."

I heard Newton's words but deep down inside myself I said, "The hell with that. I ain't gonna open up. I might stop drinking if I can, but I ain't gonna tell anybody about myself."

John asked me whether I would agree to go to The Meadows. The truth is, I was tired of having problems with my drinking, and I wanted to help myself. I didn't want to ruin my life. But on the other hand, I wasn't ready to admit that I was an alcoholic, and the idea of not drinking at all seemed very distant. I just wanted to "control" my drinking, whatever that meant.

"Hell, yes, I'll go," I told him.

"Bob, I'm not going to kid you. It will be the toughest thing you've ever done. Much tougher than making the major leagues. That was easy compared to this. People will tell you things about yourself that you won't like. You'll be angry, lonely, sad, miserable, sometimes you'll want to quit. But it will help you save your life."

Newton told me the Dodgers' medical insurance would cover my entire treatment, including transportation for my family and Mary Ellen. He pointed out that the cost would be cheap to any company, to keep from replacing a valuable employee.

Newton made a telephone call to the Dodger offices and in a few minutes we were joined by Fred Claire, a vice president of the team, who assured me the Dodgers wanted to help me, and that all the costs would be covered by their medical insurance. He said he would make arrangements for me to enter The Meadows as soon as possible, and after a couple of phone calls it was determined I could have a place on Thursday.

It was already Monday afternoon. I was supposed to fly by myself from Los Angeles to Phoenix on Thursday, but I asked John Newton to fly with me. He said he ordinarily didn't accompany people like that, but he agreed he would fly over with me but then I'd be on my own. Fred Claire assured me the Dodgers would stand by me every step of the way. Then he left, and John Newton and I took a walk.

I was a little nervous about going to this treatment center—scared, really. I had seen movies about people in encounter groups, shouting at each other, making accusations, very emotional, very revealing. I had taken a few psychology courses in college about human relationships, and I was afraid of having people try to get inside me. I couldn't have put into words what I didn't want to share. There was some inner core I was afraid of having people see—the part of me that was afraid, the part that wanted to cry, the part that hurt when people looked at me the wrong way.

I didn't know it at the time, but I thought if people knew me, they wouldn't like me. I was already planning my defenses, my escape mechanisms. If somebody asks me about myself, I'll give him a flip answer. Or I'll cut him off with a stare. I was practicing my moves in front of a mental mirror, just the way I'd practice my pick-off move to first base.

John Newton and I strolled around the neighborhood. People like to make jokes about there not being a downtown Los Angeles, but actually there are tall buildings, hotels, and even office buildings, just like in any downtown. John pointed out an older brick building which I hardly noticed at first, saying it was the California Club, so exclusive that you have to prove you can come up with a million dollars in cash before you can belong.

We walked another block to the Los Angeles Public Library, where the derelicts were getting their rays on the front lawn. These guys were wearing rags and their hair was matted and their faces were dirty. Most of them were sipping lunch.

"Most people think of alcoholics as being Skid Row bums," Newton said. "But actually only around 2 percent ever reach Skid Row. Most alcoholics hold their jobs and their responsibility while they destroy their lives slowly. When they die of alcoholism, the doctor does them a favor and lists the death as heart failure or something else.

"The great majority of alcoholics seem to be normal people, not bums," Newton continued. "We are the businessman down the block, the housewife across the street, the kid on his way to high school, the athlete in the sports pages."

We walked uphill over the Fifth Street Bridge. John pointed down at the thick foliage under the bridge and I saw a few guys sleeping on cardboard boxes, newspaper wrappings, old rags. There were bottles everywhere.

"Every so often the police come and carry away a body," John said. John wasn't exactly saying I'd wind up living under the Fifth Street Bridge, but he was suggesting I might die if I continued the way I was going. I wanted to live.

Chapter Sixteen

◆◆◆◆◆◆◆◆◆◆◆◆◆◆◆◆◆◆◆◆◆◆◆◆◆◆

Holding Back

◆◆

I stayed with my friend Mike Josephs in Burbank from Monday through Thursday until it was time to leave for Phoenix. I had met Mike through Lance Rautzhan, my Dodger roommate. Mike is a businessman, a few years older than me, and he was very supportive at the time I needed it. I was scared and I was entertaining second thoughts about going to Arizona. I kept telling myself that the master salesman John Newton had put one over on me, talked me into joining the club.

The little tin god that resides inside every alcoholic kept telling me, "You can handle it. You just have to drink in moderation. You don't need a treatment center." One night I had a couple of beers and nothing much happened, but I know now that was just luck. Mike kept me from listening too carefully to the whispers that I could handle it. Mike's approach was unique. He reasoned with me: "What's going to happen when you're not playing baseball and you have all that time to drink?" That was scary to think about. I called Mary and told her I was committing myself. At first she wasn't comfortable about thinking of me as an alcoholic, and she tried to deny it, but after we discussed going for treatment she told me it was a good idea.

On Thursday I traveled to The Meadows—flew to Phoenix with

John Newton, drove to Wickenburg with Pat Mellody, saw the little old dude ranch on the hill, hauled my luggage from the driveway, where Pat had left it, showing me I was no guest but rather part of the group.

After I checked in at the business office and informed the nurses I was not really an alcoholic—they knew denial when they heard it—I was given a tour of the main building. Everywhere I looked there were posters: "The Twelve Steps of Alcoholics Anonymous," "Don't Ever Quit," "Don't Look Back," "To Love Somebody Is to Hang with Them." You got a feeling of caring from the posters, plus from the nurses—good women, full of love.

I wandered into the main dining room, with a huge fireplace at one end. At every table there was a box of tissues, which I wondered about at first. Later I would understand the need for them. In a few minutes, the afternoon meeting broke up and people streamed into the narrow kitchen to help themselves to juice, soda, tea, or coffee. (The coffee was decaffeinated, I found out later. In my thirty-six days at The Meadows, I started drinking ten cups of coffee a day, which didn't bother me until I went home and had a couple of cups of the real thing. Talk about getting a buzz on.)

I was watching the patients and their families sitting around the tables, some talking, some staring into space, some happy, some sad. Many of them had sorrowful, wrinkled faces, reflecting years of sickness and worry. Having just arrived, I felt extremely conspicuous, felt everybody was staring at me. I guess I was a little nervous about being recognized. Part of me wanted to be Bob Welch the baseball player, so I could convince myself I was different, not like these old drunks. Part of me wanted to fit right in, to be just plain Bob. Later I found out there was a rumor that a baseball player was coming in, and everybody figured it was me.

I didn't know what to do next until this tall blond kid, no more than fourteen years old, with his long hair feathered on the side—a California beach-boy type—came over and said, "Hi, my name is Chris."

"Mine is Bob. Bob Welch."

"I thought it was you. I live in Lakewood."

"I stay right near there, at Huntington Beach. What the hell are you doing here? How old are you, anyway?"

"Fourteen."

"You're too young to be here, man."

"You don't have to be old to be an alcoholic. I'm an alcoholic and I smoke dope, too, but I'm giving it up."

I couldn't believe it. I thought I was too young to be an alcoholic, but here was this kid, hardly into his teens, and he was calling himself an alcoholic. We sat around and shot the bull about California and baseball and getting drunk and girls—all the stuff that really matters in life. He had been there two weeks and was telling me about the Twelve Steps, how you progress by telling people about yourself. He was proud of himself for passing the first two steps already and he said, "This place is really good. I've learned a lot. If I can help you at all, let me know." I felt much more comfortable knowing Chris was around.

Later that first day I spent time with my counselor, Lynn Brennan. She asked me a few questions for my evaluation chart, like why I was there, how I felt about my family, things I had done because of alcohol. I found it easy to talk to Lynn. She is a blonde with green eyes, around forty years old, I guess. She would fasten those eyes on you and you couldn't escape, but she was not threatening, either.

If she had been a man, I probably would have fought harder. There was a male counselor, Fred, a very aggressive guy. I admired the man for the way he ran the family week but I could never feel as comfortable with him as with Lynn. I'd always be holding something back with him. There is just something more comfortable about talking with a woman. Even when I was drinking, I could talk with a few guys on the club like Rick Sutcliffe or Dusty Baker or Red Adams, the pitching coach, but it was always easier to sit and talk with a woman. Maybe I didn't feel I was competing, the way men compete.

Maybe it was from being close to my sister, Diane, when I was younger. I always felt I could be more open with women. Their personalities are softer, they're more in touch with their feelings. Men just don't want to show their feelings for one reason or another. Of course, when I say that, I'm talking about myself. I never used to sit around and share my feelings with men. With a few of my friends like Jimmy Penzabene and Bryan Carley back in Hazel Park, we can talk about what we're going to do, and why we're going to do it, but even with them, I think there's always something held in reserve.

It's the *macho* thing, I guess. Men are supposed to be tough. When you sit in the movies, you don't want to show you're crying, not even to your girlfriend. You shove it down. At The Meadows they would eventually show me how I held my feelings back, even around Mary Ellen. I suppose I had learned those lessons when I was very young, but my way to ignore my feelings was to get drunk. That was the only way I could do it. At The Meadows, they stressed feelings all the time. They asked how you felt about everything. If you said you weren't feeling anything at the moment, Lynn would say, "I don't believe you."

From the first day, Lynn warned me she could be tough. When I began attending family week sessions, I realized she was like a guided missile waiting to strike. One week she was working with a guy who was a military officer and refused to open up his feelings. His family revealed some things about him that he had never disclosed after weeks at The Meadows. She shouted at him and called him a liar and told him, "Right now I don't like you at all." She concluded her dressing-down by telling him he would need another full session at The Meadows if he didn't straighten out, and she snapped: "I know you can afford it—Captain!" Her tone was so angry, you could see his head jerk back.

The guy straightened out and began talking more openly the next day. Lynn's nuclear warhead had done its job.

Lynn never yelled at me like that. She was tough but she also was gentle. I felt comfortable working with her, as if she were my sister. While I was working on this book, somebody commented that Lynn is an attractive woman and I realized I had forgotten about that. I had gotten to where I love her as a human being, enjoyed being around her, without feeling any urge to seduce. That is a tribute to Lynn as a professional. From our first talk together, I trusted her. I knew she would listen to what I said. I also knew she picked up on all my signals.

I wasn't all that trusting of everybody. I did not like the psychologist who examined me. I realized the man was just going to meet me once and make a judgment, so I screwed around with him, gave him stupid answers. We were like two bulls locking horns and getting nothing accomplished. I'm sure he thought I was full of anger.

One of the first days I was there, they made me attend a lecture on sex, given by one of the nurses. She kept using the same words over again, how men consider it a compliment to be called a "stud," or even think it is a sign of strength to be called a "prick," but that the term "pussy" for a woman is considered weak, derogatory. I didn't care much for that lecture and showed it, but it made me stop and think.

I did not love it when they finally found a set of blue cotton pajamas to replace my jogging suit and made me wear the pajamas until I was considered medically healthy. They also made me sign a slip that I would not touch alcohol or any kind of drugs, even aspirins, while at The Meadows. I did not appreciate it when they said I had to make my bed every day, and change sheets every Thursday. Eventually I snaggled some of the aides to help make my bed, but mostly I did it myself.

The Meadows was very strict about using the telephone because they wanted you to concentrate on your own feelings and not be swayed by your friends or your family. The only way you could use the telephone was to ask permission in the office. On my second day they asked if my parents knew where I was and if I wanted to call them. As far as my mother and father knew, I was out in California.

I tried to act cool while I made the call because I was speaking from the nurses' station, and people were coming and going all the time.

"Mom, it's me, Bobby. Guess what? I'm not in California. I'm at The Meadows, an alcohol rehabilitation center in Arizona. I'm getting dried out with a bunch of alcoholics. A guy in California says I am an alcoholic."

I had thought my mother would be surprised or worried when she heard the news, but she said:

"Well, that's great you're there. I'm so glad you're doing that."

I told her the entire family would have to come out in a couple of weeks for family week, and she said they'd be happy to do it. Then my father got on and said, "Hang in there. Just remember, we're here, we'll do anything we can. Write us a letter."

When the call was over, I felt they had both been giving a sigh of relief, which I was doing, too. They must have thought I was an alcoholic all along but couldn't put it into words. I was full of feelings at that moment. I was ashamed for putting them through this but I also was relieved that I was getting help. I was sad to be so far away from them but happy they were so positive.

My composure broke down as soon as I hung up the phone. I had been so cool talking to Mom and Dad, but now I was blubbering like a baby, sobbing away in the nurses' station.

"That was a bitch, but my parents gave me their support," I told the nurses.

I tell you what: If you're going to have a crying seizure, that's the place to do it. A couple of those nurses came over and gave me a hug and then Lynn put her arms around me and gave me a squeeze and told me everything would be all right. I told her, "That was the hardest thing I ever did."

In those first hours at The Meadows, I broke down and cried in the shower until I made up my mind that I did have a serious problem and would deal with it one day at a time. Also, I was very competitive. I did not want to go back to Los Angeles and say, "I could not hack it." I just hated to lose at anything. Always have, always will.

The next morning I woke up and realized how beautiful it is in Arizona. The sun was rising over the mountains in the east, and the bigger ranges to the north were shimmering purple. Just sitting on the patio and looking at the land made me want to jump up and sing a few stanzas of "America the Beautiful." It was so peaceful, so isolated, that I felt good just being there. The beauty of the land helped me face the first full day of group sessions.

I was put in with a group of patients who had been there a few days or a few weeks. Before each session began, they'd sit around talking about somebody's problem, or telling drunk stories from the "old days"—meaning a few weeks ago. I had nicknames for each of them in short order. The Silver Fox. Tom T. Hall. Pappy Jake.

A lot of the stories concentrated on places to hide their booze. The Silver Fox was a yard man. He would hide his bottle under the leaves while raking up the backyard. Every twenty minutes he would take a hit from the bottle while his wife looked out from the kitchen window and thought how healthy and safe he looked, working in the yard. Another guy kept booze in a Listerine bottle. Another guy hid his bottle in the water tank of the toilet. Me? I remembered when I was living at home, hitting on the whiskey bottle my father kept in the kitchen pantry, and after I took my gulp, I'd pour in some water so they wouldn't suspect anything. Or so I thought.

I loved the stories but did not care for the group sessions. Lynn had me introduce myself, and the guys started asking how I felt. I flared up at that. It was one thing to open up to Lynn, but quite another to open up to a bunch of patients sitting around in a circle of folding chairs. We were not allowed to bring food or drink or cigarettes into the room because they didn't want you ducking out of participating by puffing or chewing or drinking. You would sit in the circle, no place to hide, and somebody would ask, "Bob, how do you feel today?" If you wouldn't answer, they would ask, "Well, you must feel something. Are you mad, glad, or sad?"

They did not want to know what you thought. They did not want your judgments about how things should be. They wanted your feelings. I would never say I was sad or mad because then they would want to know why you felt that way. I would say, "I'm glad because I'm here at The Meadows getting help." That would satisfy them for a while. I was trying to sneak through. If they prodded me, I'd get ticked off and feel the urge to tell them to jump in the lake.

From the first day, Lynn picked up on my anger. She would say, "Bob, you're mad because people are asking how you feel." If I .denied it, they would point out little physical signs like my eyes blinking or my arms folded across my chest or my legs crossed.

I knew they had me. I had taken a couple of classes on interpersonal relations back at college and I understood what they were saying. Lynn said my voice was choppy, like I was choking off my feelings, and she would urge me to spit out my feelings. That first day, when people told me how I looked, it was like having somebody poke a stick deep into my stomach. I felt I was being personally assaulted. But what could I say? Where could I go?

In Lynn's sessions, the mood was very positive. Some guys thought she was very tough, very *macho*, but I thought she was considerate and gentle, always wearing soft colors, her hair always neat, her voice soft unless she got mad at somebody. Then her voice could cut.

It was hard to put things over on the counselors because most of them considered themselves addicts of one kind or another. A few had problems with alcohol, one of the men had consistently tried to seduce women, one of the female counselors considered herself a co-alcoholic because she had made it easier for her ex-husband to drink. Another counselor said she had been addicted to sugar, that anything sweet could bring on a buzz of energy that kept her from confronting herself. From the first day, they let you know they understood addiction.

When you were not in a group session, you attended lectures on grief or family structure or the effects of alcohol upon your body. Just by sitting there, you would learn a lot. I was scared to hear that alcoholism is a progressive disease, just as John Newton had told me in Los Angeles. I realized this was not just a theory he had invented. The lecturer said you could lay off for ten or twenty years and be worse than ever if you started drinking again. They stressed that there is no such thing as a "former alcoholic." Once an alcoholic, always an alcoholic. You could be a "recovering alcoholic" but there is no such thing as a "recovered alcoholic."

I also learned there is such a thing as a "dry drunk," somebody who has stopped drinking but still acts like a drunk—argumentative, irrational, noisy, impetuous. That person has not yet learned to cope with his or her feelings, even though he or she has stopped drinking for the time being.

One thing I heard over and over again at The Meadows:

"Every addict thinks of himself as a garbage can—no damn good. Here we learn to get rid of our garbage."

I heard people talking about their resentments toward their parents, about resentments to brothers and sisters, fear of dying or growing old, fear of having children, resentments over divorce. Just in those first few days I heard people sobbing about things that happened to them years before. Sitting there in my cute little blue cotton pajamas and my tennis sneakers, I felt like a front-row spectator at some improvised play. Get up onstage and recite some lines myself? Not me, buddy.

Chapter Seventeen

✦✦✦✦✦✦✦✦✦✦✦✦✦✦✦✦✦✦✦✦✦✦✦✦✦✦✦

Part of a Family

✦✦

After I'd been at The Meadows a few days, they let me get out of my pajamas and join the human race. Because I had been dry for a couple of days before I came, and because I was a lot younger than many of the patients, I didn't have medical problems the way a lot of patients did. You'd see people nodding out on couches in corners or trembling as they walked, until they got all the alcohol and drugs out of their system.

One woman was being medically treated for alcohol withdrawal but her family never bothered to mention her pill addiction. An upper-class woman, she had badgered about ten doctors and pharmacists into letting her have pills, and she damn near died before the nurses at The Meadows figured out her complications.

On my first Monday, I began taking part in the patients' group session in the morning and joining a five-day family group session in the afternoon. I was expected to share my feelings about other people and about myself.

The leader of family week was a counselor named Fred Downing, an intense-looking man around forty-five years old. I always thought he looked like a small model of Johnny Cash with the same wavy black hair and that wild look in his eyes. Fred is a minister but he

147

didn't fit my image of one. I had always figured ministers to be soft-looking people with their hands folded in prayer and maybe a pipe in their mouths—gentle types, father figures. Fred was not like that at all. He looked tense and combative—like a guy who'd get into fights in a bar, or some tough football coach.

Fred had a favorite ministerial expression when somebody was not being honest. He would say, "In purely theological terms—bullshit!"

The truth of the matter was, Fred looked as nervous as any of the patients and described himself as "an addict" when he introduced himself in the morning session. I later heard he told some people in his group that his addiction had been women—particularly the women in his former congregation. I had never thought sex could be an addiction the same as drugs or alcohol, but after some of the patients talked about it one day, I could see how it could. Sex could be an addiction if a man needs a woman or a lot of women to feel better about himself. Fred said he had taken treatment for his problem and I could see he was now a highly effective leader of family week. Not everybody loved his tactics. The man is a bulldog who will sink his teeth into the shins of anybody who does not cooperate. I would discover that in due time, and so would my family and my manager, Tom Lasorda.

"We use addiction to prove we are somebody," Fred once said. "Once we discover our needs are not being met one way, we try to meet them another way."

He added, "The biggest problem with the treatment of alcoholism is the idea that it is a moral problem. That may be the reason people deny it. But it isn't a problem of being immoral. It's a problem of feelings."

Fred said family week would be crucial to the treatment of the patients and their family members because "this is when things come together. It's a week for miracles, when the old becomes the new, when people turn from death to life, when water is turned to wine, just like in the Bible. This is what the world is all about.

"An addiction is a disease—a spiritual disease, a physical disease, an emotional disease, a familial disease—and a learned disease," Fred added. "I think we treat all five of these aspects at The Meadows."

Fred described how he had set up the week on a religious format, with Wednesday being Crucifixion Day and Thursday being Resurrection Day and Friday being Forgiveness Day, when people give up the pain they have received from others in the past. Most of these terms were from the New Testament, but Fred would quickly shift gears if a Jewish person enrolled at The Meadows, which often happened. He would use examples like Adam and Eve being banned from the Garden of Eden or how the Israelites had to wander in the desert, or how the Jews were put to death by religious fanatics, called Zealots. Whether Fred was working in the New Testament or in the Old Testament, his message was forgiveness and healing.

I remember one Friday on Forgiveness Day, a woman had tried hard to get rid of pain from her first husband, but was still feeling sad on Friday. She felt that she had given up a family by giving up her husband, and wanted to feel that she had gained another family at The Meadows. The entire family group stood up in a circle and hugged her, one by one, as she walked around the circle. Everybody was weeping. It was like a religious ceremony, only even more beautiful because it was spontaneous. People really felt it.

I hadn't bargained on The Meadows having religious overtones when John Newton talked about it. If I had realized it, I don't know if it would have turned me off or not. They didn't have any big statues around or crosses on the tops of buildings like they do in churches, and the language of us drunks was hardly religious. Some of the counselors did not stress religion, but the two people I was closest to, Fred and Lynn, gave off a strong sense of religious commitment. They never preached but I always got the feeling they believed in something.

It was just enough that I could be comfortable with. My family had never gone to church much and I remember my sister, Diane, trying to get me to go a few times when I was a kid. I'd put up such a fuss she had to let me leave. I still didn't like going to church that much, but I didn't feel uncomfortable when Fred talked about the Higher Power (they used that term more than "God").

Sometimes Fred would say something like, "An alcoholic cannot be an atheist because an alcoholic creates his own god—himself. He definitely believes in a Higher Power." He kept stressing that family week was a time of forgiveness, a time of miracles.

I know I wanted a miracle. I wanted to get out of The Meadows as quickly as possible and never take another drink. I wanted my family life to be better. And I wanted my relationship with Mary to grow without alcohol. I sat there watching these other families confront each other, and I felt a little jealous because the patients had arrived at a point where they could deal with the troubles in their own families while I had to wait my turn. But they wouldn't let me hang back. I was expected to give these people feedback.

We sat in a big circle in plastic chairs. Fred was a demon on making sure those chairs touched because he wanted contact all the time. At first I thought it was corny, how we'd start off each session standing in a circle and putting our arm around the person next to us. I felt funny making contact with people who were strangers to me. I was used to hugging Mary and some friends and relatives, but this was different. It wasn't like after a victory, when the Dodgers would come over all sweaty and give each other hugs. Lasorda was the greatest at that—big back-pounding hugs if you pitched well. But away from the field we would never touch. Here at The Meadows you always touched.

You'd start each family session in the circle, everybody standing up, your arms behind the person on either side of you. You'd feel the rolls of fat or the pitiful ribs of a skinny old drunk, man or woman, it wouldn't make any difference. Or you'd hold hands while everyone recited the Serenity Prayer, which is used by Alcoholics Anonymous. I had never heard it before coming to The Meadows but after a few days I could recite it by heart:

> God grant me the serenity to accept the things I cannot change—the courage to change the things I can—and the wisdom to know the difference—living one day at a time.

I remember the first time I held hands with a man at this session —feeling a big, rough hand with calluses and hair all over the back, and thinking to myself, "Damn, last week I was just a drunk, now I'm holding hands with a guy." But after a day or two, it didn't make a difference anymore. You'd squeeze the hand and feel the squeeze back. We were all in this together.

But I've got to admit, I'd pick and choose when hugging time came around. Sometimes before a session, they'd announce we could have six or eight hugs and I'd maneuver my way around the room to hug with Lynn or some of the women patients.

After we got through hugging, Fred would ask, "Who wants to work today?" Work meant one of the family members would confront the patient with the ways they had been hurt by the drunken behavior in the past. They'd move one plastic chair into the circle, facing the family member, and the patient would have to sit there and listen—no answering back. Fred knew all the tricks.

Fred had a way of breaking down people until they showed their deepest feelings. The first couple of times I saw people open up, I couldn't help but think they were acting, that they were putting on some kind of show for us.

A woman might be insisting she was not mad at her husband for sleeping around when he got drunk, insisting she was liberal or tolerant or whatever, but Fred would ask, "How do you really feel?" She would say she felt all right but Fred would keep at her until her face started to quiver and tears would be gushing from her eyes. It was then I realized why there were boxes of Kleenex all over The Meadows. While she was starting to cry, somebody in the circle would be passing the box toward her. And Fred would ask, "How do you feel?"

Pretty soon she would say, "I feel hurt. I feel sad."

"And that makes you feel . . . ?"

In most cases that meant angry. The alcoholics were angry at things that happened to them in their youth, and the family members were angry over things the alcoholic had done. That scared me because I sure as hell didn't want to share any of my feelings with strangers. I might give feedback but I wasn't going to say how I felt —if I really knew.

From the start, the counselors felt I was some kind of raving madman. A couple of them commented on the look of anger they detected in my eyes. It was the kind of anger that would come out when I was drinking—the insults Mary said I would give her, the way I picked a fight with players on the field in San Francisco at the end of the season. It was there, and the people at The Meadows were going to do their best to find out why Bob Welch had anger in his eyes.

They have a way of dealing with anger at The Meadows that I saw in the first family week. There was a young man who had a lot of anger at his parents, but the counselors couldn't get him to express it. Fred finally got him to admit he was mad.

"How mad?" Fred asked.

"Pretty mad," the guy admitted, his face starting to tighten up.

"Tell your parents how mad," Fred suggested.

The guy just shrugged and stared. He couldn't put it into words.

"You must be pretty mad," Lynn said. "Your arms are twitching. You should tell your parents how mad you are."

"I'm mad," the guy said.

"I'm so mad I could . . ." Fred said. "Are you mad enough to hit someone?"

Before the guy could answer, Fred reached behind an easy chair and pulled out a hard plastic bat with handles, something like those ninety-nine-cent whiffle bats you buy in the toy store. Fred put the bat in the guy's hand.

"This is a *bataca*," Fred said. "Show how mad you are by hitting the chair."

Gripping the bat with two hands, the guy tapped an empty chair.

"You can hit harder than that," Fred said.

The guy whacked the chair again, harder. Then he started swinging in rhythm, blow after blow, looking first at his father, then at his mother, starting to curse and telling them how they mistreated him as a child. The parents looked stunned but they didn't cry or argue, which told me he must have been touching some kind of truth. You could see the sweat pouring off him, but he was in pretty good shape and he went on for about five minutes, really whaling away at the chair. Finally he put the bat down and said, "That's enough." The guy was close to my age and it made me wonder if I'd be like that in a few weeks when my parents came.

I could see these sessions were good for people because the young man seemed to get along better with his parents after that session with the *bataca*.

The counselors had a technique for everything. A woman was having trouble confronting her husband. She'd lose her train of thought and start smiling nervously. Fred picked up on this right away.

"What's the matter?" Fred asked.

"He's telling me to shut up," the wife said. "He's dominating me with his eyes, like he always does."

Fred ordered the guy to turn around, to face the other side of the circle, and the wife began laying it on him, how he dominated her for years. That guy gripped his seat with his hands, and his eyes bugged out in anger. The only person I could think of when I looked at this man was Charles Manson. I was looking straight at him and thinking, I'd hate to meet this son-of-a-bitch in a dark alley or even see him in a batter's box at sixty feet, six inches. Later the guy tried to answer some of his wife's remarks, but Fred cut him short.

"Shut up!" Fred shouted. "You are dying of a disease and this woman is trying to save your life. Just shut up and listen for once."

The guy clamped his jaw shut but his eyes were blazing with rage. I was afraid of him, and wondered how they'd ever crack this hard case. But in the next few days, all kinds of stuff came out about this guy, and his family, and his feelings toward his parents. Within four days, the anger had left the man's eyes. We wound up having coffee together a few times and he was a regular guy, smart as hell. I saw him leave with his wife and family, and they looked like the happiest people on earth. I remember thinking, "Oh, man, I want that to be me."

Those were the words I used. On a deeper level, it was a prayer. I was taking up Fred's idea of giving up control, turning it over to a Higher Power whose name I could not even use yet. I was putting myself in other hands in hope that in four or five weeks I could walk out of The Meadows with Mary and get back to the beach in California to get ready to pitch again. But a lot of changes would have to happen before I could get out.

Chapter Eighteen

✠◆◆◆◆◆◆◆◆◆◆◆◆◆◆◆◆◆◆◆◆◆◆◆◆◆◆◆✠

First Steps

◆◆

For my first few days they made me sleep in the detoxification unit in case I had any physical problems but pretty soon they let me move to Room One, the last in a wing of four rooms perpendicular to the main building.

I would sit outside the cabin in the evening, put my feet up on a wooden railing, and stare off into the mountains. It was rainy season and there was a river flowing in the bottomland. Sometimes you'd see horses roaming out there, and jackrabbits, and all kinds of birds. I would take a dip of Copenhagen and spit as far as I could over the railing, toward the cactus.

They tried to keep you busy so you wouldn't get to wanting a drink. I've got to say it was easier on me than on a lot of other people, from what I could tell. I didn't get the shakes or get all nervous because I couldn't have a beer. The truth is, I wanted to get out of there as soon as possible, and not drinking was the best way. Still, we'd talk about drinking all the time. It was our common heritage.

At night they would schedule lectures or movies, but mostly you would sit around reading or playing cards or talking. They let you watch television until eleven o'clock, later on weekends. They also had a workout room where you could lift weights and play Ping-Pong. One time Chris and Brandy, these two young guys, started belting each other around with the plastic bats used in sessions to get your anger out. I laughed and laughed while Chris and Brandy slugged each other with these things. Very therapeutic all around.

I kept in shape by running on the grounds of The Meadows, a mile or two between sessions. Twice a week the Dodgers sent up their Phoenix scout, Gene Holmes, to see how I was doing. I would loosen up my arm and pitch to Gene or a catcher he brought with him sometimes. I wasn't looking for special treatment because I was a ballplayer but the Dodgers would call to check up on me, which bothered some of The Meadows staff, I think.

The counselors want you to remain isolated from your other life until you're ready to deal with it again, but Gene's visits were good for me. He is a guy who never drank or smoked, and he encouraged me about what I was doing. Also, his visits helped remind me of my goal to straighten myself out so I could resume living. Some people might get caught up in The Meadows as a substitute for their own lives, but I always knew I was there to prepare myself for the world outside.

After Gene's first couple of visits, people stopped paying attention to my workouts. They knew I was a Dodger and that was cool, but mostly I was just another patient.

The staff couldn't do much about the Dodgers' checking up on me but they could enforce the rules about calling out. After the call to my parents on the first full day, they wouldn't let me telephone Mary for a week. We had always talked on the phone every other day, and I missed her more than I ever realized I would.

My feelings were wide open by that time. It wasn't easy to talk about myself, but I wanted to make some changes in my life. Since my second night at The Meadows, I had introduced myself as, "I'm Bob—I'm an alcoholic," the way they do in Alcoholics Anonymous. I knew I had alcohol problems and I was glad I was getting to them at twenty-three. I could see more damage in people even five years older than me.

To go through The Meadows' program, I had to move along the Twelve Steps of Alcoholics Anonymous. The First Step is to get up in front of your group and admit you were powerless over alcohol, that your life had become unmanageable. You have to show you are sincere about admitting your loss of control. Just thinking about things I had done, I could see how I would have been in worse trouble if I had less money or more bills to pay.

Some patients would take three or four weeks before they could admit they were powerless over alcohol, but I was ready to do it after a week. My group told me to make up a list of things I had done while I was powerless, called a Drunkalogue. On Thursday, January 24, we sat in our circle and I told them how I got messed up at my high-school basketball game and how I tore up the hotel room in Japan and how I got drunk on the last trip to San Francisco. I told them as much as I could remember. Rick Sutcliffe would supply more details a few weeks later.

The men and women in my group just sat there while I read from my list. I felt they were on my side but they were not supposed to show any emotion while I talked. It was my show. I was gaining control over my life. I must have talked for half an hour, and at the end I started crying, just thinking how ugly, how sad I had been. I've seen some guys just break down but I knew I could finish this one out.

When I finished the San Francisco episode, Lynn said, "I feel you have really gotten in touch with your feelings."

Around the circle, my fellow patients nodded in agreement. A few made some comments but basically they accepted what I said. Then Lynn came over and gave me a little pin, a replica of a camel. She said that anybody at The Meadows who feels for the First Step receives a camel because a camel can go twenty-four hours without drinking. Once you admit your powerlessness, you know you can last twenty-four hours—or twenty-four seconds when you really need it—without giving in to that first drink.

I was proud of that camel. I still am. I wore it as long as I stayed at The Meadows. Later my mother gave me a beautiful gold camel which I wear on a chain around my neck.

By the time I had been there a week, I was adjusting to almost everything except the hours. Breakfast was from seven-thirty to eight-thirty. On my baseball schedule, I hadn't seen that time of day in years. I told them I would just as soon skip breakfast and go straight to the first meeting, but they requested the pleasure of my company at breakfast.

The time between the sessions was good. Little kids—seven, eight, nine years old—would come and talk to me because I played for the

Dodgers. We'd sit at the edge of the patio and toss pebbles and they'd tell me what was going on in their groups. They would say things like, "I wish my mom and dad would get back together," or "I wish my father would stop drinking," or "My mom looks happy this week." You think kids don't know what's going on? These kids had seen some pretty bad things in their homes, and they grasped what The Meadows was trying to accomplish. I think it was good for them to see a ballplayer admit that he was an alcoholic, that he was screwed up, too. They could see their mother or father wasn't the only one in the world.

Weekends were different. You didn't have the group sessions. Mostly you'd just sit around and talk about your feelings, give each other hugs, tell a bunch of drunk stories, play catch, go for a swim, or have cookouts in the evening.

I think I would have been happy just hanging out and partying and not drinking, but Monday would roll around and you'd have to work again. I didn't do shit for the week after I took my First Step. I just sat around and let other people open up. Sometimes I'd give good feedback—tell other people my impressions of them—but I wasn't giving away much of myself.

I was jolted out of that pattern during my second full week by a little sweetheart named Joan from Texas. She had been there before me and was about to go home. We had gotten along well, and I always sneaked over and got a few extra hugs from her, to tell the truth, but I wasn't prepared for her words on her last day in the group.

"Bob, I'm leaving today and I'd like to see you do some work. You haven't done anything yet," she said.

I felt weak in my knees, trapped, like I wanted to get out. Plus, I felt angry that she had come after me like that. Maybe in a way I felt betrayed, thinking that we had been friends, so she shouldn't confront me. At The Meadows, this is called "getting somebody to be in your army." I thought I had enlisted her, but she was operating independently.

"What do you want me to say?" I snapped.

"Bob, I feel sorry for you," Joan said. "It looks to me like you're living for one thing. You just think of yourself as a baseball player. You don't realize that you're just like a piece of meat to them and they'll use you and when they're done they'll throw you away."

I felt sad and angry when she said that. I knew I was losing respect

in the community and in my family relationships, but the thing that
had hurt the most was knowing my baseball career was dwindling
because of my arm and my drinking.

Other people in the circle chimed in with the same thing. They
said I was just living for baseball, that I didn't exist for myself. I listened to this for a few minutes and then I realized it was true. I saw
myself as a player, but didn't fit in with anybody as a person. I said to
myself, "Well, hell. You might as well work. They're not going to let
you off the hook anyway." So I started talking.

I told them how I had felt as a rookie, that I didn't belong, how I
had been afraid to talk to people, the other players, and even to
sportswriters. How I couldn't look people in the eye. I didn't want to
say something and have the older players say, "Who is this young
guy? What the hell is he talking about?"

I said it wasn't anything to do with my background, because there
are a lot of players who don't come from rich families. It was just
being a rookie, being new, wanting to do my job, wanting to be
respected for being good. I wanted to be liked, yet my drinking lost
me respect. I hurt my arm and got drunk and got all fucked up.

"It sounds to me like you wanted to fuck up," somebody said.

"Maybe."

Lynn mentioned that I'd gotten drunk around the Dodgers a couple
of times, particularly where Tom Lasorda could notice. She wanted
to know whether I wanted to make Lasorda angry. Was I mad at him?

"Even though I volunteered for the bullpen, maybe I was mad at
Lasorda for putting me there," I said, "or maybe for telling me I
could still drink but to cut it down. I don't know. Maybe I blamed
him for other things."

A couple of people in the group said I looked angry while I was
talking. They pointed out how my jaw was tense and I was choking
off words in my throat. They said I was rubbing my hands, another
sign of anger. I tried to look calm, but the more I tried to relax, the
more I crossed my legs or folded my arms.

"Don't be a bump on a log," somebody said. "You look like you're
angry about something else. Tell us what it is."

I didn't know why, but tears started to form in my eyes.

"Bob, we love you as Bob Welch the person, not Bob Welch the
ballplayer," somebody said.

I started sobbing now, feeling that nobody liked me for myself,
that they saw me only as a kid who could throw the ball hard. And I

had felt the same way about myself. When my arm was hurt, I stopped liking myself, stopped seeing myself as having any value, started drinking more and more to dull the feelings.

I talked a little bit about it, not much, but it was the most I had done so far. It was like my initiation into a new circle. Joan came over and gave me a hug and said she was glad I had finally done some work. And I gave her a couple of hugs for being there, for caring enough to prod me. From then on I got into the swing of it, started to take responsibility for other people.

I learned another lesson my second week when a couple of teen-aged patients sneaked out of The Meadows and got smashed on some wine they bought in Wickenburg. I could tell they were bombed because I could smell it on their breath when they came back and were playing Ping-Pong in the recreation room. The only thing I said was, "You better do something about your breath because I can smell wine."

I thought maybe I had scared them, but a few days later they did it again and were caught and thrown out. When the patients in my group found out that I had known about the first episode, they really got on my case. They said it was wrong not to turn in somebody right away, because if a patient saw somebody else drunk, he might get the idea to get a buzz on himself. The counselors were upset with me for not telling. I made up my mind not to let another patient go down the drain.

I got my chance a few days later when Pappy Jake gave signs of going over the wall. There were certain people you'd get attached to, and Jake was one of them. He had been through treatment two times before, but he insisted this time it was going to turn out all right.

Jake and I got along good. I liked his grouchy sense of humor and all his drinking stories. He was my roommate for a while except he snored too much. Jake and I used to sit around figuring out how we could beat the system and get out early without going through all the process. Typical drunk talk. Sometimes in the sessions, people would get on me for not opening up, and Jake would come to my defense.

One day somebody turned on him and said, "Jake, why are you always defending Bob? You should stop acting like his damn father and let him speak for himself." The way those groups work, a couple of other people jumped right in and told Jake to stop acting like my father. They said he would hang around and watch me work out, and talk about baseball and act protective of me.

"Hell," Jake said, "I like the young man. I'd like to see my daughter marry somebody that nice."

After that everybody called him "Pappy Jake," even me. I was getting to appreciate The Meadows, and could see it was good the way they were poking me.

One night, down by the cabins, Jake called me over and said, "I knew I'd get it right the third time. I've gathered a lot of material and I know I'm cured and I don't have to stay anymore."

He'd been there only three weeks and he hadn't gone through family week, and I told him he ought to stay. He gave some kind of excuse about having to help other members of his family, but I knew better.

"Jake, you're full of shit," I told him. "You just want to go out and get drunk."

"No, I'm sober now and I'm all right," Jake insisted. "Just give me ten minutes to get out of here and don't tell anyone."

For a guy who was supposed to be my father figure, Pappy Jake was putting me in quite a dilemma. There's a rule at The Meadows that you're supposed to report any violation of the rules, and I remembered how they had jumped all over my ass for not reporting the kids for drinking. But Pappy Jake had been working hard to enroll me in his army, by treating me like a son. I left his room for a few minutes but realized I could not turn my back on what he was doing. I ran back to try to stop him, but he was already gone.

I grabbed Chris, my fourteen-year-old buddy, and we ran down the hill after him. We got to the main road, figuring he'd be hitch-hiking, but we didn't see him.

"He must have gone to Wickenburg," I told Chris. "Let's go get him and make him come back."

Chris reminded me of the rule at The Meadows that once you leave, you can't come back, but I figured we could get Jake and come back before anybody missed us. We hitched a ride with some hippie and in two minutes we were in Wickenburg. It was the first time I had been off The Meadows since I got there, three weeks earlier. We ran up and down the main street, looking in every coffee shop and bar to see if he was getting drunk or maybe trying to call somebody, but we never spotted him. We stood on the corner and looked both ways. No trace of Jake. I started cursing at him out loud. I could feel anger working up inside me, anger at Jake for hurting himself, also a feeling that he had betrayed me, too.

"You jerk," I shouted. "You damn fool. You're just gonna get drunk again and screw up your life."

Chris cautioned me to keep quiet, not to attract attention, because somebody might figure out we were a couple of patients from The Meadows and make a telephone call that could get us in big trouble. It's funny now that I look back, but even when Chris and I were searching the bars for Jake, we never discussed getting a beer for ourselves. We wanted to play it straight, so we got a ride back to The Meadows from Chris's mother, who was staying at the motel, and we sneaked into the dining room in time for supper. I reported that Jake was missing, and nobody knew I had gone after him.

I haven't seen Pappy Jake since. My hunch is that he had already planned his getaway and had somebody waiting on the main road outside The Meadows. Every so often I'll get a telegram at the hotel and it will say, "Nice game" or "About time you did something," and it will be signed "Pappy Jake." Jake never adds whether he's drunk or sober, but I hope he's staying away from alcohol, because it will kill him.

For every patient who left, there was always another one to take his place. People showed up at The Meadows in all kinds of ways. I heard they induced one woman from Phoenix by promising her a special ice-cream store. One thing she liked as much as whiskey was ice cream. When the car got to Wickenburg, she spotted an ice-cream parlor and demanded a huge cone with double dips. She was still licking away at the ice cream when her family deposited her at The Meadows.

Some people came kicking and screaming. I know one young woman who tried to kick in the door of the infirmary when they started to test her for drugs and alcohol. A lot of patients would arrive smashed. The counselors and nurses would tell the family to get the person to The Meadows any way they could—even if they had to toss a bottle of booze into the back seat and let the patient drink until they drove up the hill. The nurses could usually detoxify a patient in a couple of days, although I did see people pass out or start to hallucinate when they began to withdraw from their drug of choice. It was scary to see someone just crumple to the floor or start to make statements that were not true. You would see how alcohol or drugs could destroy a person over the years. The old ones were the saddest—puffy, wrinkled, slow, coughing, unwilling to eat. I did not want to be like that.

Three nights a week they would hold meetings of Alcoholics Anonymous. One night it would be open to anybody staying at The Meadows, and another night it would be open to just the alcoholics. People were nice, passing out cookies and coffee (always decaffeinated), lighting candles, giving hugs. They would have a prayer to the Higher Power.

At The Meadows we heard about the Higher Power from the Reverend Wick—a pastor from Wickenburg, a real cool dude in western clothes and a string tie. You could talk honestly with the Great Wick.

When I was in a bad mood, I would say, "Wick, I hate this place. I've got to get out of here." He wouldn't act offended, as if you had been disloyal. He'd give you a rap about "existentialism." Really, it was the AA concept of living one day at a time. He would say, "The deal is today. You've got to live in existentialism." I started off being afraid he was going to preach to me, tell me I had to believe this or that about God. But mostly he listened and told me to be cool.

After I had been there a few weeks, the Great Wick invited me to his church—I can't remember what denomination—for Sunday morning services. It was the first time since I had arrived that I had legally been off the premises of The Meadows. Around communion time they passed out the wafers and also a little tray of wine glasses. I thought, man, wouldn't it be weird if you got a buzz on in the house of the Lord, but I should have realized the Great Wick would turn wine into grape juice for his special clientele from up on the hill.

The next legal time I left The Meadows was going to the stores with Marie. She had arrived two days after me, looking terrible, to be honest, skin bad, hair tangled, clothes sloppy, face all puffed up. Within a few days, once she got the alcohol out of her system, she started to look better, move better, act happier. She'd have lipstick one day, a new hairstyle the next, then she'd lose a few pounds and out would come the tight jeans and the pretty blouses. I noticed these things, and I knew they were indicative of more important things going on in her sessions with women patients.

Because Marie and I had arrived at about the same time, we became good friends during the sessions and in the free time. On the Friday before Valentine's Day, we were attending the weekly graduation, when Lynn got up and announced that Marie and I had been selected peer leaders for the next week. The counselors pick the peer leaders, a man and a woman, each Friday. It's like a pat on the back, but it also means you are responsible for making a list of jobs to be done by the patients. Who sits up at night with the new arrivals, who cleans up, things like that. It also means you keep an ear out for problems from the other patients. It was an honor, but if it had been an election instead of a selection I doubt if I would have declared myself a candidate. The best part of the job came on Saturday, when we got to go shopping in bustling Wickenburg.

On Saturday one of the nurses drove us to a shopping center on the edge of town and we had a ball poking around a drugstore and a Hallmark card shop. I don't think I've ever had a better time than buying tobacco and shampoo and tampons and shaving equipment for all the patients, plus sneaking a few quick looks at the *Playboy* magazines on the shelf. We went into a Seven-Eleven store and it never dawned on me to sneak a couple of coldies.

Another thing I noticed was that I didn't feel the compulsion to make a pass at Marie. It's not that I wasn't feeling horny. The better I felt about myself, the more I started to miss Mary Ellen, lying in bed at night. Or when the guys would sit around talking about cold frosty beers and nice cuddly women. But in reality—at The Meadows they stress facing reality—I didn't feel the need to snag Joan or Marie when we were alone together. We could sit and talk about our feelings without my need to prove myself by trying to seduce one of them. And I was so wrapped up in writing letters to Mary Ellen and thinking about our relationship that I could be friendly with other women. I missed Mary. Missed her a lot.

Chapter Nineteen

◆◆◆◆◆◆◆◆◆◆◆◆◆◆◆◆◆◆◆◆◆◆◆◆

Letters to Mary Ellen

◆◆

The main idea at The Meadows was to prepare myself for recovery, to get into my own source of pain, to isolate myself. The counselors didn't encourage much contact with the outside world other than the first call to my parents when I got there, and my first call to Mary a few days later.

With so much free time on my hands, I got to thinking about Mary—I'd sit on the railing by my cabin at night just staring at the mountains in the moonlight and when I'd start thinking about Mary, I'd just start crying, tears streaming down my face. I'd get the feeling that if I could only be with her, everything would be all right.

Of course, that was bullshit, pure alcoholic escapism. The counselors told me—and I came to believe them—that until I got myself straightened out, I couldn't afford to see Mary again; otherwise, I'd try to use her all over again—get a buzz on, talk mean to her, start to push her around. I had to find out why I did that. We'd work on that in sessions, people trying to get me to describe what I saw in Mary, why we chose each other. I became more aware of her than ever before.

I wanted her to know it, but the only way I could was through letters. Like most people, we were better at talking on the telephone

164

than in writing letters. They say letter writing is a dead art, killed by Alexander Graham Bell, and I guess it's true. When I was in California and Mary was in Michigan, or when I was on the road with the Dodgers, it was easy to dial a phone number and say, "Hey, Mary, I wish you were here in bed with me now." That was easy and intimate. At The Meadows, every time I got sad or lonely or happy or horny, I couldn't get to a phone because I had made my one damn phone call for the week. So I'd have to pick up a pen and paper and write a letter.

I don't want to sound like I'm bragging, but I used to be a pretty good writer back in grade school, before I discovered sports. I had gotten a little lazy about writing in later years because I had learned to rely on my alcoholic verbal agility, telling lies while I had a buzz on. At The Meadows I began to revive my lost prowess with the pen and paper, dashing off a page or two to Mary whenever there was a lull in the activities.

I think Mary was amazed at my output. She was in classes back in Kalamazoo and couldn't answer every one of my letters. I'd pour out my heart and soul to her—my romance, my lust, my pain, my anger. I didn't realize it at the time, but Mary Ellen Wilson collected the famous love letters of Robert L. Welch. And one day not long ago, she reached into the closet and pulled them out.

I was amazed to realize how emotional I had been in the first couple of weeks at The Meadows. As I reread these letters, I realized how my mood swung from rage (feeling I didn't really belong with all those drunks) to emotional dependence on Mary (promising to marry her) to jealousy (several times fearing she would find another man while I was confined, and that she would write me that final Dear John letter).

But I could see midway through my stay at The Meadows how my mood started to stabilize. Even my handwriting started to become neater. And at some point I stopped referring to myself as Bobby and became Bob. I could see myself becoming more rational, more moderate.

At first, I was a little embarrassed about printing these letters (and so was Mary), but I've come to realize they are a good barometer of what was going on at The Meadows. My letters show a kid quivering with emotions and realizing how much he loves his girlfriend. Later the letters even show a possibility that the kid might grow up to be an adult and have respect for this woman to whom he is writing.

What follows are my letters to Mary in January and February of 1980, with some comments by me and Mary, written early in 1981:

Friday, January 18

MARY,

Hello my love, how are you? I miss you very much and we will soon be in contact with each other and I do mean contact. This place is a scary joint. There are drug addicts, alcoholics, emotionally disturbed individuals and I mean to the max. I am an angel in this environment and I contemplate leaving, but I will try my best to stick it out.

Some terrible shit goes on because all of these people are from broken families, divorces, and typical chemical-related problems. I miss you a whole bunch and I have cried a lot but life is going to get better 'cause I'm going to share it with you. I love you Mary and I know you are beautiful 'cause I've thought very much lately. How much do I love Mary Wilson? I love Mary more than I ever thought I did.

See Ya Soon. Love, Bobby

Saturday, January 19

MARY,

It was beautiful hearing your voice today. Not being able to call you for four full days was very difficult, but knowing you're being the little goodie-two-shoes in K-zoo, I felt at ease. Ain't that a bunch of shit? Mary Wilson's boyfriend is locked up in a cuckoo's nest and can't call to check up. She's out with the next-door neighbors playing leapfrog at two a.m. You probably wonder how in the hell he found out but you blew your cover, miss goodie-two-shoes.

Tonight I will write you two letters 'cause I'm writing this one before I go to bed, and I have to get up at four a.m. to babysit for an incoming patient. Sometimes patients who arrive are given Librium to ease the pain and possible DT's or convulsions so us big, strong men have to babysit and my time happens to be 4–5 a.m. How sweet it is. Please, Lord, don't let the man go into a convulsion.

Mary, I love you a whole lot a shakin'. Please stay in tune with your boy 'cause I need to feel your love across the mountain range that surrounds the beautiful atmosphere of The Meadows.

You could start a great soap opera in this place. Tell me what's happening in 'ALL MY CHILDREN' if you ever get any spare time to write in that illustrious schedule of yours.

Please get all A's for once. If I can go through this place, you can get A's. But don't forget our little slogan: I AM SOBER TODAY.

Mary, I love you much. I'm gonna call it quits for a couple of hours so I can get some shut eye.

MARY ELLEN: *I can't imagine what was going on in Bob's mind. Was I going to find another man in five weeks? He says he called and couldn't find me in. I don't remember the incident. It must have been in his mind, early in The Meadows.*

Sunday, January 20

MARY,

Hello sweetheart, how are you? It is seven a.m. and I am babysitting for a heroin junkie and wishing you were here. Mary, I love you very much and we are gonna have a great time together beginning this year. In about four–five months we are no longer gonna have a big load in the back of our minds.

We will have no set date to say good-bye to each other and that will be a beautiful experience, something we have not faced. But then again, I really can't handle you for such a long period of time so I guess we will have to put in a couple of good-bye dates just to stay familiar with that same ole routine.

Mary, the phones are hooked up to tape recorders so I guess it really doesn't matter what you say 'cause everything comes out anyway. All the garbage that has ever been a hang-up comes out someplace at The Meadows.

Every time I write you a letter I end up writing about the boring shit from The Meadows. ENOUGH IS ENOUGH. Can't go on like this anymore. . . .

BOB: *I only had to get up a couple of times, once for a heroin junkie who was nodding off, and once for an alcoholic to make sure he didn't have the DT's.*

MARY,

Hello baby. I love you a whole bunch and miss you just the same. I have so much time to sit around here and think. We are supposed to read a lot of books and stuff but I can only handle so much until I begin to drift off towards Mary Wilson.

This place has a unique way of arresting your problem. Everything is based on feelings and emotions. They want you to show these feelings when you're in group therapy. The first step they want you to take is telling your life story on your drinking and break down and cry when you're into conclusions about all the people you have hurt while drinking. They want you to include how you've become powerless over your chemical dependency and admit that your life has become unmanageable.

My life is not unmanageable, that is a fact. And I can only think of a couple of times when I've hurt someone; when I went to the ball park in San Francisco loaded and when you say that I pushed you around and scared you. But for me to say that I am powerless over alcohol and my life is unmanageable . . . somewhere the rules have to bend or RLW is gonna go crazy. This place is a cuckoo's nest and I am a fucking member. That makes me cry every time I get into the damn shower.

I would like you to come for a week if you could. February 11 is my family week and if things are gonna be tough with school then don't worry about coming. But I would love to see you even though I can't spend any time with you at the motel. By that time I will no longer have any existence with the outside world because they want you to become totally aware of your own feelings and pretend that nothing else is happening. I am lucky with the problems that I have 'cause these families around here have been ripped apart by alcohol or drugs. I have a beautiful Ma and Pa, sister and brother. Don worries me right now. He may have a serious problem. The whole Welch family—Lloyd, Dougie, my uncles may have had a problem with alcohol. I will no longer have a problem. I will but it will be arrested. I feel good with no more hangovers but I miss you, Mary, very much and I need some letters so please write now. It is very important that we write because my calls are limited.

The weekends are a bitch. No meetings or nothing, just stories from other drunks and addicts that are driving me to drink more tea with honey. I have become hooked on it. I am still in my pajamas which is sort of a rookie kick but I will be out of them soon.

But the biggest problem I have is you. What am I gonna do about it? I can't do anything now except tell you we are gonna have a great life and my love for you grows every day so if you are gonna drop me please write me a letter quickly so I can make a quick phone call to L.A. I get worried that I can't talk to you for that security. You're the greatest and most important person in my life. Please don't run off with another man 'cause I don't want anybody else but you.

Bye. I love you. Bobby

BOB: *I don't know why I wrote that. Mary had never threatened to find another man and I really wasn't worried she would. It was just something to write. I was horny, I guess. That's what you write when you're horny.*

Tuesday, January 22

MARY.

Gee whiz, how is this gonna sound? Give me the biggest steak you have and a bottle of club soda. Hell, I want a big ice cold mug full of chilled to perfection, frosty, my mind is going nuts. Please bring me a can of Copenhagen.

Hey sweetheart, your little boyfriend is combatting the COPE SYNDROME with little luck. It is tougher than not having a beer. Everyone around here smokes cigarettes. They are a terrible stink.

Mary I love you and I will hug you like the dickens when I see my little baby. Say hi to the people in K-zoo but don't tell them I'm at the funny farm. Press conference held for Feb. 23–25 where I am going to introduce myself to someone who I haven't had a chance to meet: MYSELF.

I love you. Talk to you tomorrow. Bobby.

P.S. I am sober today.

Wednesday, January 23

MARY

Hello once again from the beautiful confines of The Meadows. Tell me the name itself doesn't sound a little freaky: *THE MEADOWS*. What a name for a drunk hall. My counselor is Lynn, you spoke with her, a sweetheart. She is super intelligent and very observant on the non-verbal cues. Although I may seem very arrogant, I did receive an A in Non-Verbal Communication at E.M.U.

Today I saw the psychiatrist and he asked me how I would describe you. This is the list I gave him:

> loving
> caring
> understanding
> intelligent
> lovable
> pretty
> small
> sharing

Then he asked me when we are loving, what are your feelings' priorities:

> hugging
> kissing
> sleeping close

Man I sure could give you a big hug right now. The other patient in this room is snoring his ass off. Every day in our group sessions we hug each other before our therapy begins. We only have three ladies in our group but I'm getting my hugs in and a little extra. They may be hugs but they are the only thing us men have. No signs of hanky-panky or else your tail will be out of The Meadows.

Tomorrow is a big day, my first week, and I'm making my first-step attempt. You begin by telling your history of addiction and show your feelings such as my stint in Frisco, and how it has made me powerless and my life unmanageable over alcohol. It's gonna be 15–20 minutes of hell and an exhibition of courage I have yet to come to grips with. But to get my feelings out will be one hell of a relief 'cause while I write this letter they are coming out. Sadness. Tears. I love you Mary. I'm going to bed. Please write me, babe. I need it from you.

I love you with all my heart. Bobby

Thursday, January 24
MARY.

Hello, my dear. I took one giant leap today. I passed my first step. I let go of about ten pounds of feelings. Mary, it feels great and I am learning more every day how to let go of my feelings no matter what: sad, anger, guilt—thousands that we both can feel better from. Mary, I love you very much and it's so cool to be able to do that. Now I will know better ways to show my love after I have let go of this garbage inside. Family week is gonna be great. I'll be able to see the ways I hurt Mom, Dad and you—whoever is gonna be here. It is very scary to think that but it will make everybody feel better if they get it off of their chests so we can love each other more. I know that our love has not come to a dead-end 'cause I love you different ways than I ever knew about until I came here. This place is beautiful. It brings families together every week, families who were way ᴗut in the distance. I can imagine what it's gonna do for us.

Baby doll Mary. I love you. The first nursery rhyme that comes into your head, write it down and send it back in a letter. If you love me you'll write daily. If you don't write every day, I'll kick your ass when you get here. Study hard, Mary. I'm with you all the way. Good luck.

I love you with all my heart. Bobby Welch

Friday, January 25

Mary.

We have a break before graduation ceremonies so I'll drop you a quick line of love. Mary Ellen I love you very much and it is beautiful outside today—very clear. The mountains are super and the sun is beating against them. Time is flying by. When you get this letter I will be in double figures, working on two weeks. I love you and miss you very much.

Bobby.

P.S. Weekends were made for Michelob . . . no, milk.

Friday night, January 25

Mary

I am sitting here on a Friday night enjoying a big ole bull session with the boys. What a hell of a time. I want to tell you something that is very unique. I have come to realize that you are my favorite individual in the whole world. Mary, if I never play another baseball game or pitch again I want you to know you are my mistress. For a long time I lived for baseball which I do love but I showed baseball more love than I did for you and that makes me feel very sad. I love you Mary and I will be able to feel it more than ever after we both go through family week. We will be able to get our garbage out and beneath that garbage will be a whole bunch of love if you follow and believe in The Meadows' process. You will love everyone involved in The Meadows 'cause these people are the most lovable and caring people I have ever met.

Please, if something comes up with another man, don't be afraid to write a Dear John. If ya do, it would hurt but I'll still love you so damn much. Wait, though, because I can. Mary, I miss you. The boys are rapping about good ole drunks and we do have some laughs, crying laughs. I love you very much. Take care and behave.

Ten days without a belt but don't forget we alcoholics take it day by day—one day at a time. With all my heart—Bobby Welch

Saturday, January 26

MARY.

Hello Mary Ellen. Boy it was sure good hearing your voice today. Long distance is the next best thing to being there. I love you Mary. You're a wonderful woman and we will be together again in a little bit enjoying, loving, and sharing our love like never before.

Betty the night nurse took some of your negatives and I will have some photographs of my love to look at and sleep with next week. Mary, you're so precious, I'll dance at your wedding. How about this for a little gift?

Tomorrow if I get up I'm gonna go to church for a bad reason: to get out of this place for a couple of hours and look at some sane people.

I love you Mary, more than yesterday. Bobby.

Sunday, January 27

MARY ELLEN.

Mary Ellen Wilson, I love you and I have stayed sober today. This has to be the longest I can remember without having a beer or two. I feel very good and look better. No hangover to cope with, drunk guilt feelings to worry about. I feel better all over. I even feel better about you. Sometimes I would not even pay attention to what you would say to me. I would siphon out the good stuff and let the bad shit rip me up inside. Now I'm learning how to cope with both sides and it is a beautiful feeling.

Mary I love you. You're a very big part of me and I can feel your presence with me every day. What a super feeling to have your heart with me when I go to bed and it's right there when I wake up in the morning. Thank you for being so nice and lovable all the time. I can still see you crying at the train station and that is beautiful knowing you love me that much that you can express it on a feeling level. You're a beautiful woman and I'm beginning to find out how lucky I am to be able to share my love with you.

I'm just kicking back on a Sunday and watching some boxing matches and checking out the new families who have come in for family week. Family week is not just for me but for you, too, to express your feelings and learn about alcoholism and drugs and how it affects the co-alcoholic. This place is the greatest experience I have ever come across in my life and I have been through some crazy and wild happenings. None of them come close to the love I receive from everyone here at The Meadows.

I love you Mary. You're a beautiful girlfriend and we will have a beautiful week together. I miss you much but my heart is with you.

All my love. Bobby.

Monday, January 28

MARY.

Suppression of any one stage could mean failure in overcoming the anguish of grief. Denial of these feelings due to one's false premises results in a person carrying around in his or her gut an unbearable pain for life. Some of the false premises are as follows:

I'm an adult . . . I can't let down. (OK Superman)
I shouldn't feel that way. (But you do)

I have to act like my old self. (But you're not)
My life is over. (True, if you don't change)

These are some of the problems we touch upon relating to alcoholism. They are true, we have felt that way before. We want to be able to control grief without alcohol and here we deal with that in group therapy.

Last week three families grew and began a new love. The process works for ripped-apart families. Can you imagine how much my family will love each other when we leave? A lot of my friends are graduating and I will miss them especially Joan and her great massages on the extremities. Don't get upset about the massages. Joan and I are here at The Meadows to love each other to help our diseases. Those massages are of therapeutic value only.

Your pictures are coming soon. Can't wait to see you again.

I love you. Bobby

Tuesday, January 29

MARY.

Another day at The Meadows and this place is getting old. Boy I sure could use my family week today. All of my close partners are leaving this week and I'll be one of the senior peers after Friday. What the hell, I'd be catching a buzz and spending money in L.A. so this is sort of a place to train 'cause I'm just about fed up with the feeling shit. I'm ready to spend my life with you and I have to ask you something when you arrive here. It's important to me that you listen very carefully. Mary I love you and I want you to be my wife if you get my drift.

The third week here at this place and after the first they start to repeat everything and keep pounding these lectures into your head. Mary I have to tell you that after my sobriety you come first. You're beautiful and I have chosen to share my love with you and no one else. I may look but no other woman could half measure up to your caring and friendship.

all my love. Bobby.

MARY ELLEN: *He's proposed to me before. In 1979 he got confused about which year was leap year and he told me we'd get married the next year on February 29. I realized there is usually no February 29, but then I remembered that 1980 was leap year and I told*

him. He backed out of that one. It's the same thing with his letters from The Meadows. He talked about getting married and then he backed off, but I don't think that's important at this point. We're young and we're growing together. That's what counts.
BOB: *Can I plead temporary insanity on that one?*

Tuesday, January 29

MARY.

I am coming to realize that a lot of people I know are my friends because of Bob Welch the Baseball Player in L.A. I know that is not the way to be and I do not want to put up a wall and fight away everyone 'cause some of my friends are not that way. I'm growing here every day and I'm with you. I love you Mary, more than yesterday. Bobby.

Wednesday, January 30

HELLO MARY.

How are you, babe? Yesterday I was laying by the pool and I was as low as you can go. I was thinking to myself why I have to be away from you so often. Then I started thinking about a lecture we had on Mature and Immature Relationships. I'm away from you 'cause we have a mature relationship. When we are together we don't worry constantly about when we're going to be away. We enjoy each other to the maximum when we are together and that is beautiful.

The minute I was thinking about that, Betty came down the steps with your pictures and I started to cry because I knew they were your pictures and how much I needed them.

When you get this letter we will be a few days apart and you will be present again. You're a very big part of me and I want to love you the rest of my life and I will.

Love. Bobby

Thursday, January 31

DEAR MARY ELLEN.

Every Thursday we get new sheets but we still have to make our own beds or we get demerits and if you get so many you are put back in your pajamas. It is 8:45 and we are off until 10 so I made my bed, changed sheets and wrote you a letter. I have run out of Copenhagen so here goes—I'm gonna try to kick it.

Mary, I love you very much, and not because of your big build, either. I sure could use a good night's sleep with you all tucked up next to me.

All my love. All of it. Bobby

Bob: *I used to tease Mary Ellen because she's slender. After a couple of weeks at The Meadows, I began to realize I wanted to see Mary Ellen Wilson, not some* Playboy *centerfold.*

Thursday, January 31

I LOVE YOU.

How do you rate to start a letter with 'I love you'? Remember, a person cannot become an alcoholic unless there is conflict between his behavior and his values.

Mary, these people around here really care about me as a person. The only one outside my family and long-time friends who I have belief in is you. I love you with all my heart.

Ivan and I are reading a bit before we go to bed and it's only 10 pm. I just ran a bit, skipped some rope and boy do I feel good.

Joan gave me an experience about the Lord in the footsteps the day she left. I miss her and some other good friends who I've met. Mary, if you get a chance, go to an Al-Anon meeting before you come out for family week. I believe it will help. Al-Anon is for husbands, wives, friends—anyone whose life is associated with an alcoholic. Mary, I love you very much and when you arrive we are not allowed to share our love in a bed. It will be very hard but when the right time comes, it will be so beautiful, like we never have loved before.

I miss you much. All my love. Bobby

Friday, February 1

Mary Ellen.

During our graduation ceremony, Gabriel just fainted over in the hallway. Things happen around this place without amazing me. Mary, I love you with all my heart and you'll be in my arms for many years but only one day at a time.

See you soon. I love you. Bobby.

Friday, February 1

MARY.

Hi. The weekend is here. It has been a long week and I'm
tired of all the feeling shit. I need some time with you up close,
so I can show you how much I love you.

We spent the first group work today talking about you and I
was asked what nursery rhyme came to mind. I'll be damned if
I didn't say "Mary Had a Little Lamb" and all hell broke loose.
I was in the hot seat for an hour. We talked about whether or
not I was your little lamb and if I felt you controlled me. I said
we worked together and we do. I am only a little lamb when
you give me that little smile and I explained that I would do
anything right now to keep us growing and loving. And I was
asked if you love me 'cause I'm Bob Welch the Dodger and of
course I said no.

Mary, I love you very much and you're very special to me and
I want to marry you when I get up the nerve to ask. I would
love for you to be my wife and it will happen. Mary. I love you.
Bobby.

Saturday, February 2

HI MARY.

Saturday evening at six o'clock. The sun is beginning to set
and the view of the mountains is picturesque. It was seventy-five
degrees and the evening temperature is Arizona weather at its
best. We had a cookout tonight by the pool and I was the chef.
We have an AA meeting tonight and tomorrow I'm going to
church. I also have to babysit at 4 am for a patient. This is just
a short note to say how much I love you.

All my love. Bobby

BOB: *We had two cookouts, on the second and third Saturdays, real
good blasts with burgers one time and steak another. Just a bunch
of alcoholics sitting around telling drunk stories and trying to
push each other in the pool, without being drunk.*

Sunday evening, February 3

MARY.

Hello beautiful. I had a nice Sunday, laid out by the pool and
caught some rays. Mary, when you receive this we will be only a

few days apart. See how time flies when you're in love. Today I laid in bed and looked at your pictures and got to feeling really sexy, just before going to church.

I will love you any way you want me to, how's that for communication? Mary, I love you and you better not get too tipsy coming from Chicago but hell, it's on the Dodgers, so knock 'em dead.

I love you. Bobby.

Monday, February 4

MARY.

I will be able to give you a big hug and kiss when you arrive before you rip me apart in group. I love you Mary, so take it easy on me if you can. No, don't do that. Tell me how it was, when, how, be specific. You're here to grow just as I am. The process here will work for you, too.

You are a beautiful person who I want to share my life with if you get the drift. The program here includes an aftercare program which calls for *no* major changes in the next year . . . for instance, new jobs, terrific weight loss, and that other one which they feel is important, divorce and m . . . . . . I won't say that but it looks like I'll make it to twenty-four.

Take care, Mary and behave. Love, Bobby.

Tuesday, February 5

MARY ELLEN

How are you doing in your schoolwork? Tell me. I want to know if you're gonna get 4.0's 'cause you're capable of getting them just as anyone around. Mary, you're a sharp young woman who, I believe, is only five or six extra hours a week away from A's.

No more school discussion. That is your matter to handle and I know you are doing your best. (Aren't you?)

I was asked this question: Name one thing you feel you always felt you had control over and discuss.

I said I felt I had control over our relationship, that some day we were gonna reach a stalemate, but now I know our love will never come to a halt. We will continue to grow for the rest of our lives (together).

I love you more today than yesterday. Bobby

Tuesday, February 5

MARY.

Mary, I hope you do not goof up your grades when you come here to see your alcoholic boyfriend. We are lucky we have no children and I'm not thirty-five and have been giving you hell with the bottle for 15 years. Some of these families here are torn apart. We are gonna have a beautiful life wherever it may be 'cause we will make it work together.

Well, I have some news for you. My hair is finally growing a bit and my scalp is sunburned. It looks pretty neat but I have scars all over my head and the damn shave cost me $11. You'll like it—a new Bob Welch—Hare Krishna. We can walk along the beach at Laguna and play the tambourine and pass out cookies.

We have such a good time whatever we do. Don't be too hard on me during family week but when you do confront me with your list, get into the feelings so I can see how I hurt you and see that the pain and hurt was evident. You should make a list of the incidents when I caused you pain due to my drinking.

Four more days and the weekend will be here. I love you.

Bobby

BOB: *I was just trying to make a joke. We had been at the beach that summer and seen some of those Hare Krishna people selling cookies, so I made a joke about cutting my hair to show how cuckoo I had become at The Meadows.*

MARY ELLEN: *I didn't think it was true when I got the letter. I couldn't imagine Bob shaving his hair off. I figured he was throwing the bull, and when I got to The Meadows I found out that was the case.*

Wednesday, February 6

DEAR MARY ELLEN.

I was gonna write you a long, sweet letter last night but I pooped out right on the toilet seat, so I wrote the rest this morning. We have an hour off between 9–10 'cause the women have a MENOPAUSE MEETING or something like that. If you get this letter on time, you'll probably be on your way here the next day.

Mary, I want you to know a few facts: Twenty teenagers a day die in alcohol-related accidents. Fifty percent of all automobile accidents are alcohol-related. Alcoholism is a disease, the number two killer in the United States and yet it is the least studied, cared or whatever disease in the country. 62–66% of all heart failure is alcohol-related. There are twenty-five million alcoholics in the United States and the number is growing every day. I could go on with some more stuff that should keep you from drinking. We live in an alcohol society, where drinking is accepted. Mary. I love you very much and I'm so happy I'm here getting this nasty disease arrested.

DON'T MISS YOUR PLANE. Bobby.

Thursday, February 7

MARY.

Hello beautiful. Lynn and I just had a one-on-one rap session and boy I love you. I have an idea that Bob Welch is growing and changing and learning so much about myself that when I uncover this individual, a real nice, caring individual is underneath.

We talked about a question that popped up occasionally with you: Does Bob Welch have fear about living with Mary Wilson for the rest of my life? You and I have talked about this. I was so fearful of the September, October, November, etc., that I was projecting in the future and not loving and growing with you on a daily basis. I will have no problem sharing my fearful months if I allow myself to grow and share on a day to day basis.

Mary, I love you and I am learning to control my projections. I love you right now and if I don't take advantage of our love then we will never be able to cope with the fear.

I miss you. Bobby.

Chapter Twenty

Family Week

I was looking forward to my family arriving but I was also scared. I had been taking part in other people's family weeks since I got there, and I was getting pretty good at offering feedback to them, if I thought somebody was denying or rationalizing or protecting. Now it was going to be my turn.

I couldn't wait to see my mom and dad and Donnie and Diane, and I couldn't wait to hold Mary Ellen again, but I was scared of them seeing me in that place. Since I was a little kid, my family had seen me as a star athlete, the kid who was going to make them all proud. Up to now, my being at The Meadows was very distant to them. They were not going through it. Would they see me as just another alcoholic? Or would they be able to see the growth in me? Would they participate?

Actually I wasn't sure how much I wanted them to participate. In all other family weeks, I had seen family members arrive with all the pain the alcoholic had caused them. I had heard some pretty horrendous stories—guys stealing money from their families, people sleeping around, parents beating their children. I knew my family had been hurt by my drinking, and I knew it was supposed to come out. But suppose I had done things during a blackout that I did not

remember? Suppose I didn't like having my old actions thrown back
in my face? I was joking with Mary Ellen in my letters about taking
it easy on me. Maybe I was trying to give her a signal to let me off
the hook. Part of me wanted to slide through family week, with no
feelings and no pain, but I didn't believe the counselors would let it
happen.

I was also worried about what other people would say to my
family. I had been through those sessions. Family week is supposed to
hold a mirror to yourself, so you can take a good look at yourself, but
it's also for your whole family. I recognized there is a tradition of
drinking in my family, that my father and Donnie both drink, and I
had a suspicion that somebody would confront them about their
drinking, force them to take a look at themselves. I wasn't sure how
my father and Donnie would react. I had seen people really blow a
fuse at The Meadows. I knew of one family where two brothers
stormed out, and accused their sister of getting a percentage of the
fee, because people were urging the two brothers to sign themselves
in as patients. On the other hand, I had seen people come as family
members and in the middle of the session admit they were alcoholics.
Sometimes the sessions went overboard, like a witch-hunt, in my
opinion, and I had seen a few of the counselors accuse people who I
did not believe were alcoholics. How would it be with my family? I
did not know.

My family was due to arrive on Sunday, February 10. They were
flying into Phoenix from different places—Mary from Kalamazoo and
Chicago, Diane and my parents from Detroit, and Donnie from Los
Angeles. They were supposed to meet at the airport, where a rented
car was waiting. The total cost was over five thousand dollars, which
the Dodgers were paying. John Newton had assured me that large
companies don't mind because it saves them money to rehabilitate a
valuable employee rather than have to hire and train somebody new
because they had to fire an alcoholic.

Mary has since told me that the ride from Phoenix to Wickenburg
was a little awkward because the five of them were tense about being
so close together on their way to a treatment center. She says my
mother was the only one who did much talking as they followed the
famous alcoholics' trail northwest into the foothills of Arizona.

They checked into the Rancho Grande Motel, the best one in
Wickenburg, and drove up the hill to The Meadows. I had been
pacing around, nervous, early in the afternoon and had finally gone

for a swim, so I was just toweling myself off when they knocked on my cabin door.

"Welcome to the Cuckoo's Nest," I said, making an elaborate bow.

I could see them all staring at me, to see if I had changed in any spectacular way. I was trying to show them I was still the same guy I had always been, but also that I had learned to be more communicative. I gave each of them a full Meadows hug and we talked. My mom said she could tell the difference in me, that I was more loving, less shy.

The first thing my mom said to me was, "Bob, I'm really glad you're here. I don't care if you never play baseball again in your life, so long as you don't drink." This was exactly what people were saying in my groups, and my mom had already figured that out in her own mind.

After the first greetings we all sat around and traded gossip, news of back home, all that stuff. Then I began telling them what was going to happen. They should have received some written material from The Meadows preparing them for family week but for some reason it had not arrived, so I tried to tell them. I said they would be in a family group in the morning and with the patients in the afternoon. I told them they would have to confront me with all the things I had done when I was drunk.

I said, "You've got to let me have it. All the stuff I've pulled. If you don't, the group will get on your case for letting me off easy. It will be pretty rough at times, but the whole idea is to get rid of your pain this week." I could see my mom nodding, and Mary Ellen.

Donnie and Diane were at a disadvantage because they could only stay two days each. Donnie had to be back to work on Wednesday and Diane had to watch the kids because her husband, Paul, had to work the night shift at the factory. It was hard to prepare them for the week, knowing they would be there only two days. My father seemed quiet, waiting to see how things developed.

We took a walk around The Meadows, introducing my family to my friends from the group. My mom admitted later that she had said to herself, "No, Bob can't be like these other people, all sick and lost." But when she started talking to them she realized they were human beings. They had problems that could be solved, just like mine. None of my family had been through any counseling or therapy session. It was as new to them as it had been to me four weeks earlier. I could see my mom looking around checking the place out.

Mary didn't say much with so many of my family around. We talked a little about how we missed each other, but the truth of the matter is, we wanted to be alone.

I had prepared Mary by letter for The Meadows' ban on sex. There are good reasons for the rule, since the patient is there for a self-examination and isolation, before trying to renew old relationships and old habits. Mary and I looked at each other a few times and decided some rules were meant to be broken. I told everybody that Mary and I had to take a walk before it got any darker outside, so we could inspect the marvelous rock formations and varieties of plant life to be found in the desert.

Hand-in-hand, we tiptoed through the cactus and the tumbleweed to a quiet place I had staked out earlier in the day, and we made love in the out-of-doors like Adam and Eve, with one important difference: Nobody intervened from the heavens to banish us from the garden.

I didn't regret what we had done, but Mary started to worry on Monday morning in their first family session. One man got up and complained because he wasn't allowed to have sex with his wife, who had been a patient for four weeks.

Mary told me about it at lunch. She said one counselor had called the guy selfish for thinking about sex, and another counselor had asked the wife, "How do you feel about your husband thinking about sex while we're trying to save your life?" The counselors also reminded patients they could be thrown out for violating the rule.

This bothered Mary, but I was a hardened Meadows yardbird by this time. I said, "Mary, the guy was an asshole for mentioning it. If he and his wife wanted it so badly, they could have managed it without telling anybody. The guy made it seem important because he talked about it. Like it was the only thing on his mind."

I suggested we could put love in its rightful perspective by not blabbering about it. Still, Mary seemed apprehensive, so I agreed we would abstain from loving each other until further notice, which we did, for at least a few days. And on that note, family week began.

Chapter Twenty-one

xxxxxxxxxxxxxxxxxxxxxxxxxxxxxxxxxx

Family Week–Monday

◆◆◆

The five days of family week are divided in half. In the mornings the family members meet in a group to talk about their problems, and in the afternoon the patients join the group to be confronted about what they have done to cause pain to their families.

I went to my regular patients' group on Monday morning while my mom and dad and Diane and Donnie and Mary Ellen all joined the family group. They told me later that Fred had talked a little about himself and about the plan for family week, leading from Crucifixion on Wednesday to Resurrection Day on Thursday to Forgiveness Day on Friday.

Fred also made it clear that family members had to work hard, open up their own feelings, to help save their patients' lives.

My mom told me Fred had said, "Think of the things they have done, the feelings you had when they did them. Not only does this put the addict in touch with reality, it frees you from your feelings. Don't assume they remember what they did when they were drunk. Start all over again and tell them here. Write it down before you go to session, so you won't forget. What they did. How you felt."

Mom and Mary were writing things down at lunchtime, and I could see my family was apprehensive about bringing up all the bad stuff. My mom said later she had always found it difficult to discipline me because she had been pretty tough on Donnie when he was younger. She said, "Maybe I overlooked a lot of things about Bob, but I didn't have to go to school very often because of him. Maybe I didn't notice things about his drinking."

My mom also said she had never found it easy to talk to me because I didn't show my feelings, because I wasn't a good conversationalist. Somehow, our family never learned to communicate, to talk over our feelings. I could see she wanted to do it here, but none of us really knew how. At The Meadows, they say 95 percent of all families are dysfunctional, because they don't know how to open up their feelings honestly. I wanted to tell her this is where it begins.

She was feeling pretty guilty about maybe contributing to my drinking, but I told her, "Ma, this is where you leave the garbage. Whatever you say here, you leave here. These are good people here. Nobody will repeat what you say. Just put the butter in the pan and turn on the heat and let it spread."

We went into the afternoon session, in the big den with no windows, but with a door that opened up into the garden. Sometimes they'd leave the door open for fresh air and you could see the hummingbirds flitting around a couple of cactus bushes. I used to sit by the door until somebody informed us that addictive personalities tend to seek out escape routes in any room. After that I tried to modify my behavior by sitting somewhere else in the circle, but I must admit I'd usually have my eye on the door.

There were two other families in the group, about sixteen people totally, which is small for family week. I could see where it was scary for my family, not knowing what was going on, to sit in a room, in a circle with ten strangers, and talk about me and about themselves. Everybody's kind of staring around saying, "I'm not going to say anything in front of these people." But the idea is to trust the other people because they're there for the same reason you are.

I could see everybody was pretty well petrified at the start of the session, when Fred looked around the room, half smiling and shrugging his shoulders as if to say, "Well, who wants to go first?"

Nobody said anything, so I thought, "You guys want to stay sick, fuck it, I want to get healthy. I'll go first."

So I grabbed my chair and scuttled into the center of the circle and everybody hiked their chairs a few inches forward to narrow the circle, so everybody's chair was touching.

It was up to me to choose which family member would confront me first, so I moved my chair facing Donnie. I knew he had only two days at The Meadows and I wanted to make sure he got his work done there. Donnie and I had not been close in recent years. He had already been out of the house by the time I was in high school. We were a generation apart, really. He was a teenager in the sixties, part of the "peace and love" generation. He had eventually moved out to California, inspired by the song "California Dreamin'," by the Mamas and the Papas. That's the way things were in the late sixties, when one song was enough to lure you from Detroit, with its snow and ice, to California, where all your dreams could come true.

Donnie had dreams of writing songs, too, but things don't always work out in California, and he wound up inland in San Bernardino, which he describes as a "cowboy town, more Texas than California, where the Saturday night hotspot is a cowboy bar in a Holiday Inn."

Donnie had tried a couple of jobs which hadn't worked out because he didn't have the right schooling. He'd get to a point and there would be no advancement. His first marriage had just broken up, and he had been through some hard times. I don't think it was easy for Donnie to have his kid brother, seven years younger than he, move out to California as a pitcher for the Los Angeles Dodgers. Still, Donnie had taken the call from Dale McReynolds, the Dodger scout, the summer before and tried to talk to me about my drinking. Donnie acted like big brother in that case, and I wanted him to get the chance to confront me right away at The Meadows.

It's kind of a hairy thing, being that close to somebody. To sit facing somebody, just a few inches apart, is really across the privacy line that most people prefer to maintain. The feeling is, "Get away from me. I'm not going to get that close to anybody." But we were supposed to break down those barriers, so my brother started bringing up things I had done.

"Remember the time you and Mary Ellen came out to my house and we all got drunk?" Donnie asked.

I kind of shrugged because a lot of my drinking tended to blur.

"You had some beers and you smoked a few joints and you went outside and knocked on my next-door neighbor's door and started cursing and insulting him."

I started to open my mouth to tell Donnie it never happened, but Fred cut me off before I could say a word.

"Bob, this is your turn to listen," Fred said. "It's Donald's time to talk."

Donnie continued, "You made such a fool out of yourself, banging on my neighbor's door. I was really embarrassed because you woke the guy up."

Donnie told me a few more examples of how I had gotten bombed and how I had acted. Most of them I could not even remember. When he was finished, his voice started getting husky and he said, "I don't remember the last time I told you this, Bob, but I love you very much." He put his arms around me and hugged me and I started to bawl like a baby. I don't think anybody from my family, or Mary Ellen, had ever seen me cry like that. Just sobbing, to know that my brother loved me and could tell me so in front of a whole group.

I wanted Diane to go next because she had only two days there. Diane is a real sweetheart. She had seemed a little down at lunchtime and I later discovered that one of the counselors had pointed out that Diane seemed hesitant, insecure. They found that Diane had never been encouraged to go to college, the way we boys had been, but that she had married and started a family in her early twenties. The counselor told Diane that my family valued sports highly and probably placed Donnie and me ahead of her. She was feeling a little sad about this, and I wanted her to open up.

"Bobby, when you are living at home, if you get into trouble by wrecking the car or getting drunk, you usually ask me to straighten it out," Diane said. "I feel sad when you're in trouble and I get involved. I'm tired of having to take care of those things."

"And that makes me feel . . ." Lynn said.

"Upset," Diane said. "Hurt. I guess you'd say angry. Sure. I'm angry when I have to help you because you got bombed the night before."

Somebody in the room—I don't remember who—made the observation that Diane might have encouraged my using her, because she always mothered me when I was little. At The Meadows they have a name for a daughter who takes on a lot of responsibility in the family. Little Mother. They were saying that Diane played the role of Little Mother, and that I inevitably took advantage of her.

Diane seemed sad as she realized that she had been taking care of a younger brother at the same time she had been trying to be a wife and mother in her own family.

"Bobby, you're still my baby brother," she said, "and I love you as much as ever, but I'm going to let you grow up. I don't want you to put any more responsibility on me. I want you to do things on your own."

I could feel the tears streaming down my face as I nodded to her. Then I gave her a hug for loving me so much.

Next it was my mother's turn. She was very outspoken about the things I had done to hurt her. She said she had really been scared, from the time I had started college, that I might have a drinking problem, but she had been afraid to say so.

"You would frighten me by wrecking the car," she said. "I never knew when I went out in the morning whether there would be any gas in the tank, or whether I'd be driving to work and hear beer bottles rattling under the seat. I was always afraid the police would stop me and find bottles in the car and I would get a ticket."

My mom was crying openly now, and I was crying, too, knowing that she had probably been hurt the worst of all, waiting up at night, not knowing if I had hit a cement underpass with her car, or gotten in a fight in some bar. It was sad to me, knowing that I hadn't given a damn, really. That's what it came down to.

My father said he couldn't remember anything specific I had done. The group had been getting on my case for about thirty minutes, and they wanted to move ahead, but they told my father to write down some specifics for the next day. My father was holding some mimeographed instructions in his hand, and he had rolled them into a long cylinder, like a bat. He started tapping me on the knee with the paper as he said, "Bobby, I just want you to know we're with you 100 percent to help you fight this disease."

Somebody said, "Rupe, this week isn't just for Bob. It's for you, too."

I got the feeling my father might be in for some prodding in the days to come.

Mary was the last to go. She mentioned a few times I had gotten drunk and she said she was afraid that my drinking habits would get passed on to her. They said she would have more of a chance to talk on Tuesday, and they moved on to another family. My folks seemed pretty relieved at getting it over with, that they had laid some of my actions at my feet. But that was only the first day. They would be pushed themselves soon enough.

Chapter Twenty-two

●✕✕✕✕✕✕✕✕✕✕✕✕✕✕✕✕✕✕✕✕✕✕✕✕✕✕✕✕✕✕✕✕✕●

Family Week–Tuesday

●◆◆◆●

When I joined my family for lunch on Tuesday, I noticed they were pretty agitated. Donnie was so mad he could hardly talk. He just ate his food and looked off into space. Later, Diane told me that Fred, the counselor, had suggested Donnie had an addiction problem.

I had been afraid something like that would happen. They do a lot of prejudging at The Meadows. Sometimes they're right and sometimes they're wrong. I know Donnie used to drink a lot and I knew he had gone through some rough times, but I was not convinced he was an alcoholic, even under their terms of somebody who uses an addiction to hide feelings.

A few people in the morning group heard Donnie say he saw nothing wrong with taking Valium to calm down, and they urged him to take a serious look at his habits. Donnie did not react well at all to this suggestion. He figured he was not the patient, he was there for only two days, and he did not come there to talk about himself. Sitting there at lunchtime, he looked mad enough to punch somebody in the nose.

It turned out that Donnie was ticked off at me because he thought

I had set him up for some of the criticism. Fred had brought up some things in the Tuesday morning session, when I was not present, that Donnie thought had come from me. For example, Fred knew I had cosigned a loan for Donnie and that I was mad because he was falling behind on the payments.

The people at The Meadows will call around and find out details about patients and their families. By the time Donnie got there, they knew more about him than they ever learned from me. I know how this works because one time I was in Lynn's office and saw a photograph of a couple dressed elegantly, with a fancy bar in the background of their expensive home. During the week, Lynn mentioned the home and their life-style to make the point that these people were upper-income drinkers with the same problems as somebody getting loaded in a gin mill somewhere. The Meadows also had learned a lot about the Welch family, and wanted to confront us with some of the information, which had my brother seething as we went into the Tuesday afternoon group.

In the afternoon, Fred and Lynn started right in about how my family called me "Bobby." They said my family was keeping me like a baby by calling me "Bobby." Donnie blew up at this, saying, "Wait a minute, who is the President of the United States? We don't say 'James Carter' or 'Robert Kennedy.'" Fred and Lynn just said, "You're keeping him a baby."

Donnie snapped, "Jimmy Carter's whole family, even his mother, calls him 'Jimmy.' You get in the habit after twenty-three years."

But the counselors insisted that my family did not want me to grow up. If my mother slipped and called me "Bobby," one of the counselors would say, "Lou, he's not 'Bobby' anymore. He's 'Bob.'"

It was as if I were going to stay sick because people called me "Bobby." My mother said she sometimes felt she was on trial at The Meadows but she also understood what the counselors were doing and she took their perceptions seriously. It was not that easy for my father, and I knew the "Bobby" stuff was ridiculous.

I got really ticked at the counselors for picking on my father, especially because I thought Fred was using my father to get my anger out. Anger comes from guilt, sadness, and fear, and when you get your anger out, you find out what's underneath.

Fred really got on my father, saying, "Rupe, you don't even have a list of complaints for your son. Don't you want to help him? He's dying—he's got a fatal disease—and you're not even willing to tell him how he hurt you."

I could see what they were trying to do. They were trying to help my father. I know he drinks, and I know I probably pick it up from him. But I never considered my father to be an alcoholic, and I got mad as they kept prodding him.

"Take a good look at yourself, Rupe," Fred said. "Ask yourself if you've got the same disease as your son."

My father had known I was having trouble with drinking but he had never been able to bring himself to talk about it. They were wondering if he had ever been hard on me, but really it was the other way around. He had never criticized me about my drinking, and I found it hard to criticize him. He hadn't written down any memories of when I had gotten drunk. He was just sitting there, real quiet, feeling like shit because he thought people were blaming him for me being messed up. Meanwhile, Fred kept coming at him.

I must admit, there were a few moments when I felt like jumping out of my chair and blasting Fred, but I remembered slugging that cabbie the summer before, and I checked my anger. I felt that I was the one who had fucked up, so why was Fred picking on my family? But that's what they do at The Meadows. They try to find out where you learned your behavior and that's why they kept after my father.

I didn't like it, though. I felt very protective of him. He's not at all verbal, like a lot of people at The Meadows. He's always been kind of shy, keeping his feelings hidden, and of course I could remember times when he'd drink a lot, particularly on Saturdays after work, when Donnie or Diane or I would have to open a can of chicken noodle soup for him. But my father is one of the most disciplined, neatest people I know. He always taught us to keep things orderly and to work hard and try to make something of ourselves.

I was looking over at him while the group was getting on him, and he seemed to shut off even more. His eyes turned down toward the floor, and he didn't know what to say next. His pride was wounded, and being from the South, his pride is very important to him.

Then they got on Donnie again because he and Diane had to go home after Tuesday. They kept giving Donnie the feeling, "If you really loved your brother, you'd find a way to stay." Maybe Donnie had wanted to stay, but not after what happened on Tuesday afternoon, when Fred accused Donnie of being an alcoholic.

Donnie said, "I could give up drinking for a year if I wanted to."

Fred said, "I bet you can't."

Donnie snapped, "My salary against yours."

Fred started laughing at him, and said, "It's a bet."

I had tried to tell Donnie this would happen, that the counselors liked to confront people, but Donnie thought he'd been set up by me. That afternoon when they got on him again, Donnie said he could handle drinking his own way.

I remembered how when I was a teenager, my parents were yelling at me for drinking, and how I said to them, "Donnie does it." I didn't want to bring it up now, because Donnie had enough troubles at the moment. I probably should have said something. (Months later, Donnie told me he had the same memory, along with guilt feelings that maybe he had contributed to my being an alcoholic.)

After the session, Donnie went back to the motel and locked himself in his room. He wouldn't even come out for dinner. The next morning, my mother drove Donnie and Diane to the Phoenix airport, so they could get back to their obligations at home. Donnie hardly said good-bye. I felt real bad about Donnie, and at the time I was afraid my family might have been hurt rather than helped by this week at The Meadows.

Chapter Twenty-three

▶◀◆◀◀

Family Week–Wednesday

◆◆

I woke up Wednesday morning feeling bad that Donnie and Diane had to go home and miss the rest of the week. The five days of family week are laid out so carefully that they would never understand what the first two days meant if they didn't go through the other three.

Wednesday is called Stuck Day or Crucifixion Day. Even while I was attending my patients' group, I knew the lecture my parents would be hearing. They were being told that 95 percent of all families are dysfunctional because their emotional needs are not being met—the need to be loved, the need to feel worthwhile. Often this happens because one of the parents is not giving emotional attention to the other family members.

I remember one of the counselors describing a family with a huge elephant in the room, but nobody in the family will mention it. The counselor said, "You could be up to your ears in elephant shit but if you mention it, the family members would say, 'What elephant?'" This is what happens when one parent cuts off feelings and the other has to take over both roles.

In the Wednesday morning lecture, they would tell family members some of the roles played in dysfunctional families:

Super Spouse: The parent who holds the family together by running interference for a parent who is drinking or addicted to work or to television.

Scapegoat: Somebody who distracts the family focus, a rebel.

Clown: The member who provides humor but also distracts people.

Lost Critic: Somebody not involved in the family, aloof.

Little Mother, Little Father: The child (usually a girl) who takes on parenting roles because the Super Spouse is too busy with other problems.

Hero: The overachiever who provides the family with its self-worth, who lets the family say, "We must be all right because so-and-so is part of us."

When I first heard of those categories, I tried to fit my family into those patterns. I could see where my father was quiet and didn't talk too much about himself, how my mother fussed over all of us, how Diane took me under her wing, how Donnie had been the first to move away from the family.

I also could see myself falling into three of these roles. Clown, early in my drinking, when I'd be funny, laugh my ass off. Scapegoat, when I fucked up, got into trouble. Hero, when the shop foreman could pat my father on the back and say, "How do you manage to keep your feet on the ground, having a son pitching for the Dodgers?"

In the morning lecture, they would show how these roles got passed down from generation to generation unless families learned how to communicate. It made a certain amount of sense to me, but I had a hard time blaming my parents for my alcoholism. I saw my father as a hard-working man who never missed a paycheck and who had high ambitions for all of us, and I could see my mom as being the best mom imaginable, giving me a sense of right and wrong, helping me in every way. But this would be a week for the Welch family to look inside itself. On Crucifixion Day, my father began to open up.

They had been getting on him about his own drinking, and about admitting he knew about me. When I got into the session in the afternoon, he had written down a couple of things on yellow paper. I sat facing my father and he said:

"I started noticing you were drinking too much a few years ago, when I saw you weren't just drinking a shot of whiskey, but a whole water glass. One time over at your aunt's house, you filled a water glass to the top and just gulped it down. I should have said something right then, but I didn't."

I looked at my father's face. He was staring at the floor and his voice was soft, but I knew he was feeling a lot because I could see muscles working in his face.

"How did that make you feel, Rupe?" Lynn asked him.

"I was sad because Bobby was hurting himself," my father said. "Sometimes I'd lay awake at night worrying that he was in a wreck driving home from Ypsilanti. We went down to Kentucky for a funeral and one of my brothers-in-law said to me, 'Hell, I couldn't tell when the man was drinking, but he sure can drink!' I always used to drink with Bobby around. Kept it in the refrigerator. But I never thought he'd drink as much as he did."

"And that made you feel . . ."

They tried to pin down my father's feelings, but it was too tough. He seemed to be sad that I was an alcoholic, and they asked if he felt guilty for my drinking. They also asked if he was more mad at me than he would admit, and questioned him about the extent of his own drinking, suggesting he might want to take a look at the Alcoholics Anonymous program. He said he would think about it. I could tell he was affected as my mom took her turn.

My mom really came to work each day. She let me have a few more examples of my drinking and she said she was mad at me for making her worry. The counselors told her to remain stuck on being mad from Wednesday to Thursday, that she would get positive results if she concentrated on her mad feelings overnight. She said she would.

She also said she was feeling guilty about my drinking. She was acting like a typical mom, trying to figure out if it was her fault for not telling me about the operation on my testicle when I was little. She was trying to find out if I developed any complexes from finding out I had only one testicle.

"Hell, no, Ma, that ain't it," I said. "I never used that as an excuse. I probably would have, the way I was going, but I swear it never bothered me."

Still, somebody in the group said I seemed to have a fear of death and injury. I think all athletes are more sensitive about injury because their livelihood depends on everything working just right. I know I got resentful and began drinking more in 1979 when I went to the bullpen and my arm was injured.

In baseball, when somebody is sent to the minor leagues or is released, ballplayers often use the term "he died." That's what it is. If you can't make the team, you're dead. You don't exist. You become like millions of other people and you vanish from memory and sight of the clubhouse, losing esteem in everybody's mind, including your own. When my arm was hurt, I had visions of my own premature "death," and that may have pushed me along the scale of alcoholism, although it was always there, sports or no sports.

People in my groups were saying something else, though. They detected a fear of the real death, the ultimate one. They said I would really suck up my words when I talked about death. On the Wednesday morning of family week I had completed my Fourth Step, talking about my fear of dying. I remember one time a relative died and we were at the funeral home. My cousin and I wandered down in the basement and this guy was showing us different caskets and telling us one of them was for me. I didn't like that much. So maybe I was linking my forty-two-day fever and my testicle operation and my sore arm into a greater fear than I would admit. The counselors told me to get in touch with my feelings on Wednesday night.

Then it was Mary's turn. She had been pretty quiet the first two days while Diane and Donnie worked on some things, but now the group wanted to hear from her. Somebody in the group expressed the perception that Mary didn't open up much because she liked to mother me and maybe she hadn't wanted to face my drinking problem. Mary replied that she never knew much about alcoholism, never thought of it as a feeling disease. They asked Mary to tell me ways I had hurt her.

"One day I was cooking dinner while the Dodgers were playing a day game," Mary said. "I had the dinner ready when you were supposed to get home, but you were a couple of hours late. Finally, you got home and I asked where you'd been. You said you had to drive some guy all the way out to San Fernando Valley, but you never even called me. I had cooked lasagna and had candles all set, but everything was ruined by the time you got home. You insisted you only had a couple of beers."

Mary started to cry, great tears rolling down her cheeks.

"And that made you feel . . ." Lynn said.

"Hurt. Sad. Angry."

I was embarrassed at seeing Mary cry and I tried to jolt her out of it by making a joke.

"Hell, if you had to eat Mary's cooking, you'd know why I came home late," I announced to the group.

One of the men did not think it was funny.

"Why are you laughing?" he snapped at me. "Don't you know how serious this is?"

Mary might have started to smile at my joke, but the caustic tone from the man froze the smile off her face. Lynn asked Mary why she let me get away with my behavior, over and over again.

I was surprised to hear Mary say how she had felt caught between her mother and her father when she was growing up. Her father used to work in a factory and so did her mother, until Mary was in the eighth grade. Then her mother went back to high school and got her diploma and started college for a degree in early-childhood education. Now her mother teaches emotionally disturbed kids in Detroit. Mary recalled how she had learned to do the dishes and clean up, because she wanted her parents to be happy when they got home from work and from school. Apparently she had talked this over in the morning group, but Lynn wanted her to discuss this again in front of me.

Mary faced me and said she had always wanted to feel needed, and that she was afraid to show her emotions, of expressing herself, for fear of being rejected. This holding in of emotions was exactly what Lynn had been working on with me for about three weeks. Now she was discovering that Mary also held herself back.

Lynn got this big look of surprise on her face and she asked in dramatic tones, "Boy, how long did it take for you two to discover each other?"

One of the things they believe at The Meadows is that there are few coincidences in life, that you plan more than you think. Lynn reasoned that Mary and I had been looking for each other all our lives. I wasn't sure I believed it at first, but later Mary told me that when she was in the tenth grade in chemistry class, her first instinct was, "I really like the guy. He's a kind person, a sharing person, not a typical jock all stuck on himself." The joke was that once I started acting like a jock, she went along with it for years—Little Mother seeking Hero-Scapegoat, and vice versa.

Somebody in the group asked Mary what her favorite nursery rhyme was. I had already written to her how the group called me "a follower" for answering "Mary Had a Little Lamb," but Mary didn't heed my warning. She blurted the first thing in her mind: "Mary had a Little Lamb," and they jumped all over her for that, because it was obvious I was the little lamb who followed her around. They said she had to stop protecting me, give me room, make me face my drinking and my behavior.

Then somebody asked me my favorite rhyme and this time I was prepared. I said "Humpty-Dumpty," because obviously I had taken a big fall—from the pitching mound into drinking bouts and finally to The Meadows.

That seemed to satisfy everybody—but it wasn't the truth. That was not the first nursery rhyme that came into my head. The first was "Twinkle, Twinkle, Little Star," only I wasn't about to admit that. I did not want to answer a lot of piercing questions about why I wanted to be a star, why I thought I was better than anyone else, whether I had an identity crisis—"How I wonder what you are."

I did not want the group interpreting lines like: "Up above the world so high." Or "Like a diamond in the sky."

A diamond. Not a baseball diamond but the real thing, something rare and valuable. I was afraid of telling my group that I wanted to be a star. How could I get up in front of my parents and my girl-friend, the counselors and the two other families—hard-working people with jobs in offices and factories, with money problems, with little chance of being famous or knowing they were near the top of their business—and admit that I wanted to be a star? I wanted to win twenty games a season, wanted to pitch in the All-Star game, wanted to pitch in another World Series, wanted to win. Deep down I wanted to "twinkle, twinkle" like a star. But I choked off the words, choked off the feelings.

Lynn and Fred told Mary to stay stuck Wednesday night in her pain of being used by me, of being afraid to show her own feelings. They told me to stay stuck in the pain of falling from my own private wall, and they urged me to identify the feelings behind the fall.

It was not easy to focus on the pain that evening. It was so good to be with Mary and my parents again, in the Arizona desert in February. I had raged against The Meadows at times, wished I could run away, fought the process, but physically and emotionally the place had become like home. I strolled around the grounds with my parents, put my arm around them, sat and talked about what we would do when I got out. Then around dinnertime, they would go back to the motel and leave me alone with Mary. We would sit on the patio and talk into the evening, laughing or serious.

A lot of people at The Meadows commented how happy my family looked. Most of the families there had been broken apart by alcoholism or other addictions. People had hurt each other so badly that it showed in their faces and the tentative way they began to deal with each other. You could see family members wondering whether they dared trust the patient again, trying to find the good things.

I had not been an alcoholic that long, had not done all the terrible things I eventually would have done. The Dodgers and Union Oil and The Meadows and the Welch family were helping me stop a fatal disease before it progressed too far. While most families had decades of pain to be cured, we only had a few months or years to patch. I was eager to start. I couldn't listen enough about Mary's schoolwork or her plans after graduation—things I never cared about before. I realized Mary was special to me, and I wanted to know more about her. On Wednesday night I tried to focus on my pain—but it wasn't easy at all.

Chapter Twenty-four

◆◆◆◆◆◆◆◆◆◆◆◆◆◆◆◆◆◆◆◆◆◆◆◆◆◆◆◆◆◆◆◆◆◆◆◆◆◆

Family Week-Thursday

◆◆◆

Thursday at the Meadows is called Resurrection Day, the day on which you begin to recover from your pain. Each member of the family is supposed to go back to the motel on Wednesday night and remain stuck in pain until Thursday. They promise that changes will take place if you let yourself remain stuck overnight.

It was hard for me to work at being stuck in pain because I was feeling so good at not drinking—four weeks now—and because my family was feeling better every day. But the counselors have their ways of bringing you back to the source of your pain.

At lunchtime Mary Ellen told me how they had been working on her because of her relationship to me. They wanted to know why she allowed me to insult her. Somebody in the morning group had suggested that allowing me to drink was a way of controlling or manipulating me. Somebody suggested that Mary was afraid of letting me know her true personality, that maybe she was inadequate and insecure. This is a pattern they talk about with alcoholics: They will often be discovered by somebody with a mother image or a martyr image.

Like most people who come for family week, Mary had assumed she was coming to help me, but the program goes far beyond that.

I've got to say this for Mary Ellen Wilson: Once they began concentrating on her, she opened herself up. I've seen people who cut and ran the first time anybody prodded them, but Mary listened to their feedback. Sitting opposite her at the lunch table, I could see Mary was thinking it over.

"They got on me again about the nursery rhyme 'Mary Had a Little Lamb,'" Mary said. "Somebody asked if I felt the need to be punished for something."

"What did you say?" I asked.

"I didn't know. I don't know. I'm all confused."

They did not leave Mary in that state for long. After lunch, we had a family session with the patients, and when they asked who wanted to work, I said, "Hell, I'll go." I turned my plastic chair around to face Mary, because I knew she had been hurt a lot by my drinking, second only to my mother.

Mary told a couple more stories about my drinking that I hardly remembered, how I'd passed out in rest rooms or nearly crashed my car. But there was a difference in Mary on Thursday. She was not showing that tentative half smile of hers. She seemed sadder, angrier than the day before.

Lynn picked up on Mary's mood and commented that Mary seemed hurt by my actions. Lynn also reminded Mary how she had often mediated quarrels in her own family. When Lynn picks up verbal cues like this, she leans forward, her jaw seems to jut out, her green eyes seem to darken, to penetrate like lasers.

After watching that woman at work for a month, I'm convinced that Lynn has a sixth sense for women's emotions, that she can zero in on them. It's not that she's oblivious to men's problems—in many cases, they're the same problems—but I have the feeling Lynn has suffered in family relationships and man-woman relationships, and she can detect that suffering in other women. I've seen her be really tough with men—with me, as a matter of fact—but she is gentle with women. Gentle and accurate.

"How does that make you feel when you have to take care of other people?" Lynn asked.

"I don't know."

"Are you angry?"

"Yes. I guess."

"I think you're angry. Let's see how angry you are."

Then she placed Mary between two people who reminded her of a father figure and a mother figure, and had the two people tug at her hands.

Lynn told Mary to remember how she had felt when she was caught between family members as a child, feeling she had the responsibility to keep the peace. Mary's face grew taut with anger.

"Mary Ellen, you look angry," Lynn said.

"I am."

"How angry are you?"

"Really angry."

"Angry enough to . . . angry enough to scream?"

Mary nodded.

"Well, then, scream," Lynn said. "Let it out, a good scream. Show how angry you were at having to be the peacemaker. Show how angry you are when you have to mother a friend who's always getting drunk, when you just want to be a college student, a young woman growing up. How mad are you? Can you scream?"

Then Mary Ellen Wilson, sometimes known by me as Miss Goody Two-Shoes, sometimes known to herself as Mary Had a Little Lamb, took a deep breath and let out a scream from deep in her stomach, a scream that cut into my own guts.

I had never heard Mary scream like that, not when I wrecked the car, not when I got drunk, not when we were in bed, not when she thought I'd been out with other women. Mary was screaming to let out the pain she had never shared with me or anybody else, or even with herself. She was letting out the garbage, just as they tell you to do. When the scream ended, Mary was crying, sobbing, really, and people were dabbing tissues to her eyes, and hugging her.

"That was good," Lynn said. "Let it go. You don't have to hold things inside. You can be yourself. You can be Mary Ellen. You don't have to mother this guy. Let him take care of himself."

Mary nodded, taking this moment in.

Then Lynn turned her attention to another member of the group, fastened her piercing green eyes on somebody else who needed a little work, Little Bobby Welch, the kid from Hazel Park.

"Bob, what about you?"

I shrugged. What about me?

"How do you feel?"

"Glad. Glad. I'm glad because we're getting stuff out."

But Lynn kept insisting that I looked angry but wouldn't let my feelings out. She had been working on me for days, and the more she bugged me, the angrier I got, but I had made up my mind I was going to swallow it. I wanted to get out of The Meadows as easily as possible.

"Bob, you say you're not angry, but your face looks angry to me," Lynn said. "Your arms are wrapped around your chest like you're holding something in, and your head is down like you're trying to force something down your throat. Why don't you let it out?"

I didn't know what Lynn wanted me to say. She knew it.

"I think you should be mad," Lynn said. "Everybody's using you."

"What do you mean?"

"Everybody's put you up on a pedestal. Your family's using you. Their younger son is playing for the Dodgers. Your father can talk baseball with the men in the shop, your mother sees your success, your sister and brother might be jealous of you, but they can boast about you. People look up to them because of you."

I remembered the diagram on the blackboard about the dysfunctional families, how people play the roles of Clown or Little Mother or Super Spouse or Hero.

"You mean I play the role of Hero in my family?" I asked.

"Not just Hero," somebody said from across the circle. "You're also the Scapegoat."

"That's right," somebody else said. "Bob, you're always saying how you got a buzz on so you could get fucked up. But I think you mean you want to fuck up. You want to lose."

Somebody asked me if I felt guilty about playing with the Dodgers, about making the major leagues. I couldn't describe all the images that flashed across my mind—about going back to Detroit after the 1978 World Series, the parades in Hazel Park and Ferndale, everybody making a fuss over Bob Welch. But then I'd go visit all my buddies at their little houses, guys I'd played ball with in high school or college, guys who got stuck in the minor leagues, guys working in factories.

In my mind, some of them might be thinking how much money I was making from playing ball, wondering why I had all the success when everybody's buying foreign cars and the auto industry is laying off workers in Detroit.

I remembered going into the Rainbow Bar and hearing guys throw remarks like, "Hey, Bobby, Reggie really scored on you in the last game," good old Hazel Park verbal abuse, and how I'd laugh and toss down a few more beers just to show I was the same old Welchie, hadn't changed a bit.

"Bob, how do you feel right now?" Lynn asked.

"A little sad," I said.

Feelings. I was getting in touch with them now. I realized this session was rapidly becoming a Bob Welch session, and my mind began planning some form of escape. I was too far from the door to run for it, and I knew that if I tried to duck the questions there'd be half a dozen addicts like myself waiting around the circle to pin me down. I was stuck with my feelings of guilt for getting a chance to play in the majors.

Deep down inside I knew it was more than that. I didn't want to punch the time clock. I didn't want to work nine to five. I didn't want to pinch pennies. I wanted to play ball, and I had worked damn hard to get there, cleaning the fields for Ron Oestrike back at Eastern Michigan, pitching in summer leagues when other guys were swimming at the lakes. I had wanted it, but now I also felt a little guilty about having some success.

"What about the Dodgers treating you like a piece of meat?"

"But it's filet mignon and not ground round," I replied.

I thought about the guy in Albuquerque trying to sucker me into signing a cheap contract. I remembered how they put me in the bullpen when my arm went bad. I knew this was how baseball operated, but I also knew the Dodgers even had a program to help alcoholics like myself.

"The Dodgers have a big investment in you," somebody said. "Look, they even sent a scout and a catcher up here to The Meadows while you're under treatment for alcoholism. They wanted to keep an eye on you. You're valuable to them."

I wanted to explain how the Dodgers were a family organization, but the people in my group were digging in, linking my job to their jobs, equating me to working on assembly lines, in offices, in corporations, where your personality was not as important as what you did.

The weight in my stomach grew heavier as I remembered how I felt when I lost a ball game, the feeling that I'd let the company down. I had the feeling that nobody really knew me, that nobody really cared about me. And when I got a buzz on, when I got all fucked up, the feeling I got was, "How could you do this to us, to the company?"

"How do you feel right now, Bob?" Lynn asked.

"A little sad, a little angry at being used by everybody."

I felt like I was swallowing hard, trying to keep something in my stomach. I was aware of choking off my words, afraid of what was going to come next.

"How sad? How angry?"

I didn't know.

"You are so angry you could . . ."

I didn't know. I couldn't talk.

"Could you hit something?"

I thought of the cabbie I had hit. I thought about wanting to deck Fred for picking on my father on Tuesday. I thought about my anger toward Lasorda, my anger toward college coaches who criticized me for drinking. And I looked across at Mary Ellen, tears in her beautiful dark eyes, and I remembered her telling how I had abused her when I was drunk. I was angry at myself, angry at others, tired of being everybody's Hero, everybody's Scapegoat. I remembered the kid swinging the bat at a chair in my first week at The Meadows, but I didn't want to hit anything. I didn't want to use my hands. My pain was deeper inside, down in my stomach.

"Are you mad enough to scream?" Lynn asked.

I thought, well, damn it, anything to get these people off my back.

But I didn't know how to scream. It was like having the dry heaves, wanting to throw up but not being able to do it. I made a few dumb noises from my throat but that didn't satisfy anybody.

"It's all right, Bob," Lynn said. "Let it go. Don't hold back."

The next thing I knew, my head was down between my knees, and my body was curled forward, like in a sitting fetal position, and I let out a sound that seemed more of a moan than a scream—a moan from deep in my guts. The moan was equal parts:

Anger—at being prodded by Lynn and the group.

Anger—at being used by other people.

Fear—of never getting out of The Meadows.

Sadness—at being an alcoholic when I wanted to be a pitcher.

Guilt—for making my family and Mary come here, for giving them so much pain.

Relief—damn right, relief. Relief that somewhere in that half-assed moan I loosened a hundred pounds of tension, let it fly through every opening in my body.

I knew I was crying, but all I could say was, "My hands and arms feel really light."

"Bob, you've got so much of your feelings tied up in your arms and hands," Lynn said. "Now your arms feel light, the pressure's off you, Bob. You don't have to be a pitcher for people to love you. You got your self-worth from pleasing other people, from pleasing crowds. You are loved right here, not because you're a baseball player, but because you're Bob."

While I was sitting there weeping, Mom and Mary Ellen came over and hugged me, and a few other people from the group, people who had been strangers a few days before, but who now held tissues to my eyes and put their arms around me.

And I was thinking, "Man, you're on your way. You're saving your life."

When that session was over, people gave me an extra hug and told me they were proud of me for working some of my anger out. I sat down by the patio and gazed at the purple mountains in the distance, the river rushing through the bottomland, the horses moving around the corral. I felt limp, exhausted, at peace with the world, particularly myself.

Now that the emotion of the group was over, I felt as if I had left many things behind. I could see myself going back to Hazel Park as Bob Welch, love me or leave me, and let somebody else buy a round. I could see myself going back home for the holidays and being a better son, a better brother, a better uncle.

I could see myself going back to the Dodgers and busting my ass— for them, but also for me. I wasn't giving up booze to satisfy the Dodgers. Maybe it started out that way a month ago, but now it was for myself. They were going to profit from it, though. Instead of a kid with a vacant stare, they were going to have an alert, sober, adult pitcher in a few weeks.

Maybe even a star. I thought of my blue satin Dodger jacket and I pictured a big white star on it, just as in the nursery rhyme I didn't dare tell my group about, "Twinkle, Twinkle, Little Star." I could see myself back in Dodger Stadium, striking out the last batter of a game, not only for my teammates or the Dodger management or the fans in the grandstand or my family or even for Mary Ellen.

For me. I still wanted to be a star for me, Bob Welch.

I wanted to win.

Chapter Twenty-five

▰◆◆◆◆◆◆◆◆◆◆◆◆◆◆◆◆◆◆◆◆◆◆◆◆◆◆◆◆◆◆◆◆◆◆▰

"Thanks for Being a Drunk"

◆◆◆

On Friday my family finished with a morning session where they wrote down their plans for following up their experiences at The Meadows. My mom wrote that she wanted to be "more considerate of others' behavior. If I can't change them, not be demanding." She also promised to start attending meetings of Al-Anon, a group of people related to alcoholics. Mary Ellen wrote that she would work on letting go of her angry feelings, that she had to recognize the good things about herself and also "to let Bob be responsible for himself, letting him grow." My father agreed to take a closer look at himself. I wrote that I would work on a "feeling of inadequacy about myself, feeling that if I really show who I am, no one will love me."

We turned our statements over to the counselors, who read them during lunchtime. Early in the afternoon they held a graduation where every family presents himself or herself with a Meadows medallion for participating in family week. It's happy and sad at the same time, seeing people you have grown to love, knowing you won't see them again. One by one, my family got up there and said they had gained a lot from the week. I wanted to be up there with them but I had another week to go.

My parents and Mary were staying for the weekend and I was

rewarded with a weekend pass, starting Saturday morning. I joined them for a drive around the desert to some Indian shops and a museum and an old gold mine.

On Saturday night we had dinner at the Golden Nugget Restaurant in Wickenburg, the first meal I had taken outside The Meadows in almost five weeks. People were drinking at the tables around us but my folks did not order any drinks, even though I told them to go ahead.

"Hell, I've got to live out in the world," I told them. "I can't expect everybody to stop drinking just because I'm an alcoholic. Some people can handle it. Don't let me stop you. Hell, I'll buy a round."

Clearly, they did not want to put alcohol within my grasp, but there was no way I was going to drink that night. After dinner Mary and I checked into our own motel room, a whole lot better than the floor of the desert.

On Sunday I was due back at lunchtime, so I said good-bye to the folks, and Mary drove me up the familiar hill. We were crying because we would not see each other for a few more weeks. She was going to Kalamazoo for her final semester and I was going to California and then spring training.

I felt I could leave right then but the counselors insisted I needed another week of work. I felt desolate as I watched Mary drive off but I had to get ready for my second family to arrive. The Dodgers like to think of themselves as a family, and in a lot of ways they are. They are owned and operated by the O'Malley family and try to make the players feel part of the organization. The counselors thought it was important for some people from the Dodgers to spend a week with me, to help me explore my feelings about myself and my work.

The Dodgers had been calling down to check on my progress, and Don Newcombe had visited for one day a few weeks earlier. Newk had given his talk on alcoholism, telling about his life the way he had done in spring training of 1978. Whenever Newk talks, he stresses the idea of becoming a "somebody" by not drinking. Some counselors and patients at The Meadows did not agree with this philosophy. They believe you are a "somebody" already but you have to learn to stay sober.

Newk is such a powerful man that he tends to come on strong. He was dressed in a suit with an imitation diamond stickpin and he talked about his connections in the government and private industry and who he played golf with. He wanted to contrast this with the star pitcher who had become a dangerous alcoholic, threatening his family, losing all his money. He wanted to show himself as an example of how you could rebuild your life by staying sober.

I could readily understand Newk's competitiveness, his pride. The man had been the Most Valuable Player in his league and out of major-league baseball four years later. He was proud of his new success. Some people may have been jealous of seeing that big, articulate black guy talking about success. A few people commented that he had never gone through Alcoholics Anonymous or any other program to stop drinking, but he was good about praising what AA could do for others. Some people might have felt he was not in touch with his feelings, or the feelings of the patients, but I could relate to his pride, the pride of a warrior who struggles against an enemy. I knew I needed The Meadows and AA—but I was also glad to have Don Newcombe's example. Now I had to find some other Dodger people for my second family week.

I had called Rick and Robin Sutcliffe, who had become friendly with me and Mary Ellen in 1979, the year Rick won seventeen games and was Rookie of the Year. After not getting to know Rick very well in the minors, I had come to like him a lot—so much that I honored him by making him my drinking partner and chief defender.

He had been calling me all winter before I checked into The Meadows, leaving messages at my home, but I was too messed up to call him back. When I reached him in Kansas City from The Meadows, I beat around the bush until I finally said, "Rick, I have a problem. I'm an alcoholic." Rick sounded shocked that somebody as young as me could be an alcoholic. He kept saying, "Are you sure?" and I said, "Hell, yes. This place would like you to come down for a family week. Can you and Robin come down?"

Rick and Robin arrived Sunday afternoon. I watched the expressions on their faces when they spotted a couple of our older drunks shuffling around, having a few withdrawal tremors. Neither Rick nor Robin had ever experienced anything of alcoholism except for mine, so the whole concept was a shock to them.

I watched their faces for a moment more, then popped out of the shadows and asked, "How does it feel being around all these drunks?" They seemed a little taken aback by my words but they seemed even more shocked when I gave Rick a big hug. Robin started off to give me a handshake but I did not invite Robin Sutcliffe all the way from Kansas City for one little old handshake. I grabbed her and gave her a Meadows hug, too. I told them, "You're in for a big week."

The counselors and the Dodgers had thought it would be a good idea if Tom Lasorda would come down, so we could get to know each other better while I was in a sober state. He did not arrive on Monday, and family week began without him.

Rick and Robin got a quick dose of family week that first afternoon when Fred Downing did one of his bloodhound numbers on an alcoholic and his wife. Fred asked the woman, "How do you feel when your husband drinks?"

She answered, "Well, he hurts me sometimes."

Fred replied, "What do you mean, 'sometimes'?" The wife started crying because apparently her husband had hurt her deeply. Fred usually knew when people were in pain and needed to let it out. I could see Rick and Robin look at each other as if to say, "What have we gotten into here?"

It was hard for Rick to confront me when they asked him what I had done. He acted shy, as if he didn't want people to know bad stuff about me, but people said, "Look, if you want to help Bob, you can't protect him."

By this time, I thought I had heard every bad thing about myself, so I said, "Hey, Rick, tell it to my face." He and Robin started scribbling stuff down on yellow legal paper, to be armed for the next day. It would be a shocker to me.

"Bob, I remember how we went roller-skating in Venice last summer on a day off," Rick began on Tuesday. "My family was out visiting me in California and we wanted to show them a good time. But you started drinking heavily and started tearing around on roller skates, throwing yourself around in the sand, cutting your elbows, laughing, and cursing. We were playing catch with a Frisbee and you went out for a pass and didn't even look where you were going and you ran into a parking meter at full speed. You fell down and your whole leg was cut, so we figured we'd better quit. We drove you back to your house and there were still a few hours of daylight left but the whole day was ruined.

"And you felt . . ." Lynn prodded.

"Hurt. Mad. Sure, I was angry because you ruined the day for us by getting drunk. Then there was the time we went to Disneyland during the day and you suggested we carry vodka in a shaving kit.

We were drinking it in the bathroom with all these kids around, pouring it into Cokes.

"We kept drinking and when we got to your house we were playing Ping-Pong and we must have been making too much noise because somebody called and complained. Right after that, Bob, you went into your bedroom and just passed out while the dinner was cooking. Just passed out, and we had been planning to go out for a movie. It was only eight o'clock but Robin and I went home. We felt like the day was ruined."

"How did you feel about that?" Lynn asked Rick.

"Terrible," Rick answered. "I realized later I was being led into drinking more. I was embarrassed at drinking in a bathroom at Disneyland, afraid some kids would recognize two Dodgers drinking vodka out of a shaving kit. I was really mad at you, Bob."

Later when somebody asked how I felt about Rick's story, I had to tell the truth. I did not remember it. Rick seemed amazed when I told him that, but it was true. I vaguely remembered going to Venice, and I vaguely remembered going to Disneyland, but I had no memory of the details.

"Bob, you've been having blackouts for at least a year," somebody said, making me realize my alcoholism was worse than I had believed.

Then it was Robin Sutcliffe's turn. She is a very attractive woman with a little-girl voice, who sounds as if she wouldn't say anything bad to anybody. She told me about the time she was visiting Rick in St. Louis and I got smashed before dinner.

"Bob, you were so drunk, I did not want anything to do with you," Robin said. "I did not want to go out to dinner with you."

That hurt me a lot, the idea that a friend would want to duck me. I had to ask myself how many times this had happened, how many people had been turned off by my drinking.

On Wednesday, Rick came up with some more times I had hurt him. This was Crucifixion Day, and he was feeling stuck in pain from the time I got drunk in San Francisco. He started supplying details I had never known before, like my challenging Terry Whitfield of the Giants to a fight that time in Candlestick Park. The more Rick talked, the angrier he got.

"Bob, what really hurt me is that I covered up for you, started drinking more because of you, almost got into a fight with Terry

Whitfield, and had to yell at Burt Hooton to get away from you while you were cussing at him. I did all these things for you, but you never even said thank you."

Just a few inches from my face, this great big man with red hair started to cry. He was really letting loose his pain, sobbing, his face all wet. People reached over and held tissues to Rick's face. It tore me up to see him cry, realizing I was the cause. I couldn't think of anything else to do except put my arms around him. I just reached out and gave him a hug and told him I was sorry.

It was a very touching moment for both of us. The counselors told Rick and Robin to remember their pain Wednesday night, that they would be able to release it Thursday. I could see how much respect everybody had for the Sutcliffes, who had come to help me but also were working on themselves.

It was not that easy for Tom Lasorda. He arrived for the morning session on Wednesday, missing the introduction on how to confront me with the way I had hurt him.

Tom Lasorda is a fascinating baseball man who often recalls how the Dodgers kept him in the minor leagues so they could bring up another left-hander named Sandy Koufax. But Lasorda loved baseball so much that he worked in the minor leagues and the Caribbean leagues, pitching and scouting and coaching and managing. He became extremely loyal to the Dodger organization, always talking about the "blue Dodger blood" in his veins.

When he was the Dodgers' third-base coach under Walter Alston, Lasorda used to do his monologue on the "Game of the Week," telling about the Great Dodger in the Sky. He can hold his own with professional entertainers. You just look at the autographed pictures on his office wall and you see the worlds of baseball and show business overlapping. I've walked by his office and seen Frank Sinatra, Don Rickles, other big stars. They are his friends, not just his acquaintances. The man runs in some big company.

I think Tom Lasorda came to The Meadows trying to live up to a certain Dodger image in his mind. Some members of the staff said he was giving out autographed pictures of himself in the office when he arrived. Because he had not been there for the start of the week, he didn't realize that people wanted to know the real Tom Lasorda, not just the man in the celebrity pictures.

I wasn't there on Wednesday morning when Tom joined the

family group but people have told me about it. He said, "I'm Tom Lasorda, the manager of the Los Angeles Dodgers. I've got the best job in baseball, and I'm the happiest guy in the world."

Fred Downing turned and said, "Tom, I don't believe it."

A few other people said they thought Lasorda looked mad at being at The Meadows. It is my feeling that some people had been waiting for Lasorda to arrive, annoyed that he hadn't been there Monday. He was set up in a way, and people didn't like it when he wouldn't talk about his feelings. Apparently he talked about drinking as a moral issue, a matter of self-control.

When I joined the group for the afternoon session, Tom seemed upset, maybe even threatened by the way people were responding to him. They were urging him to tell me how I had hurt him but he did not want to do it. He wanted to encourage me, to give me a pep talk, that he was on my side, but that isn't the way it works at The Meadows. You act on somebody's side by confronting him with what he did to you. And the truth is, I had challenged Lasorda a number of times by getting drunk, but he didn't want to bring all of that out.

He found an ally in the group, the mother of another patient. She also refused to talk about her feelings and sided with Lasorda when he declined to participate. She would become one of the few people to spend a week at The Meadows and not get a Meadows medallion on graduation day.

Lasorda did not last until Friday. On Thursday morning he and Fred Downing got into an argument. It must have been tough for Lasorda, who has to balance twenty-five guys, all itching to be stars, to be put into a situation where he was not the boss. Fred was the boss of family week. He called the signals. People told me their argument continued in Fred's office at lunchtime. Later that day Lasorda and I talked, and he offered to stay on if I wanted him to or thought it would help, but we agreed that it would be pointless. The next time I saw him was at spring training.

I was not mad at Lasorda for not coming for the whole week. But I also think he could have gotten more out of The Meadows than he did. He could have gotten more in touch with himself and with other people. It probably would have been good if we had talked about why I tried to make him the scapegoat for my going to the bullpen and getting a sore arm in 1979. By the time he came to The Meadows, I did not blame the man for my troubles. I took responsibility myself, but it would have been good to get that stuff out in the open.

As it was, it took a long time for us to be comfortable with each other, which we are now.

For Rick and Robin Sutcliffe, the week was a success. On Thursday both said their pain could have been handled better if they had confronted me earlier. Both promised to be more honest with other people in the future. Both said they could see examples in their marriage where they did not pay attention to each other's feelings, where they would carry anger inside.

The staff at The Meadows had great respect for Rick and Robin. I could see that. Neither of them had an alcohol problem but they had used the week to work on their feelings. On Friday, Rick and Robin both awarded themselves medals. Rick said he would be able to be a better husband and friend because of the week. Robin said she knew herself better.

She got up there in front of the group and said she was very proud of her medal. She added: "This is a nice gift. I don't know what else to say except, Bob, thanks for being a drunk."

I was still laughing when it was my turn to be graduated. It was my last hour at The Meadows after thirty-six days—thirty-six big ones out in the desert.

I thought about all the other people I had watched at the Friday ceremony, and now it was my turn. I started mumbling something about getting in touch with my feelings, learning how to save my own life, meeting some wonderful people. And I finished with a little bit of Meadows honesty.

"Actually, I came here trying to bullshit everybody and just get through the process," I said. "But everybody knew it, and wouldn't let me. I award myself this medal for learning to be more honest about my feelings, for not hiding out."

Everybody applauded and a few came over and gave me hugs. Lynn stood up and congratulated me on the progress I made. She said she was sad I was leaving but felt I would be able to deal with my feelings now.

We talked a little bit about what I would do when I got out. People were trying to give me advice about how to get back into daily life again. I listened politely but I was eager to leave. I had done my work. I wanted to get back to my life.

Chapter Twenty-six

XXXXXXXXXXXXXXXXXXXXXXXXXXXXXXXXXX

Spring Training

◆◆◆

John Newton met me at the airport at Phoenix and congratulated me on going through The Meadows. We flew back to Los Angeles together, and I had my first opportunity to slip off the wagon when the stewardess came around serving drinks. The airlines make it really easy for somebody to drink. As soon as the plane is off the ground, just wave a few dollars and you can have a couple of shots. Now that my eyes were open, I was becoming aware of what an alcohol-oriented society this is.

"Would either of you gentlemen like a drink?" the stewardess asked.

John gestured to me, giving me the option to make up my own mind. I ordered a glass of club soda on the rocks with a twist of lemon. In my mind, I expected her to shrug and say, "What, you don't drink?" and people to turn around and look at me strangely because I wasn't following the custom. But the world didn't end when she handed me the plastic glass with the bubbling soda in it. I was just beginning to discover what nondrinkers already know: You do not have to drink. Nobody is making you.

John and I talked all the way back about my next steps. I had a few days before spring training opened, so I was going to stay with

216

my friend Mike Josephs, who had taken me in just before The
Meadows. I attended AA meetings in Burbank almost every night
until going to Florida.

I was curious if anybody had talked or written about my going to
The Meadows, but he said it was a big secret, even in the Dodger
organization. Even if the rumor had gotten around that I was taking
the cure, The Meadows would never confirm it had even heard
of me.

I was already making my plans for spring training. Now that I had
gone through the process, I had the enthusiasm of any new convert.
You want the world to know. You are on a super high, better than
any buzz from alcohol. You want to tell the world how you feel, how
much you love being alive. You want to shout, "I don't have to ruin
my life. Here's what I did."

I anticipated that some people—my teammates or sportswriters—
might notice a difference in me. I remember some of the sportswriters suggesting that my mind was in outer space most of the time. If I
seemed to be more clear-headed, some of them might start asking
questions. And I wanted to be able to tell them.

"What should I do?" I asked John.

"Well, AA does have a step of making amends to people you've
hurt," John said. "If you've screwed up in front of your teammates,
or given a bad impression to people, it's probably a good idea to tell
them you're sorry."

"The best time would be right away in spring training," I said.
"Tell my teammates first and then hold a press conference. Get it all
out of the way."

"Before you do that, consider this. If you hold a press conference,
it will go all over the country. It will be like making a commitment
in front of millions of people. You don't owe them anything. You're
not staying sober for other people. You're doing it for yourself."

"I know that, man. But I'm not afraid of pressure. I've pitched in
the World Series."

"I know that," John answered. "But look at it this way. If you go
public, there's going to be a lot of people rooting for you to fail.
Think about the player or club official who has drinking problems
but doesn't want to face them. He's going to want you to fail so he
can say to himself, 'See, Welch can't make it and neither can I.' They
might make it harder on you in some way."

I thought about the sportswriters sitting up in the press box. I knew that some of them have problems, just as in any profession, and I wondered how they would treat the story.

"That's right, Bob," John said. "The best story some of them could get would be when Bob Welch gets drunk in a bar some night and they can come up with the lead that says: 'Bob Welch fell off his stool at Sloppy Joe's Bar and Grill last night.' There will be some guys making comments and jokes because they feel threatened by what you're doing."

"How do you know that?" I asked John.

"Look, Bob, I'm not kidding you. I know a few executives at Union Oil who get down on their knees at night and pray that John Newton is out getting smashed. That would mean they don't have to face themselves, or try to get help for their wives or kids. There are people who want to see failure."

"I'm sure you're right," I told John. "But I personally know that Lyle Spencer of the *Herald-Examiner* and a couple of other guys will listen to me and write a fair story. They know I've got a drinking problem. When they hear what I've done, they'll be glad to write about it."

We decided that I would take care of the matter as soon as spring training started. I stayed with Mike and went to my meetings and joined the club for the flight to Vero Beach. For the first few days, just the pitchers were in camp, but all the regulars had to show up on March 1. I couldn't wait until then to hold my secret. I had to tell somebody. I decided on Sandy Koufax. This man was one of my idols. He was just finishing his career when I started to follow baseball on television, but I knew he had been the greatest pitcher in baseball until his retirement after 1966. There was only one Sandy Koufax, and I had to tell him. Rick knew, of course, and it had been important to tell Red Adams, our pitching instructor.

I used to see Koufax once in a while around Dodger Stadium when I first joined the Dodgers, slender and dark-skinned and very quiet, shy. He had tried broadcasting after retirement, but he had spent the last decade out of the public eye. He does not like the limelight, but around the players he is easy to talk with. In 1980 the Dodgers talked Sandy into becoming a pitching instructor. I was thrilled to see him wearing his old No. 32 around camp, and taking long jogs before practice. I love running, too, so I started joining him on long, slow runs across the grass.

On the weekend when all the players were arriving, I decided to try my secret out on Sandy as we jogged. I wanted to see the look on his face, and I knew the man would not give me any bullshit answer. As we were going for a run, I said to him, "Hey, Sandy, I want to tell you something. I'm an alcoholic. I just spent thirty-six days at a treatment center and they taught me not to drink. I feel a whole lot better about myself."

I waited for something to happen, for the earth to part, for Sandy to stop dead in his tracks. But we just kept loping across the grass and he turned to me and said, "That's great. Congratulations. Terrific." He actually thanked me for sharing it with him, and he said that the AA advice of living one day at a time was really something anybody could use. He said when he was having trouble with his arm, he realized all he could do was go out and do his best that day.

I felt so terrific about Sandy's understanding that as soon as our run was over, I rushed over to tell Red Adams, our pitching coach. Red cracked a big smile and congratulated me. So far I was two-for-two. Of course, Rick was around, giving me encouragement, too.

Rick said later that a few people had been asking him whether I had been drinking all winter. He didn't spill the story but he tried to prepare people for a difference in me.

I also looked up Lyle Spencer of the *Herald-Examiner* and told my story one day in advance, knowing that it would not appear in the paper until after I told everybody else. I wanted to get my story out to people I trusted first. Lyle had been supportive in the past. He hadn't seen me in a while and he commented that I looked better. My face wasn't as puffy. When he told the story accurately, everybody else would have to be more careful, which is exactly what happened.

The big day was Monday, March 3. John Newton had flown down to deliver a lecture on alcoholism to the entire team.

The guys were already in uniform around nine in the morning when Al Campanis announced that everybody should assemble in the locker room. I could see a few guys grumble when they heard they were in for a lecture, but as soon as John started talking, almost all of them listened. That man has got a gift for gab. He must have been a piece of work when he was drunk. He brought up all the diagrams and his visual aids—the thimble, the beer can, the shot glass. He told his famous story of taking a nap in the fast lane of the Santa Ana Freeway. The guys laughed at that.

Then John told how he had joined AA and learned not to drink, and how his entire life had improved—his family relations, his work, his health. He told how the Dodgers were tying up with Union Oil in a treatment program for the entire organization, and he gave his room number in case any of the players wanted to reach him privately. John's talk took about half an hour.

Then Al Campanis got up and gave a little talk about using The Meadows, how the Dodgers' medical insurance covered any employee and immediate family. Al was praising the process at The Meadows and then he paused and said:

"One of your teammates went to the center last month."

You should have seen heads turn. Everybody was looking one way to see who it was, as Campanis continued:

"I'm very proud of him for having the guts to go through with it, and I'd like him to come forward now."

Silence. Nobody moved but a lot of eyes were darting back and forth. I waited a few seconds, enjoying the suspense, but finally I got up and walked to the front of the room. Then I turned to face everybody and I asked:

"Who did you think it was?"

That made everybody laugh, broke the ice. They turned a lot more serious when I added: "I'm an alcoholic. I always will be an alcoholic. But now I know how to stop drinking one day at a time, and that's what I'm going to do.

"One of the things they teach us in Alcoholics Anonymous is to tell people you're sorry for hurting them. Most of you guys remember last September when I got drunk in San Francisco and made a fool out of myself on the field and in the clubhouse. If I offended any of you, I apologize. I was so drunk I did not remember a lot of it. I was having blackouts. That's how bad my drinking is. I cannot remember what I do. So if I have ever torn up anybody's house while I was drunk or insulted your wife or acted like a fool, I want to say I'm sorry."

I had never been a very confident public speaker, but after The Meadows, I felt pretty good about facing the guys. The reaction was good. Guys came over afterward and patted me on the back and told me they were proud of me. They said it took guts to do it. I told them how Rick and Robin had come to Arizona to be with me, and I thanked Rick in front of everybody else.

Then I went out and did it all over again for the press. They had been assembled for a conference, not knowing what it was all about.

They were all terrific, asking questions and wanting to know the background of alcoholism and what The Meadows does. Some of them went to Rick and Robin to get their version of it. And the stories the next day were excellent. The *Santa Ana Register* wrote that I used to be a "reticent man-child . . . who watched the floor when he talked." It recalled that "when his arm failed him, he began snapping at reporters' questions, at one point grabbing one by the shirt and threatening him."

The reporter noted that in 1980, "To those who knew Welch before, they are aware of the changes he has undergone. He looks directly at you when he speaks. He answers questions as best he can, even if the answers are still tinged with sarcasm."

Davey Lopes, who had been captain of the Dodgers, was quoted in the papers: "Bobby went through the transition from a World Series hero to obscurity in one year. I don't think a lot of people realize how tough it is. You're seeing a man develop now. You'll see a much more mature Bob Welch.

"I think everybody was touched. I could see some guys were shocked, but the reaction was kind of positive. There are very few people in the world able to accept something negative about themselves. I don't think I would have."

Davey continued: "I think there will be more positive vibes around the league than negative. He knows he's going to take a lot of hell from some ignorant people but he's ready for it. He can handle it now."

I did notice that some people seemed uneasy being around me—until they realized I wouldn't crusade and preach to them. I told people over and over again, "I'm not into crusading. Shoot, I'll be the first to pour them a glass of beer if they want."

I remember right after March 3 I went out to play golf with Rick and a couple of other guys. Afterward we stopped in the clubhouse and ordered two beers for them and a Coke for me. Rick does not have an alcohol problem but he had cut his drinking down since The Meadows, and I could tell he was hesitant about drinking in front of me.

"Isn't this going to bother you, us drinking like this?"

"Hell, no. Don't change for me. That would hurt my feelings. Don't do anything you don't want to do."

I still feel that way today. I don't have anything against alcohol. I'm sitting here talking about a cold glass of beer after a game of golf and, to tell you the truth, I wish I could drink a glass of beer. But I can't. If I drank one glass of beer, I would drink fifteen or sixteen or seventeen of them, and they'd have to throw me out the door when the bar closed. I would probably stop at every place on the way home and try to drink there.

The fact is, I'm crazy when I'm drunk. There is every chance I would have been dead by now if I were drinking. Somebody would have shot me or kicked my ass or I would have been killed in a car accident. I don't want to sound too dramatic, but alcohol could kill me. I do not want that to happen.

Chapter Twenty-seven

❖❖❖❖❖❖❖❖❖❖❖❖❖❖❖❖❖❖❖❖❖❖❖❖❖❖❖❖❖❖❖❖❖❖❖

The Season

❖❖❖❖❖❖❖❖❖❖❖❖❖❖❖❖❖❖❖❖❖❖❖❖❖❖❖❖❖❖❖❖❖❖❖

Everything seemed easier in 1980. I was no longer going around mad at people, suspecting they were checking up on my drinking. I was running to get myself in better shape, not to burn the alcohol out of my system. I had better control of myself in every way.

To me, it was more than symbolic that I could finally throw a change of pace. Before, I never could relax enough to let up on my fast ball, to permit the ball to float toward the plate, to throw the hitter off stride. In 1980, sober for the first time since I was a young teenager, I started learning the change-up.

Even in spring training I would hear the jokes from the stands. The fans are getting tougher every year. It used to be that you'd hear bad stuff from the bleachers only in places like Detroit or New York, but now it's everywhere, because of the big salaries we make, I guess. Even in Florida, where the fans are mostly older people, all the players would hear stuff like, "You're overpaid." I would get all the drinking insults, in every town we visited.

"Hey, Welch, throw a highball."

"Let's see if you can walk a straight line, Welch."

"Hey, Welch, buy you a beer."

In the opening series at Houston, Tom Lasorda used Rick as a pinch-hitter and when he got a base hit, Lasorda used me to run for him. I got to first base and I heard a fan shout, "We're gonna win now, boys. They've got a drunk running the bases." We won that game in seventeen innings. Take that.

I didn't mind the teasing from the stands and I never really heard anything vicious from the other dugouts. I was surprised in a way because you really hear some bad stuff. I never felt any resentments from my teammates, even the ones who drink. Rick got upset one time when the Dodger bus was chugging along some downtown street past a typical Skid Row and somebody in the back of the bus shouted, "Hey, there's Welch." Hell, I would have laughed if I'd heard it. I need a lot of humor in my sobriety. I've got a sharp tongue myself. I like getting on people. Ballplayer humor cuts down on the tension. I didn't want people tiptoeing around me.

I'll give you an example of something that made me laugh. I didn't get to pitch in the opening series of the season at Houston, so I opened up in San Diego. I didn't give up any runs in seven innings but we lost after I came out of the game.

Charlie Hough had promised he would give me a present if I pitched well in my first outing. After the game, he made a big presentation—a rum cake. I took one whiff of that and rolled my eyes and everybody laughed. Then Charlie cut the cake and distributed it around the clubhouse while I drank my soda and stuck my elbow in ice, the way I always do when I pitch. The reporters came around to see how I felt and I held up my soda and told them: "You'll notice, no beer." A couple of Dodgers came by and offered me a beer just to be helpful. That's all right in the clubhouse. It might not be the right way to coexist with an alcoholic in a business office, where things are more serious, but in a clubhouse, anything goes.

It took me a while to get my first win of 1980. J. R. Richard blanked me, 2–0, and then I had another no-decision. In the past I might have become anxious if things didn't go my way immediately, but I knew I had time in 1980. My first victory came against the Giants in my favorite city. The only thing I regretted was that it was on getaway day and I couldn't go back to the Pierce Street Annex and celebrate. As soon as we had landed in San Francisco, I had gone back to my favorite bar.

I know there are some people at The Meadows or Alcoholics Anonymous who would worry about my becoming a "dry drunk," with the companions and symptoms of drinking without putting the stuff in my system. The way I see it, I've got to keep on living. The Pierce Street Annex is a live place, lots of good people playing dice games on the counter, talking a lot of bullshit, playing music, a lot of pretty women to look at, a lot of friends.

When I dropped into the Annex after our arrival in San Francisco, people congratulated me on not drinking. I'd go there at lunchtime, which is breakfast time for me, and have a quick glass of juice. Then I'd go out for eggs or fish with Gary Ferrari, one of the owners. Gary told his bartenders he would break anybody's arm if they offered me a drink, but I just laughed.

"Hey, Gary, if I'm going to drink, I ain't going to start in your bar," I told him. "I'll go to some package store and buy a beer, or I'll go into some Skid Row joint and slug one down. I'm the one who controls my drinking, and I'm not going to get drunk today. I am sober today."

Living one day at a time, I am able to enjoy most of the things I used to do. But if I'm at the Annex or any other place and people are just getting smashed, I go home early. I am getting more selective about friends and my environment.

I felt better as a pitcher, too. I had always liked being in the spotlight, holding the game in my hand, and it was easier now. Don Sutton used to tell me, "Nobody can do a damn thing until I do something." You could have the whole ball park holding their breath —you might even be holding your own breath—but the game couldn't go forward until you threw the ball. The trick was to throw it right.

Sometimes I'd forget and try to muscle one past Dave Kingman or Ted Simmons and they would hit it over a fence. But the percentages were on my side. I beat the Cubs despite a homer by Kingman, I shut out the Pirates with Steve Howe getting the final batter, I beat the Cubs again, then I pitched a one-hitter against the Atlanta Braves on May 29. I beat Seaver in Cincinnati before the Mets beat me in New York. Then I shut out the Expos in Montreal, beat the Astros in Houston, lost to the Padres, and beat the Giants. I had nine victories and three losses on July 5 and I was named to the National League All-Star team.

I really felt as if I had life in control, on the road or at home. I hope I'm not giving away any trade secrets, but I love pitching on Sunday afternoon. In the 1980 season I'd get up early, drink a cup of coffee and have a doughnut, and drive to the ball park before traffic built up. I would still have my butterflies because I'm a nervous person, but I didn't hide from it now. I'd sit around and throw the ball more easily. Some of the guys on the other team would have stayed up late after the night game Saturday, visiting friends and relatives, and some of them had probably taken a drink or two. They'd still be sweating out that last ounce or two of alcohol while I was warming up a few minutes after one o'clock. At game time, I would be ready. Get the game over by three-thirty or four, wait for traffic to clear, get home on the freeway, take a walk on the beach, and cook a halibut steak on the hibachi. I felt I was truly alive.

I did not feel so wonderful in the All-Star game at Dodger Stadium after the American League rocked me for five hits and two runs in three innings. I might have been the losing pitcher but the National League came back to win after I left. Once again, Welch had gotten off the hook.

The best part of the game was giving my All-Star souvenir bat to Bob Fenton, my lawyer, who had stuck by me in the bad times. When I gave him the bat—*macho* guy that he is—he said, "What do you want me to do, cry?" He almost did.

Things did not go as well after the All-Star break. My old teammate Rick Rhoden beat me twice for Pittsburgh, and my record slipped from 9–3 to 10–9 by the end of August. There were times when reporters wanted to do an update on my alcoholism story, and there were times when groups wanted me to speak, and there were times when I was just plain horseshit. I can't make excuses. I just couldn't put together one entire super season. I'd lose my concentration, feel it drifting away.

During the summer, two of my friends from The Meadows, Lynn Brennan and Pat Berry, who works in the business office, drove over from Arizona and met me at Dodger Stadium, along with Lynn's girl, Dawn, and Pat's daughter, Kinsey. I was groggy from having wisdom teeth pulled earlier in the day but I chatted with them out in the parking lot for a while.

Sometimes Lynn would call me and ask how I was doing, which is beyond her responsibility to former patients, but that is how Lynn is: She wanted to keep in contact with her people.

Whenever Lynn called, I would feel a surge of memories of how she had opened me up in my thirty-six big days at The Meadows, and I would talk easily to her because she is such a warm and understanding person. But for a long time I did not initiate the contacts.

Did she think I was holding back? I wondered. Seeing her at Dodger Stadium, I knew I wanted her to be my friend as well as my former counselor. It was also strange to have the two worlds overlapping right outside the clubhouse door. I was trying to blend them together, to create a life in which I played ball and continued to treat myself for alcoholism, my way.

Chapter Twenty-eight

••••••••••••••••••••••••

A Warning

••

I thought I was in control of myself as the 1980 season moved into the final weeks but something was lurking under the surface, some resentment, some anger, just waiting to tempt me.

My arm was fine but I started getting pounded after the All-Star break. Mary was living with me in a borrowed house in Lakewood after her graduation from Kalamazoo. She was looking for a job and not coming up with anything and I was getting itchy about the instability of our lives. The guy who owned the house was coming back on October 15, so we had to find some other place to live. I didn't have enough money to buy what I wanted—a little pad by the ocean —and I was feeling lousy about having to move from one place to another all the time. No different from millions of other young people, and in fact I was better off than most people my age. But I was getting itchy. I shouldn't use this as an excuse for what happened, but I can see now how I let things add up.

I started to win again on September 1, beating the Mets at home. Then I beat the Phillies at home, the Padres at home, and the Braves at home, and things were coming together for me again. But after that game against the Braves, I started feeling a pain down in my groin, some kind of pulled muscle. I went to Bill Buhler, our trainer, and he couldn't find any bruise, any discoloration, but we knew something was aggravated.

We went into the next-to-last Sunday two games behind the Astros. We got word that they were losing on Sunday, but that did not help my groin. I started warming up in the bullpen but as soon as I tried pushing off the mound, I could feel the muscle ache deep in my groin. I was so damn angry, so damn frustrated, that I tried muscling the ball to the catcher. I went out and pitched a few innings but couldn't pitch worth two cents. I got off the hook on the decision but we lost when a dinky pop fly got lost in the sunlight. We were still two games behind the Astros.

We went to San Francisco for a couple of games and the club wanted to know if I could pitch. I suppose I could have asked for some kind of pain-killer and tried pitching, but there were two reasons why I was against that.

First, I tried to avoid medication as often as possible. When I left The Meadows, I was told that alcoholics can be affected by many drugs—even those used normally by doctors and dentists, even simple aspirins and cold tablets. I know some alcoholics who will not even take Novocain for their dental work, although I tell the man, "Put me out."

The other reason I did not want a shot is that I did not want to take the chance on injuring my legs or my arm if my groin muscle made me change my pitching motion. At first I thought the club officials would put more pressure on me to try the arm, but after a few conversations Al Campanis told me, "Bob, the thing we don't want to do is mess you up for a long time."

Still, I felt terrible as we won two out of three games in San Francisco but returned home three games behind Houston. We had just picked up a kid, Fernando Valenzuela, a left-hander from Mexico, who was pitching sensationally in relief, but damn, I had won four straight decisions as a starter and I knew the team needed me. I wanted to pitch so badly and I felt guilty about letting the team down. Nobody said anything to me but there's always the feeling of guilt. Is anybody saying anything behind my back? What do they really think? Do they think I don't want to pitch? Does anybody think I'm acting differently because I'm an alcoholic? Because I'm drinking? Because I'm not drinking? Let me tell you, sitting around and watching other guys pitch, your mind starts jumping around on you. I was close to frantic, really.

The last weekend in Los Angeles was a festival, a riot, a carnival. We had three games against the Astros in our ball park, knowing we could not afford to lose one time. Valenzuela won in relief on Friday night as the fans roared like I've never heard Dodger fans roar. Jerry Reuss beat Nolan Ryan on Saturday afternoon as the fans staged standing ovations. Then on Sunday, Steve Howe, another kid from Michigan, was the winner in relief as we clinched a tie with the Astros, forcing a one-game playoff.

By this time, I was totally frustrated. The groin just did not respond. We tried everything—massages, exercises, whirlpools—but nothing loosened it up. I could not lift my left leg and push off with my right foot. The pain would just shoot up my groin. For the play-off game on Monday afternoon, Lasorda went with Dave Goltz, who had a so-so season after coming over as a free agent from the Twins. I ate my heart out as Joe Niekro tossed his knuckleball at us, and the Astros won the playoff by a 7–1 score. I tried to think positive, to root for my teammates, but in my heart I was destroyed. I kept thinking, "I should have been out there. I would have won that game. I can shut those guys out."

I don't think I realized how bad I felt until I got back to our borrowed house that Monday night, October 6. The season was over for me and the Dodgers. My groin still hurt. I had nine days to find another place to live. I could not afford the house I wanted. Mary was going to job interviews and not finding anything. And the Astros and the Phillies began playing a five-game championship round that was one of the most exciting baseball series ever played. But all I could think was, "That should have been us."

What I have just described is the old "stinking thinking." Mother told me there would be days like this. Mother Meadows. But there I was, indulging in "stinking thinking," letting events get me down, forming excuses, bringing up resentments for things that were nobody's fault. I was a prime candidate for a fuckup.

On Monday, October 13, I went out to play golf in the morning. I finished after lunch, drank enough iced tea and club soda to float the *Queen Mary*, and got in my car. But I did not go home.

Instead, I visited a girl I know, a stewardess I had met on an airplane in 1979, back when I was drinking. I had discovered that her drug of choice was Valium. That's what made her feel better.

I knew I did not want to get drunk. I did not want to drink one beer or twenty beers because I am an alcoholic and it could seriously hurt me. So I indulged in a little wishful thinking—the old "Yet Syndrome"—that maybe it was all right if I just substituted a few Valiums for a few beers.

The woman did not initiate my visit. She did not call me or pick me up at the golf course and make me an offer I could not refuse. I contacted her because I knew what I wanted. In another frame of mind, I might have visited her to talk over my blues or suggest we make love, but I did not want her body or her soul. I wanted her medicine cabinet.

I just wanted to pop a few Valiums to take away the pain. I wanted to get fucked up.

I raided her cabinet and popped a couple of pills and then we hung around for a few hours, my mind off the pain.

I thought I was all right until I got behind the wheel of my car. No, let me phrase that better. I thought I was all right until I hit somebody else's car. I was driving on the Pacific Coast Highway, going the legal speed, not weaving or anything, but when a man started to make a turn in front of me, I took my eyes off the road and got blinded by his headlights. I swerved my car and caught another car with my right front. My head flew forward, cracking the windshield, but my head was hard enough to withstand serious injury. Fortunately, the other guy was not hurt, either, but he wanted to press charges. The police arrived and I told them who I was and said I was under medication for my groin injury—good old alcoholic bullshit, hustle to get yourself out of a jam. I told the guy I would pay for his car if he did not press charges, and we worked that part of it out. Then the police drove me home. I realized I was spinning, had a good buzz on, from the couple of pills I had belted down. For what it was worth, I might as well have chugged down a six-pack.

Mary was frightened when the police drove me home, and she got really upset when she saw the condition I was in. Naturally, she thought I had been drinking. She was afraid I was going down the drain with alcohol that night, and I don't blame her for thinking that. I told her, "Damn, Mary, I just took a pill because of my groin and I got fucked up. It will be all right." I went to take a bath, still spinning, still with a buzz. Naturally, Mary was upset and I could not tell her any more that night.

The next morning, I felt as if I had died. The world had ended. I was totally sober, no after effects, no blackouts, but my guilt was making me sick. I was hoping it was a dream but I knew it wasn't. Mary kept asking me for more details and I said I was over at a friend's house and took a pill watching *Monday Night Football*, but I couldn't tell her the whole truth, not yet.

That morning, I was convinced I had lost it all. I felt I was the first individual who had ever screwed up after joining AA. I kept waiting for a hand to come out of the sky and crush me, for the newspapers to call up and start crowing, for Newton and Newcombe and the Dodger front office to read me the riot act. But nothing happened. Hours passed.

Finally I could not stand it anymore. I had to tell someone. I went off by myself and called Bob Fenton, my attorney in Detroit.

"Bob, I fucked up," I told him. "I took a pill. I wrecked my car."

"Were you drinking?" he asked.

"No, but the same thing happened."

He told me he knew alcoholics who went off the wagon, that it was not the end of the world. He started to reassure me that I could pick up the pieces, and I felt so good that I thanked him and said, "That's great. Just don't tell anybody else." But he told me I should contact The Meadows and let them know what had happened. I was scared to do it, but I knew he was right, and I called Lynn.

"I'm glad you called me," Lynn said, sounding capable and concerned. "That's a critical step, for you to call somebody. Bob, nobody ever guaranteed you would never slip, but we do say that if you follow the program you're not going to die from chemicals. You were going around thinking you had your addiction licked, but you never have it licked. Now you have to get back into the swing of the program. You were not paying enough attention to your sobriety. You were not talking about it, you were not giving up enough time for meetings.

"Maybe this is what you needed. You have to stick with your program. This is a slap in the face. When you got off by yourself after the season, you didn't stick with it."

We talked for almost an hour, with Lynn urging me to go to an AA meeting that night. We said we loved each other and promised to ke͟ in touch. As soon as I hung up, I leafed through my AA directory and found a meeting.

That night, in front of mostly strangers, when it came time for people to talk, I told how I had screwed up, tried playing God with chemicals. I described my feelings, said there was no excuse, and told how I had been afraid I was out of control, that my alcoholic impulses would control me.

When I was done, several people in the group told me the same thing had happened to them. They had tried a few beers or a few pills or a few joints or a few Scotches. Anyway, they found they couldn't handle it. They told me to work harder on my sobriety. They supported me when I needed it most. That's what AA does. Every time.

A few days later, somebody found this paragraph about alcoholics slipping up. It was from a book, *Games Alcoholics Play: The Analysis of Life Scripts* by Claude Steiner (New York: Grove Press, 1971):

> It has been my experience that every alcoholic, after some months of sobriety, drinks again. In the context of ongoing treatment, this episode need not be disastrous, but rather may refresh the patient's memory about the realities of the drinking situation. Except for the patient who goes on an extremely self-destructive binge, one or perhaps two such relapses can have some positive and salutary aspects. The nature and extent of the drinking episode is usually a good indication of whether or not the treatment is having any effect on the patient.

After three days of feeling I had thrown my life away, I started to rebound, enough to tell Mary the full story of how I visited the woman and popped the Valiums. Mary was hurt again, particularly because she was home alone while I was visiting some other woman, but I told her I was sorry, and I was. We started all over again, and day by day the pain got less.

A few weeks later, Mary and I flew over to Las Vegas for an alcoholism convention, and while I was playing golf I met some guys who run the Advanced Health Systems, a growing company with health-care centers in California. One of their specialties is treating alcoholism, and when they met Mary, they offered her a job in management training.

As soon as she began working, Mary felt like a young career woman instead of a college girl. She had her own job, her own car, her own schedule. She would grumble about waking up in the morning and I would just roll over and go back to sleep. In the evening she would come back and I'd go out and buy some fresh fish and we'd broil it on the hibachi. We were living in a studio apartment out by the ocean, and sometimes we'd feel pretty cramped, being together in the evenings. But after my slipup, we understood each other better, grew even closer.

Chapter Twenty-nine

◆◆◆◆◆◆◆◆◆◆◆◆◆◆◆◆◆◆◆◆◆◆

My Other Team

◆◆

When I say that I am combating alcoholism "my way," I do not mean I am doing it by myself. I don't believe you can do it all by yourself. You need the support of other people to bring out the positive, joyous side of abstaining from alcohol.

When I first said "I'm Bob, I'm an alcoholic" at The Meadows, there were some other alcoholics in the room to respond, "Hi, Bob." This is a custom at some Alcoholics Anonymous meetings, to let you know people are there. I need that. When I was released from The Meadows, the Dodgers and Union Oil recommended a program of three meetings a week—during the season and in the off-season—for at least eighteen months.

It has been easy for me to get speaking engagements to talk about alcoholism. That's no problem. A lot of people want to hear Betty Ford or Bob Welch talk about how they arrested their own alcoholism, because it gives a positive view to people looking for the negative. John Newton was right when he told me there are people who would like to see me fail. I haven't felt it from my teammates at all, but I have felt it from some members of the press and from the public.

There are always people who will say, "Welch—he's a drunk,"

when my name is mentioned. A friend of mine in the newspaper business was in the press box one game when I took a line drive on my hand. While I jumped around the mound in pain, one sports-writer jumped up and announced to the press box, "Oh, no, that's his hoisting hand." To me it indicates there are people waiting for the other shoe to drop.

It's important for people in the public eye to witness about their sobriety. One way you reinforce your sobriety is to give it away. I try keeping in touch with some people like my friend Chris, who helped me adjust to The Meadows. It's not easy being a teenager growing up in Southern California, where alcohol and dope and sex are even more common than when I was a teenager in Detroit. I try to show a positive example but the fact is I'm a kid myself in a lot of ways. Like my sister, Diane, says, "A little boy in a great big body." I need my reinforcement, just like any other addictive personality. I have to keep admitting I am different, that I cannot mess with chemicals. This is a lesson I learned the hard way.

As much as I might make public appearances, I have got to take care of myself first, keep that "stinking thinking" from creeping into my mind. The major step is to find an AA group I'm comfortable with. There are hundreds of groups available to anybody living in Southern California and I've tried more than a few. There are day groups, night groups, English or Spanish, closed or open to nonalco-holics, even meetings for smokers or nonsmokers.

I found that I needed meetings with a sense of humor, or meetings that are similar to The Meadows. I don't just want to hear somebody telling me, "This is the way to stay sober." I've been to some in Detroit or California that seemed like private clubs, a bunch of old-timers sitting around staring suspiciously if anybody under fifty wanders in. That is wrong. I want to be able to drop in at a meeting whether I just came from the beach or the ball park or a business meeting. I want to feel natural.

During the winter I went out and had a sandwich and then decided to drop in on a meeting not far from me. It was not until I was inside the building that I realized I was still wearing a T-shirt from my favorite bar—the Pierce Street Annex. I kept my sweater on during the meeting, figuring it might not be cool to promote a bar at an AA meeting. Personally, I fly up to San Francisco a couple of times a winter just for a good party at the Annex. In AA they tell us to face reality, and one of my realities is that people my age, a lot of my friends, congregate in bars. I've got to strike a balance.

I try to spend a part of each day reading some of the books from AA and The Meadows. I've got a loose-leaf notebook with pages of guidelines and essays about the temptations of backsliding. I also carry around books like *I'll Quit Tomorrow*, by Vernon E. Johnson, one of the founders of the Johnston Institute, whose philosophy and techniques are used at The Meadows. It's one of the clearest books I've ever seen about how to deal with alcoholism—your own or somebody else's.

Another thing I carry around with me is a list of meetings in every city I visit with the Dodgers. There are meetings at all times of the day and night, designed for strangers on the road who want to be with other alcoholics. We're not totally strangers, however. We all know why we're at the meeting. We recognize the look in each other's eyes. Most alcoholics have been through a lot. You see the suffering, the struggling they have done. I'm comparatively lucky, getting to the problem at an early age.

I go to meetings when I can on the road. I whip out my directory and find one not too far from my hotel. I like being just another young man in jeans and a sweater going to a meeting at lunch hour. Sure, it's great being recognized around the ball park as Bob Welch, No. 35. I still love that part of being a ballplayer.

Some people at the meetings recognize me because of the documentary film *Comebacker*, which was made about me during the 1980 season. It's around twenty minutes long, shows me and some of the Dodger people and Rick and Mary Ellen.

The film, by Ed Schuman of FMS Productions in Los Angeles, won the Blue Ribbon Award for the best film about addiction at the American Film Festival in New York in 1981, and has been made available through Churchill Films in Los Angeles. Different groups have shown the film, which sometimes makes it hard for me just to slip in as another AA person, which is really what I want to do.

This is what a fairly typical AA meeting is like:

I climbed the stairs of an old church hall, three flights up, to a meeting room where the Twelve Rules of AA were tacked on the wall. A bunch of worn folding chairs and wooden benches were arranged in a circle. There were ashtrays everywhere: The percentage of smokers seems high among alcoholics. Smoking may give you cancer and make your hair and clothing smell terrible to nonsmokers, but nicotine helps people get through the day. I have found out that my tobacco, which I dip between my cheek and my gum, gives me a higher chance for cancer than smoking would. I'm going to give it up, I promise myself.

At the meeting of AA, people kept bustling up the stairs, hanging up their coats, finding seats until the twelve-thirty starting time. I didn't think many people knew each other, because only a few were talking. Most of us just nodded politely—strangers with a common and familiar problem. We ranged from around eighteen to over seventy years of age, men and women, black and white. I saw jeans and I saw dark business suits.

One guy, the moderator, began the meeting by reading a little statement that AA is not a religion and supports no causes, that its only purpose is to combat alcoholism. Then he introduced the day's speaker, a man around forty, very artistic and well-spoken, who told a story that every one of us recognized.

"I was a secret drinker," he said. "Whenever there was trouble at home, I'd sneak a few belts, even when I was ten or twelve. In college, I'd stay sober when I had papers or sports events but later I'd get drunk and make a fool of myself."

He told how he began drinking more heavily after he got married and began a steady job in midtown. He described how he made scenes at work, was banned from certain restaurants, mistreated his children, lost his family and job, wound up waking up with strangers in unfamiliar beds, borrowing money, capitalizing on old friends.

People in the group nodded their heads. We had either been there or seen it coming. The man told about joining AA, how he had tested himself a few times by backsliding, only to realize he could not afford to take a drink of alcohol.

"I live alone now," he said. "At the moment, I have no love interest in my life. I used to dread weekends and holidays because I felt so alone, but now that I am really alone, I find ways to keep busy. Just staying sober, day by day, keeps me occupied."

We applauded the man when he was done. To me, the best part of that meeting, any AA meeting, is when people ask questions like a bunch of pitchers talking with the pitching coach about how to throw to the opposing batters.

One woman said, "Maybe you can help me. I've got to go to a cocktail party for business reasons in a few hours. I'm scared because my best friend slipped from sobriety over the weekend. I'm mad at her because I feel threatened by what she did. How can I deal with my feelings about her? How can I go to this cocktail party and not drink?"

The moderator replied, "Of course, you want to help your friend back to sobriety, and you don't want to stay angry at her. But you've got to take care of yourself first. Keep yourself sober. Tell yourself, 'That's not for me. I'm not drinking today.'

"As for the cocktail party, I always try to avoid them. Nothing good ever happens at a cocktail party anyway. But when I've got to go to one, here's what I do: I find the waiter with the nicest face and I tell him, 'I do not want to have anybody offering me alcohol while I am here. Would you please make sure my hand is always filled with a soft drink or juice?' And I slip the guy five bucks. It has never failed. Every waiter I pick is sympathetic and helps me out. It's worth the five bucks because the cost of my taking one drink is far greater."

We all nodded at one more tip to get us through the lineup of alcoholism. Then another woman said, "You mentioned how you have become sensitive to your health since you stopped drinking. I thought I was the only one who imagined I had every possible disease."

Our moderator smiled and replied, "I'm a hypochrondriac because for years I could not feel my body while I was drinking. I was too anesthetized to know if I had a cough or a sore back. Now I feel everything. I imagine every disease possible. It's normal."

As people tossed questions back and forth, I listened with interest, but did not feel like participating. It was good just to be anonymous, not a guest speaker. When the meeting was over, I smiled at a few people and headed for the door, leaving one set of teammates, heading for another. By now it was nearly two o'clock and I was meeting a few friends from the Dodgers for a late lunch. For some of them, it might even be a late breakfast. For me, a major part of the day was already accomplished. As I walked the city streets, I repeated to myself: "I'm Bob Welch. I'm an alcoholic. But today I'm sober."

Chapter Thirty

◆◆◆◆◆◆◆◆◆◆◆◆◆◆◆◆◆◆◆◆◆◆

Day by Day

◆◆

My house felt like an empty thirty-room mansion. I rattled around in it, with no purpose, no meaning. I had bought this townhouse near the beach to share with Mary Ellen, but now she was 2,500 miles away, and I had the stone-cold sober blues.

It was a couple of days after Christmas of 1983. I had spent the holiday with a few friends up in the mountains, but now I was sitting around my house thinking this was the time of year when you want to be with your family, with the people you love best. And I knew who that was.

Mary had moved out to California to live with me, but I had kept putting off talk about getting married, and she had decided to go out on her own. First a job, then her own apartment, and now she had moved all the way across the damn country. She was living in Westport, Connecticut, working for a payroll firm, and feeling closer to her sister in Boston and her family in Michigan, and giving me all kinds of room to grow up. Room? The space felt like infinity.

She had dropped over one evening late in the season. I had just gotten back from a game, and was packing to leave the next morning on a road trip. She was carrying her favorite rocking chair from her car, and I asked her what the heck she was doing lugging that thing.

"I'm cleaning out my apartment," she had told me. "I'm moving to New England."

At first I hadn't believed it, but she told me it was true. Maybe she had been waiting for me to ask her to stay, but I was too dense. We sat on the couch and shed a few tears and the next morning she was on her way. We spent ten days together in Rhode Island after the Dodgers lost to the Phillies in the play-offs, but now I hadn't seen her in two months.

"She really went and did it," I said to myself.

In the old days, I might have gone to a six-pack to make myself feel better, but I wasn't pulling that stunt, not today.

Fortunately, the telephone lines stretched from Huntington Beach to Westport, so I picked up the telephone and gave Mary a call. Just wanted to hear her voice, you understand. We joked around for a few minutes, me telling her about all the fun I was having, she telling me how nice New England was.

Then I threw her the shocker: "Mary, I want you to be my wife."

Shocked me, too.

"Come off it," she said. "Cut it out."

I don't think she believed me in that phone conversation, but the next morning before she left for work she called me in California. Woke me up, naturally.

"Are you kidding me, or what?" she asked.

"I'm serious," I told her.

We talked again a week later and Mary said, "You'd better be serious because I'm accepting."

We decided to meet the next day in Dallas, where I was giving a talk to a convention of college baseball coaches on the dangers of drinking. My attention was divided as I addressed the coaches, and to make my point about being sober, I said, "If it wasn't for not drinking, I might not be here today, and it's a very important day in my life because I've asked a young lady to marry me, and she's arriving here later today." I think they thought I was nuts.

Mary met me at the house of our friends Pat and Carol Rodgers, out in Plano, and we had this big emotional scene, laughing and crying, and we continued it behind closed doors until we decided to get married almost right away. We did just that, setting the date for Saturday evening, January 21, 1984, in the chapel at Boston University. Our parents flew in from the Midwest, and our friends from all over the country.

I thought I would be nervous, but this was nothing like starting a World Series game. This was fun. I stepped into the beautiful chapel, lit by candles, and took one look at everybody, particularly the lady in the white gown, and I started smiling, and so did Mary. This was *fun*. We just kept smiling at each other while the minister and everybody else did their thing. People said later they had never seen two happier people. We had finally gotten some sense in our heads, and now we could laugh about it.

We had a dinner reception at a fancy hotel in Boston, and we had a champagne toast, with nonalcoholic champagne for some of us. Somebody asked if I wasn't worried about having champagne and wine at my wedding, and I said, "Not today." And that's as far ahead as I could look.

We drove through New England, in the coldest snap of the winter, closing out Mary's apartment and staying with friends on Long Island. (We forgot our wedding cake in Marianne Vecsey's freezer, and didn't get it back until the Dodgers came to New York in 1984, and we wound up eating a few bites of it in the Sheraton Hotel in Montreal. I think you're supposed to save it for an anniversary, but the cake didn't make it.) Then we went to stay with Dan Kapstein in Beaver Creek, Colorado, where Mary went skiing and I wished baseball players could.

When we got back to California, the house did not seem empty anymore. We felt like an old married couple, except that we couldn't bear to be apart from each other even for a day. Mary went with me to spring training and on a lot of the road trips during the 1984 season. My shoulder was hurting but I led the team in victories with thirteen, and I was maturing on the mound as well as in the rest of my life.

I remembered after my slipup with pills in 1980, how my elbow tightened up in spring training and how I tried to bull my way through the pain, and wound up with a truly sore arm. I think if I was ever to go off the wagon, I would have done it then. Yet even at the depths of arm trouble, I was able to laugh and say, "Hey, it's only my career. It's only my way of earning a living. I can get by. I could go get my degree."

Things were so much better in my family. My parents moved to Paducah, Kentucky, because my father wanted to stop working and start fishing. My mother didn't like giving up her job in the florist shop, but she knew it was good for my father to make a move.

My mom has gained a lot since I went to The Meadows. She joined an Al-Anon group back in Hazel Park and became one of the officers in the group, making some of the best friends she has ever had. She says she now realizes that she has had it much easier than most of the people in the group. She has a son who was on his way to tragedy, but some of the people in that group have already suffered the tragedy.

She has met women whose husbands beat them and stole money and ran around, but this has never happened to my mother. She says she is not out to change people around her who drink, but she wants to understand herself and me better. She hears women talk about whether they showed some need to be punished, which is why when they divorce one alcoholic they often marry another one. She wants to know more about herself and her relationship with me and the rest of the family.

My father was hurt by the suggestion at The Meadows that he was an alcoholic. I didn't think he was one because I had never seen him abusive or blacking out or wrecking the car or missing work, but he did quietly cut down on his drinking, and maybe it saved his life. In October of 1984, my father needed heart surgery, and he came out of it feeling better than he had in years. He's back working a little farm I bought near Paducah, and having a great time.

My sister, Diane, could have used the entire week at The Meadows for herself. I think she got a little mad when somebody in the group said she had been shortchanged because my family put priority on boys. She realized nobody had ever urged her to go to college, and that she had been mother to everybody. I think Diane is a terrific person and a very bright woman, and I've seen her growing even more in the last few years.

My brother, Donnie, left The Meadows after two days, furious with everybody suggesting he was an alcoholic. I was afraid maybe Donnie would close himself off to us for a long time, but he admitted, "The Meadows was a good experience for me. It scared me. It made me ask a lot of questions about myself." Now when we get together, we sit around and talk easily and he'll offer me advice or tease me like a confident older brother. I love him more than ever.

Are you ready for this? All four Welch boys—my cousins Doug and Lloyd, my brother, Donnie, and I—have stopped drinking. We grew up drinking together and now we're sober together.

I've had other friends who took a look at drinking and drugs after seeing what some of us were doing, day by day. When this book first came out in 1982, I started getting letters from people who said they were looking at themselves for the first time. I know people in my business, and George Vecsey knows people in his business, who have gone for help as a direct result of this book. It's not very often that a book could actually help save somebody's life, but I see signs this one has.

Not everybody has won the battle. I had a buddy from Michigan who was spending up to a hundred dollars a week on pot and alcohol. He said, "Damn it, I've got to get off this stuff. How do I do it?" I told him to quit for ninety days to prove he could do it, and he made it for a while, but later he started backsliding and I told him, "You'd better check in somewhere while you still have a job and hospitalization and you're still alive." He checked in, and I hope he makes it—not just for ninety days, but day by day.

Before the games, most of us sit in front of our lockers in the Dodger clubhouse and open our mail. Usually, people want autographs and pictures, but one woman wrote to me to say she was applying the ideas about addiction and feelings to her own problem, which was overeating. She said she used to go out and stuff her face when she was feeling down, but now she thinks about what is really bothering her before eating extra meals—and she says the pounds have come melting off.

I've had a couple of guys in the Dodger minor-league system ask me how I stopped drinking. I know that a number of ballplayers have sought treatment, including Darrell Porter of the Cardinals and Lou Johnson, a former Dodger, after I was the first player to talk about it. Nowadays you hear more about illegal drugs than alcohol, but drinking is still the major chemical problem among ballplayers, as far as I can see. It's legal, but with some of us, it can also be lethal.

One former Dodger has a drinking problem, and he talks to me about it from time to time. I think he'd like to do something about it but he's not ready. I'm not about to put pressure on the man. We get together a lot. He knows where I am.

I feel good when I hear my experiences have reached other people, but I don't go around preaching to people to give up drinking. I don't want to be a pain in the neck to my friends, to drive them away. But if they want to talk about it, I let them know I'm there, the way Rick and Robin Sutcliffe were for me. I missed Rick when he was traded, first to Cleveland, then to the Chicago Cubs, and nobody was more proud of Rick than I was when he won the Cy Young Award as the best pitcher in the National League in 1984.

Tom Lasorda and I did not get to know each other better at The Meadows, and our relationship was still fairly distant in 1980. I'm sure he was not comfortable talking about his feelings when somebody else was the patient. I know he saw his job as Dodger manager to go down there to encourage me. He didn't seem convinced I am an alcoholic—which I am—but he seems to agree that treatment helped me, which is what matters.

When I first joined the Dodgers, I never felt comfortable kidding with the man, the way some of the guys do, but in 1981, I found I could stand around and shoot the bull with him, part of my growing-up process. He has been very encouraging about my pitching, and he and Al Campanis, The Chief, have stuck with me even when I wasn't producing.

I had elbow problems early in the 1985 season, and Campanis encouraged me to take my time until the elbow was stronger. I went to the Dodgers' farm team in Vera Beach for a rehabilitation period and had fun riding the buses with the kids, no pressure like in the major leagues, and after a few games, I was ready to come back. Lasorda showed faith by putting me back in the rotation, and I won seven straight in midseason as the Dodgers opened up a big lead. I never felt more comfortable on the mound or in the clubhouse as I looked forward to the postseason championships.

My life is so much more stable than it was when I first became sober. I am now represented by Jerry Kapstein, and there is the added bonus of his parents, Sherwin and Gladys, his sister, Deb, and her husband, Len Bronitsky, and their children, Molly and Max, and his brother, Dan, who were all at our wedding in Boston.

I have continued to speak at A.A. meetings and treatment centers, but I have not gotten involved with any one center. I think maybe when I retire I'll investigate operating a rehabilitation center, but for now I just want to live a quiet life away from the ball park. Mary and I enjoy being alone, cooking fish on the hibachi, entertaining relatives from the Midwest, and walking over to the beach.

I'm still learning. For our first wedding anniversary, we drove up north to the Napa Valley, out behind San Francisco, and spent one night in a mountain lodge. The next day we visited a few wineries with their open tasting bars and display cases of wine. I love the idea of vineyards and the different brands of wine, but all I needed were a few whiffs of wine to remind me who I am and what I am.

"Let's get out of here," I told Mary.

Next anniversary we'll try the desert or New York or Europe or somewhere other than Napa Valley.

That little anniversary reminded me that I've got to focus on saving my own life and, I hope, win a few ball games. All I know, as I finish this book, is that I am sober at this moment, and I'm going to be sober the rest of the day. Tomorrow? I want tomorrow, too—but it can wait.

When Mary and I were showing our wedding pictures to our friends, somebody pointed to the smiles on our faces and said, "Looks like a happy ending for your love story."

I don't believe in endings. Can't afford to.

"A happy beginning," I said. "Day by day."

About the Authors

Bob Welch grew up in suburban Detroit and attended Eastern Michigan University. He lives in Huntington Beach, California.

George Vecsey is a sports columnist for *The New York Times* and has previously covered such subjects as Appalachia and religion. He is the coauthor of *Coal Miner's Daughter* and *Martina* and the author of six other books and of eight books for children. He lives in Port Washington, New York.